THE FIRST BREXITEER

The Diaries of Sir Neil Marten, 1970 – 79

Edited by Tim Aker
Foreword by Anthony Marten.

© Tim Aker

Published in 2025 by The Bruges Group

ISBN: 978-1-917743-00-6

The Bruges Group Publications Office
246 Linen Hall, 162-168 Regent Street, London W1B 5TB
www.brugesgroup.com

Bruges Group publications are not intended to represent a corporate view of European and international developments. Contributions are chosen on the basis of their intellectual rigour, and their ability to open up new avenues for debate.

Twitter ❌ @brugesgroup, LinkedIn 🔗 @brugesgroup
GETTR 🅖 @brugesgroup, Telegram ✈ t.me/brugesgroup, Facebook 🅕 @brugesgroup
Instagram 📷 @brugesgroup,   YouTube ▶ @brugesgroup

For Mum

Contents

List of Illustrations	1
Acknowledgements	2
Editor's Introduction	3
Foreword by Anthony Marten	6
Part One: Full-Hearted Consent of Parliament and People	8
Part Two: The Fall of Ted Heath	71
Part Three: The Rise of Thatcher	133
Part Four: The Hung Parliament	160
Contributors	236
Index	237

List of Illustrations

Neil and Joan	124
Wartime Allies	124
Turkish Delight	125
Fête	126
Triumph	127
Gandhi	127
The Queen	128
Ministers	128
Arise Sir Neil	129
Thatcher	130
Unveiling	131
Skiing	131
Anyone for Tennis?	132

Acknowledgements

I am indebted to Anthony Marten for granting me permission to transcribe and edit the diaries of his father, Sir Neil Marten. It has been an exciting and humbling experience working on diaries that, his son Anthony aside, no one has seen before. This is history in its purest form now available to future scholars and researchers as an important primary addition to a significant period in Twentieth-Century British political history, namely Britain's entry to the European Economic Community and the catastrophic failure of the Heath administration that paved the way for Thatcherism in the 1980s.

It is fitting that the Bruges Group has accepted these diaries for publication. In the following pages Sir Neil is convinced that Mrs Thatcher was on his side when it came to 'Europe'. Unfortunately, having passed away in 1985, Sir Neil did not get to see Mrs Thatcher publicly declare her turn against ever closer union at Bruges in 1988. The Bruges Group has been at the centre of British political debate on the European Union since. I firmly believe Sir Neil would have approved of this partnership.

Anthony Marten's confidence and support in this exercise has been invaluable. I am grateful for the guidance of my PhD supervisor Prof. Simon Heffer, the advice of Dr. George Owers at Polity Press, and special thanks to Robert Oulds and the Bruges Group for publishing these diaries.

My heartfelt gratitude goes to my wife Tania for her encouragement, love, and patience. It has not been easy juggling a family life, work, my PhD research and this project. I couldn't have done it without you.

Tim Aker
Kent, February 2025.

Editor's Introduction

These diaries provide an incredible insight into the Conservative party during the tumultuous Heath administration and the early Thatcher years in opposition. The Heath years were dominated by two issues that haunted the Conservative party for some considerable time. The first, for which Marten was best known, was the battle over Britain's entry to the EEC. The second was Heath's policy U-turns from which Thatcherism sprang.

Neil Marten was Britain's first Brexiteer. He organised the most determined parliamentary campaign to oppose Britain's entry to the EEC, chaired the 'No' campaign in the 1975 referendum to leave the EEC, and continued agitation in parliament against ever closer European union. Without his activism the Eurosceptic movement would have had significantly weaker foundations. His defining moment was organising fourteen other Conservative and Ulster Unionist MPs to vote against a government confidence measure, specifically the Second Reading of the European Communities Bill in February 1972.

At the time of the Second Reading the country was in turmoil. Unemployment had passed the symbolic figure of one million. Bloody Sunday had shaken Northern Ireland, and much of the rest of the United Kingdom, that January. The miners' strike ended two days after the Second Reading. That Marten and his colleagues voted against a government confidence measure in these circumstances demonstrated their commitment to principle.

For all his rebelliousness Marten came under attack not, one might assume, from the party whips, but from his constituency Association. Indeed, during the rebellion on entry to the EEC Marten kept the whips informed of his numbers in a gentlemanly display of agreeing to disagree with his party. Nevertheless, his Association tried, over many months, to get him to alter his vote on the Common Market. Marten wrote of a wealthy 'hunting set' within his Association that put pressure on him with sniping in the press, protests, and clandestine organisation to have Marten overruled at constituency meetings and even deselected. Although he provides no evidence to support it, Marten believed that blessing for this action was given by the party chairman Peter Thomas who met with his Association chairman in July 1971 shortly before they initiated a coded censure motion against him. To rebut these constant attacks, Marten told them he would force a by-election and stand against them if they didn't cease. They did not call his bluff.

These diaries also chart the fallout from Heath's famous U-turns, the rise of Mrs Thatcher, and the challenging parliament of 1974-79. Whilst Marten was no theoretical monetarist, he saw the folly of the U-turns and dash for growth and noted, with horror, how the party reneged on each one of its election promises. The slow departure of Edward Heath is something, even after the party's second election defeat of 1974, that Marten did not consider an inevitability. Heath fought to the end.

Marten's first choice to succeed Heath was Keith Joseph. But, in his heart, Marten explored the varied, and somewhat elaborate, ways that Enoch Powell could return to the Conservative party and lead it, even as a member of the Ulster Unionists. But it must be emphasised that Marten was no Powellite. Whereas Powell thought the Commonwealth irrelevant and a folly, Marten was fully devoted to it, serving for many years in executive roles on the Commonwealth Parliamentary Association. He even privately disagreed with Powell's tone on immigration. It was Powell's opposition to the EEC, however, that brought Marten square behind him and the two became friends, even after Powell encouraged the country to vote Labour in February 1974.

Marten eventually endorsed Mrs Thatcher and his relationship with her was positive from the start. He noted how her leadership style was completely different from Heath. She reached out more. She listened to Marten on Europe as he encouraged her to resist further integration in the shape of full elections to the European Parliament. He sensed she agreed with him, as she eventually did, but she was boxed in by advisers and the Shadow Cabinet. Despite the views of those around her, Mrs Thatcher displayed an interest in Marten's position on Europe and took regular briefings from him. These instincts shone through in her Bruges speech of 1988, which Marten would have enthusiastically endorsed.

I am extremely grateful to Sir Neil's son, Anthony Marten, for giving me the opportunity to transcribe and edit these fascinating diaries. This project evolved out of a paper for *Parliamentary History* in 2023 when I visited Anthony to discuss Sir Neil's parliamentary activity. I was amazed when Anthony brought out a stack of his father's handwritten diaries and leapt at the opportunity to transcribe and edit them. Anthony's help with the transcription, and encouragement, have been invaluable in this endeavour. Any changes that have been made from the original diaries are merely stylistic. For example, Sir Neil liked to use '+' instead of the word 'and', and some longer entries have been broken up into shorter sentences to make it easier to read. He liked his abbreviations too. The two most common are CM, which stands for 'Common Market', and Cwth. is 'Commonwealth'. Other entries either noting the weather, tennis or where (and how impressively often) he went for lunch, have been edited out to maintain the flow of the narrative. I have done my best to provide commentary and biographical details in the footnotes. Any errors are purely my own.

These diaries are of a parliamentarian devoted to the cause of parliamentary sovereignty. Sir Neil Marten was a soldier, spy, politician, husband, father, and grandfather. These pages reveal just a fraction of his contribution to British politics and to his country.

Foreword by Anthony Marten

My father became an MP for the Banbury Division of North Oxfordshire in 1959 following a very distinguished war service in SOE in France and Norway. He worked in the Foreign Office from 1946 to 1957 serving in MI6 in Malaya, Egypt, Turkey, Cyprus, and Germany as well as at Broadway, the HQ of MI6. We have repeatedly tried to gain access to my father's files within MI6, but such was the secret world within which he worked that both William Hague and Boris Johnson, when Foreign Secretaries, wrote to me and said my father would quite understand that that information could not be revealed.

Neil Marten was one of the leaders of the campaign to keep Britain out of the Common Market, highlighting the loss of sovereignty and the inevitable pull towards a European Parliament acting as a continental legislature. He was Chairman of the Common Market Safeguards Campaign which was an All-Party group of MPs who were against British membership and pressed for a Referendum. Subsequently he was leader of the National Referendum Campaign which coordinated the various Anti-Market organisations. My sister, Mary-Louise, served as the only member of staff in the campaign for the 'No' side.

Over this period my father records the pressure that was brought to bear by his Constituency Association Officers and Central Office to get him to change his mind – something he resolutely refused to do. His reputation in Parliament and amongst his constituents remained high as a man true to his word and his beliefs. He continued to challenge successive Prime Ministers at Question Time and had a knack of catching the Speaker's eye.

During this time he served extensively on the Executive of the 1922 Committee under Edward du Cann's chairmanship. He was repeatedly re-elected by his parliamentary colleagues despite his anti-EEC views. He also had other key roles. He was vice chairman of the Conservative Foreign Affairs committee, Chairman of the Anglo-Norwegian Parliamentary Group, Chairman of the Space committee, also the All Party Disabled Drivers Group. In this latter role he was successful in getting much improved terms for disabled drivers so that they could commute their mobility allowance and instead lease a 4-wheel car.

He was a strong supporter of the Commonwealth and was Treasurer of the Commonwealth Parliamentary Association. This involved extensive travel throughout the Commonwealth. He was also involved in the campaign to stop the export of live animals to Europe. All this whilst leading a very active life as a popular and well-respected constituency MP with every weekend often up to four fundraising and political Branch events to attend in addition to surgeries, fetes to open, factories to visit and a family to connect with. On the sporting front he was a regular participant in the Lords and Commons ski team in their annual battle against the Swiss MPs in Davos. He was captain and organiser of the Parliamentary tennis team which, in addition to matches against livery companies and the legal profession, also involved an annual match against French Deputies in Deauville. In his constituency he organised an annual cricket match between the Lords and Commons and the Duke of Marlborough's team at Blenheim Palace.

Mrs Thatcher, upon forming her first Government, appointed my father Minister of State for Overseas Development in the Foreign Office. He was able to bring all his knowledge and strong support for the Commonwealth to bear at a time of Government cutbacks in the Overseas aid budget. He stepped down just before the 1983 General Election after announcing his imminent retirement as a member of Parliament.

His death within two years of his retirement and my inability to track down his long-suffering Secretary has meant that Tim Aker and I have had a challenging time transcribing his diaries into print. However, reading the diaries some sixty-five years after they were started has been a rewarding experience and highlighted how different the pressures of being an MP in those days were compared to now. An age without emails, mobile phones, or Special Parliamentary Advisors and with energy sapping all night sittings. Is an MP's lifestyle nowadays any more productive or personally satisfying than in those far off days without computers?

His knighthood and membership of the Privy Council were just rewards for a political career well lived.

Part One:
Full-Hearted Consent of Parliament and People

1.2.70

I hope this past week is not typical of the pages which will follow! Monday a futile debate on Nigeria and aid to Biafra raised by Hugh Fraser[1] under S.O. 9[2]. This postponed the Agriculture debate on our censure motion on the state of farming today – farmers are very angry at falling incomes and they have just censured the President of the NFU! Tuesday I left early for Brighton to speak at Sussex University at a week's seminar on the Common Market. The evening before Douglas Jay[3] had been there and spoken on the economic cost. John Mackintosh[4] also spoke – he was pro-CM. Reaction of Sir Harrison[5], just retired British Ambassador to Moscow "I have been pro CM all my life being in F.O. but having heard you and Douglas I am now very wobbly". Moral to that is we must influence the Establishment. He also said that Mackintosh had made a good speech but had given no reason <u>why</u> we should join the CM. Darted back and just made it for Question Time – I had the first question – PM back from USA having fallen on the steps of our Embassy in Washington and a big patt for the injured PM – looked <u>ok</u> to me but I commiserated with him at Question Time. Spoke at Wembley Cons. Supper in evening on CM – all anti-CM. Wed a.m. standing Committee on Disabled Bill then spoke at big anti-CM meeting at Caxton Hall 300 present with Peter

---

[1] Sir High Fraser (1918-84), Conservative MP for Stone, 1945-50; Stafford and Stone, 1950-83; Stafford, 1983-4. Fraser came last in the first round of the Conservative leadership election in 1975.

[2] Under the rules of procedure an MP can request a change to the order of business.

[3] Douglas Jay, Lord Jay (1907-96), Labour MP for Battersea North, 1946-83. Economic Secretary to the Treasury, 1947-50; Financial Secretary to the Treasury, 1950-1; President of the Board of Trade, 1964-67. Created Baron Jay of Battersea, 1987. Anti-marketeer and ally of Marten's.

[4] John Mackintosh (1929-78), Labour MP for Berwick and East Lothian, 1966-74.

[5] Sir Geoffrey Harrison (1908-1990), diplomat, British Ambassador to Brazil, 1956-8; Iran, 1958-63; the USSR, 1965-8.

Bessel[6], Michael English[7], and Frere-Smith[8]. All night sitting on Consolidated Fund Bill – I spoke at 5.20am on the proposed Oxford Motorway not that I wanted to but Angus Maude[9] raised it and as it was clearly his intention to mention my constituency on the instructions of his b...y wife I had to be there! So felt a bit jaded afterwards!

8.2.70

Tuesday lunched with Lord Campbell over the Common Market and the Cwth. Sugar agreement. Ted Heath[10] came to the Foreign Affairs Committee and gave an <u>excellent</u> account of his Far East trip. He really seemed on the top now – perhaps his win in the Hobart Race has made him feel he is a man in his own right regardless of politics[11]. On Wednesday we launched our "Common Market Safeguards Campaign" (really anti-CM but we don't actually say so!) – the aim is to group together all the organisations and people with doubts about the CM under one united group. I went on the BBC European news about it and then A.T.V. the next day. Wed. evening we had a CM dinner in the House which went well. Thursday we dined with Sir Michael[12] and Lady Wright to hear the Canadian Dep. High Commissioner and on Friday there was the annual dance of the Burford Conservatives at the Lamb. Rest of the weekend I spent working – it seems endless these days the additional burden of the Common Market.

---

[6] Peter Bessell (1921-85), Liberal MP for Bodmin, 1964-70.
[7] Michael English (1930-2019), Labour MP for Nottingham West, 1959-83. Anti-marketeer.
[8] Christopher Frere-Smith (1928-2000), Chairman Keep Britain Out, 1966. Frere-Smith and Marten did not see eye to eye on strategy and would fall out during the 1975 referendum campaign.
[9] Angus Maude, Baron Maude of Stratford upon Avon (1912-1993), Conservative MP for Ealing South, 1950-58; Stratford-on-Avon, 1963-83. Founder of Conservative One Nation group, 1950. Resigned his seat in 1958 to become editor of the *Sydney Morning Herald*. Paymaster General, 1979-81. Created Baron Maude of Stratford upon Avon, 1983.
[10] Sir Edward Heath (1916-2005), Prime Minister, 1970-74. Leader of the Conservative party, 1965-75. Conservative MP for Bexley, 1950-2001.
[11] In 1969 Edward Heath won the Sydney to Hobart yacht race on his 'Morning Cloud' yacht. Heath is the only British Prime Minister to win an international sporting event.
[12] Sir Michael Wright (1901-76), diplomat, British Ambassador to Norway, 1951-4; Iraq, 1954-8.

15.2.70

On Monday we had the Bill on Equal Pay – a bit silly but we didn't divide against it so in the evening I took Judith[13] to hear Andrezj Panufnik's[14] new composition 'Thames Pageant' – usual lively Panufnik! On Tuesday the White Paper on the economics of joining the Common Market came out – like a bombshell it gave the range of £1,100m - £100m deficit on our bal. of payments! And merely a pious unquantifiable benefit. The "pros" are very downcast and we are jubilant. I went on BBC news with Sir Geoffrey de Freitas[15] and, so I am told (!), demolished his arguments – Douglas Jay went on T.V. with Eldon Griffiths[16] and demolished him - so, on balance, we did well. The White Paper is riddled with nonsense, too. We are to debate it later. Wednesday spoke at Oxford to P.E.S.T.[17] on Common Market – really getting fed up with talking to students – most of them seem to be incapable of sensible thought. Friday was our constituency Executive and I carried them with me on Common Market – relief.

1.3.70

A dullish week except on Wednesday 18 I spoke at Cambridge University where I was well dined and had a good meeting with intelligent questions mainly on the Common Market although I was speaking on Space[18]! Thursday lunch with Jordan Ambassador and in evening went to George Washington Ball which was fun. Friday went to Bermuda to attend the annual British-American Parliamentary

---

[13] Marten's daughter.
[14] Andrezj Panufnik (1914-91), composer and conductor. Panufnik was a Polish émigré. Marten arranged his escape from Poland during Russian occupation after the Second World War. He married Neil's secretary Camilla Jessel.
[15] Sir Geoffrey de Freitas (1913-82), politician and diplomat. Conservative MP for Nottingham Central, 1945-50; Lincoln, 1950-61; Kettering 1964-79. High Commissioner of the United Kingdom to Ghana, 1961-4.
[16] Sir Eldon Griffiths (1925-2014), Conservative MP for Bury St. Edmunds, 1964-92. Minister for Sport, 1970-4.
[17] Pressure for Economic and Social Toryism. Founded by Michael Spicer in 1963, it came to embody the left of the Conservative Party. It merged with the Macleod Group and Social Tory Action Group to form the Tory Reform Group in 1975.
[18] Neil had been chairman of the parliamentary Space Committee in the 1960s.

Conference – colleagues were Tony Crosland[19], Lord Chalfont[20], Lord Jellicoe[21], Paul Bryan[22], Michael Alison[23], Alf Morris[24], Don Concannon[25]. The object was to have mutual discussions with our American opposite numbers on defence, foreign affairs, crime, pollution, law and order etc. This we did in 3 workshop sessions and 1 working dinner otherwise we were free. Great reception at Government House on arrival, tennis with Lord Chalfont in Govt. House on Sat. afternoon. Lord Martonmere[26] the Governor opened up our deliberations in full uniform which was a bit much! Banquet by C.P.A.[27] on Sat. night and lots of boozing! Sunday Michael Alison and I went by boat to have lunch with Maurice Grieg[28] and wife Peggy at the far end of the island – lovely position but it must be a very boring life for a retired Admiral. Monday afternoon tennis with Tony Crosland and Lord Chalfont and Tuesday a lazy afternoon and we then packed and had an interesting meeting with the Bermudian Government before flying back by night. A worthwhile exercise but it could have been better with better organisation. Sat in on the second day of the Common Market debate on the White Paper but was not

---

[19] Anthony Crosland (1918-77), Labour MP for South Gloucestershire, 1950-55; Great Grimsby, 1959-77. Secretary of State for Education and Science, 1965-7; President of the Board of Trade, 1967-9; Secretary of State for Local Government and Regional Planning, 1969-70; Secretary of State for Environment, 1974-6; Foreign Secretary 1976-7.
[20] Arthur Jones, Lord Chalfont (1919-2020), Labour and Conservative politician. Created Baron Chalfont, 1964. Resigned from the Labour party in 1970. Supported Mrs Thatcher in 1979.
[21] George Jellicoe, 2nd Earl Jellicoe (1918-2007), Leader of the House of Lords, 1970-73.
[22] Sir Paul Bryan (1913-2004), Conservative MP for Howden, 1955-83; Boothferry, 1983-7.
[23] Michael Alison (1926-2004), Conservative MP for Barkston Ash, 1964-83; Selby, 1983-97.
[24] Alf Morris, Lord Morris of Manchester (1928-2012), Labour MP for Manchester Wythenshawe, 1964-97. Created Lord Morris of Manchester, 1997.
[25] John Dennis 'Don' Concannon (1930-2003), Labour MP for Mansfield, 1966-87.
[26] John Robinson, 1st Baron Martonmere (1907-1989), Conservative MP for Widnes, 1931-35; Blackpool 1935-45; Blackpool South 1945-64. Created Baron Martonmere, 1964. Governor of Bermuda, 1964-72.
[27] The Commonwealth Parliamentary Association. Marten was a strong supporter of the CPA and later served as Treasurer.
[28] Admiral Morice Gordon Greig (1914-80), retired 1965.

called. Most speakers were against it – brilliant speech by Enoch Powell[29].

8.3.70

Monday dull business. In the evening I went to the PM's reception at No. 10 for the German Chancellor Willy Brandt[30]. It was far from stuffy! Lots of showbiz folk there, pop stars, footballers, press and T.V. and the usual establishment. One pop star entered, shoeless, with all the T.V. cameras going - that side of it was really too much. While it was amusing it lacked dignity for the head of another state. It got a bad press on the whole. Tuesday we had a meeting of the unofficial committee of the Chronically Sick Disabled Bill in an interview room and it was televised for BBC2 – a new departure. Was host at lunch to the NZ High Commissioner who was very anxious about us joining the Common Market. In the evening we dined with the Norwegian Ambassador – very pleasant. Wednesday, in heavy snow, went to Southend with the Estimates Committee to examine Customs and Excise HQ – not very interesting. Second day of defence debate on Thursday – Ted Heath opened and halfway through he said "One of the two things we frequently complain of is the lack of information from the Gov. – now all is change for the Member for Banbury received a written answer to his question yesterday and to it was attached the notes for supplementaries for the Min. of Defence"! Panic on the Govt. front bench, but mirth everywhere else. Ted was very good and didn't reveal what was in the notes! Awful row at the end of the debate – Healey[31] said the Conservative Party would need conscription to fulfil its defence commitments – pure electioneering and Jim Wellbeloved[32] was very angry. The Labour majority was down to 22 and he then accused the opposition of drunken behaviour and all hell was let loose

---

[29] John Enoch Powell (1912-1998), Conservative MP for Wolverhampton Southwest, 1950-February 1974. Unionist MP for Down South, November 1974-1987. Financial Secretary to the Treasury, 1957-8. Minister for Health, 1960-3.
[30] Willy Brandt (1913-92), Chancellor of West Germany, 1969-74.
[31] Denis Healey, Baron Healey (1917-2015), Labour MP for Leeds South East, 1952-5; Leeds East 1955-92. Created Baron Healey of Riddlesden, 1992. Defence Secretary, 1964-70. Chancellor of the Exchequer, 1974-9. Deputy Leader of the Labour Party, 1980-3.
[32] Alfred James Wellbeloved (1926-2012), Labour MP for Erith and Crayford, 1965-81; Social Democratic MP for Erith and Crayford, 1981-3.

– he eventually withdrew but not before he had successfully taken the eyes of the press off the slashed majority!

22.3.70

A good debate on Wednesday about B.O.A.C.'s[33] proposed take-over of B.U.A.[34] resulting in the Government's climb down and then insistence that BUA should negotiate with Caledonian to try and form a second live airline – good victory for Fred Corfield[35] who really has done his stuff as shadow aviation spokesman. Wed. evening I had the Adjournment about a teacher Mrs Green of Ascot-u-Wychwood who is being sacked, like 3,000 others, because she is "unqualified" – an N.U.T. racket to create a shortage of teachers. The debate went well - and afterward I went to the BBC to do a "Jack de Manio" programme which was well received in the constituency. This is a subject we must press. Friday morning spoke in the House on the Chronically Sick Disabled Bill 3rd reading and then home as I had to speak at the constituency A.G.M. at Blenheim. Full house of 270, Duke and all – went well, I think, and then a champagne and cheese party and then on to the Mayor of Banbury's Ball – oh! - and a surgery at Eynsham on Saturday – quite a tiring week and I look forward to Easter. The previous week we saw the bye-election at Bridgwater with an 8.3% swing to us and then this week at Ayrshire we had a swing of only 2.3% - the Labour victor was sharply anti-Common Market and this may account for his success – Scot. Nats. did fairly well but they are obviously on the wane.

29.3.70

Monday lunched with 6 French MPs from Normandy and Brittany – one interesting point emerged that they all disliked the Common Market on the ground that Brussels and Strasbourg were over 1000 km away from them while Britain was only 200kms from Normandy! They said they felt much closer to us than to CM!

---

[33] British Overseas Airways Corporation.
[34] British United Airways.
[35] Sir Frederick Corfield (1915-2005), Conservative MP for South Gloucestershire, 1955-74.

12.4.70

Certain traditional row over the guillotining of the Ports Bill to nationalise the Ports – I suppose it is good timing to have these rows. Had tea with the Swedish Prime Minister, Palme[36], on Tuesday – only 42, more like a young executive – he was anxious about the effect of some on EFTA[37] plus us joining the Common Market because of its effect on EFTA and NORDEK[38]. Mainly a quiet week except for the County Council and GLC[39] elections. We did well in the CC elections winning seats when we expected to lose them - and only losing 13 on the GLC. It looks as though an election in June is now less likely but we'll have to wait and see what happens in the Budget and the local Boro' elections. Friday we had an anti-CM meeting in Birmingham with Douglas Jay, Renee Short[40], Sir George Dowty[41] and self-speaking – went well but poorish attendance due to awful weather.

18.4.70

A busy week. Started off by speaking in the Foreign Affairs debate on the question of the Gulf saying that we should stay there and not hurry away – I think I got my point across even if we were a bit hurried. Tuesday was Budget Day and Roy Jenkins[42], having increased the employer's contribution, then "gave away" £100m admittedly quite sensibly. No pre-election vote catching here! But then with rising wages he was his own prisoner because of the danger of inflation as the result of the ending of prices and incomes policy – should never have started it! He sat down at 5.30 and I went post-haste to the A.T.V.

---

[36] Olaf Palme (1927-86), Prime Minister of Sweden, 1969-76 and 1982-86. Assassinated on 28 February 1986.
[37] European Free Trade Association.
[38] The organisation for Scandinavian economic cooperation. Proposed by Danish Prime Minister Hilmar Baunsgaard in 1968 but it did not survive as Denmark joined the EEC and Finland failed to ratify the agreement.
[39] Greater London Council.
[40] Renee Short (1919-2003), Labour MP for Wolverhampton Northeast, 1964-87.
[41] Sir George Dowty (1901-1975), inventor and businessman. Knighted for services to industry in 1956.
[42] Roy Jenkins, Baron Jenkins (1920-2003), Labour MP for Southwark Central, 1948-50; Birmingham Stechford, 1950-77. Social Democratic Party MP for Glasgow Hillhead, 1982-7. Chancellor of the Exchequer, 1967-70. Home Secretary 1965-7 and 1974-7. President of the European Commission, 1977-81. Chancellor, University of Oxford, 1987-2003.

studios to do a broadcast. Having been sent to the wrong studio, I just made it by 6pm – lousy interviewer – pro-Labour. In the evening went to the theatre with the Smedvig's[43], Newmans and the Kirbys. Wednesday went with Estimates Committee in the morning to see examples of pornography and how the Customs deal with the attempts to import it. Quite interesting and it was a good example of the moving line of the permissive society – how what was regarded as pornographic 10 yrs ago is now acceptable and normal. Lunched at the Dorchester with Smedvigs and spoke in Chelsea in the evening to their YCs. Saturday was Judith's wedding and I had to propose the toast of the bride/groom. Too many speeches in one week!

26.4.70

Tuesday at London Airport all day examining Customs and Excise for the Estimates Committee. Wednesday the 1922 Committee lunch for Ted Heath at the Savoy – sat between Earl St. Aldwyn[44], Chief Whip Lords and Tony Barber[45], Chairman of the Party – a good lunch but only a moderate speech by Ted – he did it without notes and was the sort of speech he might have delivered the previous Saturday to the Central Council – full of the usual political points which MPs don't want to hear and not enough of the uplifting philosophy which Macmillan used to give us. Received a nice letter from Anthony Eden (Lord Avon)[46] saying he agreed with me over my speech in the Foreign Affairs debate – this was v. nice of him as he is a very sick man. Thursday lunched with the New Zealand High Commissioner and in the evening on Friday went to the Conservative Commonwealth Council meeting where Sir William Powell Barker[47] was presenting a paper on the Common Market – I waded in on an anti-market speech

---

[43] Torolf (1917-77) and Nora (1921-99) Smedvig, close friends of Neil Marten. Marten met Torolf in Norway during the Second World War organising the resistance to German occupation. Torolf's wife Nora had been imprisoned by the Gestapo and Marten assisted Torolf in freeing her. They attempted to capture the Gestapo officer, but he had fled. Marten kept the German commander's hat and iron cross as souvenirs. Torolf regularly entertained Marten at the Dorchester.

[44] Michael Hicks Beach, 2nd Earl St. Aldwyn (1912-1992), Conservative Chief Whip in the House of Lords, 1970-4.

[45] Anthony Barber, Lord Barber (1920-2005), Conservative MP for Doncaster, 1951-64; Altrincham and Sale, 1965-74. Conservative Party Chairman, 1967-70. Chancellor of the Exchequer, June 1970-4.

[46] Anthony Eden, Lord Avon (1897-1977), Conservative Prime Minister 1955-7.

[47] Sir William Barker (1909-1992), diplomat and Professor of Russian.

that got a lot of support and rather set the cat among the pigeons. Alec Douglas-Home[48] replied and was very kind altho not in agreement.

3.5.70

Went to London on Sunday night in order to speak to the Anguillans at Slough – I am President of the 'Friends of Anguilla"! About 60 of them present and I spoke of my views about the future – they received them well. A charming group of people – I really enjoyed it even though it was a Sunday night! Monday visited the Stratford customs depot with the Estimates Committee - a vast place for customs clearance inland obviously ready to receive a lot more business. Tues. and Wed. we debated the Ports Bill to nationalise the ports and on Wed. evening we had a good anti-CM meeting at Caxton Hall with Arthur Bryant[49], Derek Walker-Smith[50], Douglas Jay, Reg Prentice[51] and Michael Foot[52].

Meanwhile, all the week the debate goes on about the date of the next election – polls continue to wobble at a small Conservative lead if they are averaged out. The trend is definitely to Labour if one looks at those halcyon days of a year ago with us on a 24% lead! If I were the PM I would go in June/July because by autumn the cost of living will have risen considerably. On the horizon too is the falling stock market, unemployment, further US involvement in Cambodia which shall split the Labour Party again. But we shall see how Labour does in the local elections next week.

---

[48] Sir Alec Douglas-Home, Baron Home of the Hirsel (1903-1995), Conservative Prime Minister, 1963-4. Foreign Secretary, 1970-4.
[49] Sir Arthur Bryant (1899-1985), historian. Bryant was a patron to several anti-Common Market organisations in the 1960s and 1970s.
[50] Sir Derek Walker-Smith, Baron Broxbourne (1910-1992), Conservative MP for Hertford, 1945-55; East Hertfordshire 1955-83. Created Baron Broxbourne, 1983. Sir Derek was a prominent anti-marketeer and formed 'Derek's Diner' and the 1970 Group after the 1970 election to organise, with varying results, Conservative anti-marketeers.
[51] Sir Reg Prentice, Baron Prentice (1923-2001), Labour MP for East Ham North, 1957-74; Newham North East, 1974-9. In 1977 Prentice defected to the Conservative party. From 1979 he sat as Conservative MP for Daventry, 1979-87. Knighted, 1987. Created Baron Prentice of Daventry, 1992.
[52] Michael Foot (1913-2010), Labour MP for Plymouth Devonport, 1945-55; Ebbw Vale, 1960-83; Blaenau Gwent 1983-92. Leader of the Labour party, 1980-3.

10.5.70

On Monday evening I went to see Ted Short[53], Minister of Education, about "unqualified teachers" – this is a constituency case I have been running for several months. In 1968 an agreement was made between the Minister of Education, local authorities and N.U.T. that the teaching profession should be completely 'qualified' as teachers - and that by Aug. 1970 all 'unqualifieds' should get the sack. In Nov '69 at my Witney surgery I received a delegation from Ascot-u-Wychwood about the teacher at the primary school, Mrs Green, who had been teaching since 1945 and prior to that she was from 1933-39 – but she had no qualifications. The parents, governors, and local education authority all wanted her to stay on – but when the Minister was asked he said No. So I gave the story to the *Daily Telegraph* and they published it. I then had an adjournment debate and 6 Con. MPs joined in. I then started a correspondence in the *D. Tel.* in which the new Secretary general of the N.U.T. joined in. This resulted in 70 cases from all over the country being referred to me. I then put a motion on the order paper of the Commons and got 32 signatures. The pressure began to build up. I had PQs to the Minister and eventually went to see him with 5 other Con. MPs and we each put our cases to him. We made an impression, and he has agreed to consider our individual cases and I believe he will do something about it. It is an interesting example, if we succeed, how far a surgery case can affect national policy by using the BBC, national papers and pressing a just case because the elderly teachers in the villages throughout the country have given and are giving wonderful experience and it is quite stupid to sack them; they should be phased out. When the vets, architects, engineers, dentists etc. went all professional they allowed those unqualified to stay on. On Thursday the Lab. left wing staged a debate on the USA advance into Cambodia and there was a division with 68 MPs voting against the Govt. – the left were <u>furious</u> with Michael Stewart[54] the Foreign Secretary for his support of the Americans. The PM wound up (much against his will) and was quite odious in the way he failed to support either his own Foreign Secretary or the Americans.

Thursday were the Borough Council elections – we lost one seat in Banbury and one in Norton – not too serious but there has

---

[53] Edward Short, Baron Glenamara (1912-2012), Labour MP for Newcastle upon Tyne Central, 1951-76. Deputy Leader of the Labour party, 1972-6.
[54] Michael Stewart, Baron Stewart of Fulham (1906-1990), Labour MP for Fulham East, 1945-55; Fulham, 1955-79. Twice Foreign Secretary, 1965-6 and 1968-70.

certainly been a return to Labour – the Lab. Party was very active in Banbury, too, so the party workers have obviously returned. What a change from 12 months ago – when Labour was abstaining and tearing itself to bits over Prices and Incomes and Trade Union reform – it only goes to show that the political memory is 6-9 months! Reason of the return to Lab. is pretty clearly the impression that Govt. policies over balance of payments is working and of course wages explosion means more money in the pocket.

Spent Friday with the N.F.U. and in the evening debated the Common Market with the Young Farmers with Peter Davis[55] against me. It was put to a vote and the result was exactly the national average 65% against 20% for. Peter D. was furious that there was a vote - and threatened to resign from the Conservative Assoc. – although it had nothing to do with them! It shows what a dreadful "religion" the CM is with some people.

17.5.70

Much feeling in the country that, the swing to Labour, will make the PM go for an election on 18 June – he has many advantages if he does, including 4½m people on holiday (mostly Tories!). Everyone seems to think it will be the 18th if the PM can make up his mind.

24.5.70

On Monday afternoon 18 May the PM went to the Palace to seek dissolution for a General Election on 18 June. The Polls were running strongly in his favour with Gallup giving Labour a 7% lead but others somewhere between 2 and 3%. With the fear of rising prices and the balance of payments showing signs of having reached the top, he was under considerable pressure from his own party to go for it – many of us thought he may have been lured into it by the volatile polls and that he has made a book. However, he has decided. The rest of the week was spent feverishly preparing my Broadsheet and election address and generally preparing for the fight. My betting is that either party could win by 20 seats, that the polls will swing back to us during the course of the campaign, and that my majority will be much the same as last time, possibly up a bit. Since the announcement the Cons. have been on the attack and one feels things are perceptibly moving our

---

[55] A member of the Banbury Conservative Association.

way. We were all summoned to a briefing meeting with Ted at Church House – he made an excellent speech and then we had lunch and a detailed briefing. A splendid innovation.

31.5.70

Parliament reassembled on Tues. 26 to finish off 3 days. Pretty dull stuff as there were no divisions – we tried to concoct a few rows and had some fun but all to no avail. I spoke on the Finance Bill and moved an amendment to get road fund tax exemption for disabled passengers – nearly got it but not quite – called a division and the Govt. Chief Whip was furious! Then spoke at the Chronically Sick and Disabled Bill at 1am and home to Swalcliffe by 4am! Work on election address and on election preparation generally. Afternoon meeting at Blenheim Palace, Duke and Marquis and all and 348 people – went very well. By contrast the Labour candidate had 45 at his and the Lib had 10 at his (and spoke for 1hr 45mins compared with my 30 mins!) 4 meetings on Sat. night in the villages – better attended than 1966 so far. Polls beginning to move our way Gallup lead of Labour cut and O.R.C. gives Tories 2% lead – we are on the way (with luck) but H. Wilson[56] is being quite foul in his approach.

21.6.70

The General Election 1970 is over and won by the Conservatives with an overall majority of about 30! Very interesting. The Opinion Polls went just haywire giving Labour a lead of anything between 7 and 12%! But in this constituency the canvas returns coming in (and we had a total of 52,000 canvassed) showed about a 5% swing to Conservatives – we in fact got a 4.9% swing! – this was so in many other constituencies, yet the polls never really discovered it. I would imagine that the electors had never in fact returned to Labour – the bye-elections certainly seemed to confirm this. Harold Wilson said he never took any notice of the Polls and said anyhow he had decided on the date in 1966! So he can't complain. But I am sure he was lead [sic] to take this decision by the polls and he will be highly unpopular with his own party for having taken it. Yet he was in an awkward position because the wages explosion would lead to far greater inflation by the

---

[56] Harold Wilson, Baron Wilson of Rievaulx (1916-1995), Labour Prime Minister, 1964-70 and 1974-76.

autumn and the balance of payments is likely to slow. So he hadn't much option. He fought a 'personal' campaign and a very silly one – he merely attacked the Tories, put forward no policies of his own and was devious. I believe the result was because the electorate was fed up with his lies and wanted a man of integrity with policies.

The Election for me took the usual form – 70 public meetings, canvassing in various places, "meeting the people" in the markets, etc, etc,. Spoke to 2,944 people – meetings better attended than '59, '64 or '66 altho' total slightly down due to World Cup on T.V. on some nights. Motored 1,573 miles and answered 388 questions. Glorious weather throughout – farmers mostly haymaking and many people on holidays. The first election with the 18 yrs. vote and polling until 10pm. And the result even taking these factors into account and the failure to make the boundary redistributions, was a real defeat of Labour and Wilson in particular. My result was exactly as predicted – I had forecast a vote of 37,000 Cons. all the way through the election based on canvas returns and got 36,712! This was 53.4% and a 4.9% swing to me. Labour (Booth) got 25,166 and Lib. (Fisher) got 6,859 forfeiting his deposit – my majority was 11,546, up from 4,400! No complaints being in the 5 figure bracket. Lab. really expected to win by 4,000! They based their optimism on canvassing the Brecon Hill estate in Banbury and the Smiths estate in Witney and of course in both places could expect to do well – so were totally misled. They had no organisation at all in the county, having tellers on 7 polling stations outside Banbury only (out of 97). All of ours were manned all day and supported by committee rooms and we got the voters in on the day. Liberals manned one polling station! They really have no idea. I imagine the Labour organisation collapsed completely in 1967/8 over the Prices and Incomes policy and never recovered. All neighbouring constituencies did just as well as us. Now back to battle on Common Market!

28.6.70

Spent Monday winding up affairs and went to London on Tuesday to take back all my papers and get the flat set up again. At about 5pm the telephone rang and it was No. 10 – "the Prime Minister to speak to you" – it was Ted simply to say he would like me to join the Government but there was the difficulty of my views about the Common Market – he asked if I had changed them. I replied that I hadn't and that it would be dishonest of me to say I would, just to join the Government. I said that, if I did join, I would of course have to keep my mouth shut about it as I did with Macmillan and Alec D-H but the crunch would come if there was a debate on it when I would have to vote on it. He said that would not be very satisfactory for him. Anyhow, he thanked me for being honest with him and he would think it over. The next day Wednesday 27th I was back at Swalcliffe and No. 10 came through at 6.30pm again, "The Prime Minister wants to speak to you" and Ted said he had thought it over and decided that, for the moment, it was better if I didn't join – the implication being that when the negotiations were concluded one way or another he would think again. We had an agreeable chat. I thanked him for thinking of me in the first place and said I thought he was right from his point of view! Not so sure really - he might have done better to tie me up – now I am free to campaign again and look forward to the prospect, but it won't be nice fighting our own side. The solution might well be if we can get enough Tories to guarantee to vote against it and not be persuaded to yield we could block any chance of it getting through the House – if Labour voted against it!

Thursday we gave a small dinner party for the builders who did our house last year and Friday Ascott-u-Wychwood school gave a party for us to celebrate the granting of qualified status to Mrs Green! It was a v. nice gesture and one which made it really worthwhile being an MP – I must confess I felt proud of what had happened!

5.7.70

We met on Monday 29 June to elect a Speaker. Tremendous cheers for Ted and same for Wilson! I must say that Wilson made the change, which must have been very hard for him, very well – he slid naturally into opposition. Some Ministers looked broken, others seemed to enjoy it. Robin Turton[57], Father of the House, and Jack Ashley[58] (Lab.) (deaf) proposed Horace King[59] and off he went to be Speaker again – I don't think he will stay for long – my bet is that next year he will be

---

[57] Sir Robin Turton, Baron Tranmire (1903-1994), Conservative MP for Thirsk and Malton, 1929-74. Like Walker-Smith, Turton was a leading anti-marketeer.
[58] Jack Ashley, Baron Ashley of Stoke (1922-2012), Labour MP for Stoke on Trent South, 1966-92. Created Baron Ashley, 1992. Ashley was deaf for most of his parliamentary career and, like Marten, campaigned for the rights of the disabled.
[59] Horace Maybray King, Baron Maybray-King (1901-1986), Labour MP for Southampton Test, 1950-55; Southampton Itchen, 1955-71. Speaker of the House of Commons, 1965-71. Marten was correct, King was elevated to the Lords in 1971.

elevated to the Lords and someone like Derek Walker-Smith or Selwyn Lloyd[60] will take over. Next day we signed in and in between we aligned the anti-Common Market forces and had a few meetings! Thursday was the State opening in all its glitter and pageantry – televised again – Mountbatten[61] holding the Sword of State, nearly fainted as did Field Marshal Montgomery 2yrs ago. A good speech from the throne with plenty of Conservative policy therein. Mary Louise[62] went in the Royal Gallery! The debate on the Address was pretty dull fighting the election all over again.

On Friday I had a most tedious meeting with my President John Schuster, Chairman Jack Friswell and Harry Webb who all tried to dissuade me from carrying on my anti-CM campaign. Jack F. threatened to resign! I really do deplore this attempt to influence me in political activities – it shed an awful light on all three – but enough for the moment.

12.7.70

All this week the debate on the Queen's speech continued – lots of maiden speeches – some very good new MPs certainly on our side and some on Labour's side. Labour seem very sour about being beaten at the election and are still (understandably) fighting it in the House! Thursday I had a meeting with the Disabled Drivers in the House of Lords with Lord Crawshaw[63] and others plus racing driver Graham Hill – charming person who has taken an interest in disability since his crash. Had a successful meeting on the CM with a lot of antis and some good new antis. Ted spoke at the 1922 and went over well. W/end was our delayed silver wedding anniversary – family dinner party and a really enjoyable w/end – a very happy one.

---

[60] Selwyn Lloyd, Baron Selwyn-Lloyd (1904-78), Conservative MP for Wirral, 1945-76. Foreign Secretary, 1955-60. Chancellor of the Exchequer, 1960-2. Speaker of the House of Commons, 1971-6. Made Life Peer, 1976.
[61] Louis Mountbatten, 1st Earl Mountbatten of Burma (1900-79), Viceroy of India, 1947; Governor General, 1947-8. Chief of the Defence Staff, 1959-65. Murdered by the IRA in County Sligo, Ireland, 1979.
[62] Marten's daughter.
[63] William Brooks, 4th Baron Crawshaw (1933-1997).

19.7.70

The sooner we rise the better – Parliament is in a negative state. Tuesday evening 14 July we celebrated our actual wedding anniversary with Andrezj Panufnik and Camilla at their riverside house in Twickenham – we had a ride down the Thames on twin cabin cruiser and then a good boozy supper. The only other thing of any note in the week was the election to offices of the various Committees. We had a good anti-Common Market lobby to vote in our nominees and we had a meeting beforehand to brief everyone. I wrote the agenda for the meeting and put it on the board for MPs for Derek Walker-Smith as Chairman [of Foreign Affairs Committee] – he claims he never got it – I believe he did and then left it somewhere – anyhow it pretty clearly fell into "enemy" hands and there was a substantial election with lots of "pros" turning up to vote. So I was not voted as vice-Chairman of the F.O. Committee!! But I was elected to 1922, where we have Harry Legge-Bourke[64] as Chairman (he is almost anti) and 4 antis, 6 wobblers and 7 pros amongst officers and executives. This is fairly satisfactory.

26.7.70

What a week! On Monday we debated the Royal Proclamation by the Queen giving the Govt. extraordinary powers to cope with the dock strike. The dockers are striking about the level of the basic wage when they are actually earning £30-£50 a week! The basic wage is low but if it is raised then all the other rates, etc, go up and they get a whacking rise. The Govt. is encouraging a settlement (as Wilson used to) because somehow we have got to stop these inflationary settlements. In the evening I did a BBC broadcast on Arms to S. Africa – it all arose because I signed a motion that if we did send arms for the external defence of S. Africa it would in no way imply approval of apartheid. The political commentators tried to make it seem as a split in the party and in fact it was done with the approval of Sir Alec D-H, Foreign Secy., and was completely in line with his statement. I got a lot of ill-informed letters on the subject, the right saying damn you the left applauding me – all were wrong – just shows what a few mischievous commentators can do! However, it earned me £10 fee with BBC – I did

---

[64] Major Sir Harry Legge-Bourke (1914-73), Conservative MP for Isle of Ely, 1945-73. Chairman, 1922 Committee, 1970-2.

the broadcast with the Earl of Lauderdale[65] who on the way back to the House told me an amusing story. At the last party conference he came into the hall as I was making my anti-CM speech and stood next to Douglas Dodds-Parker[66] who said to him "If Neil goes on like this he will lose his seat" - 11,546 majority compared with 4,000 when <u>he</u> last stood[67]!

On Tuesday morning we heard that Iain Macleod[68], Chancellor Exchequer, had died from a heart attack – he had had his appendix out a couple of weeks earlier and returned home and it must have been post-operative trouble. Poor Iain, at the summit of his career, after years of labour as Shadow Chancellor and determined to make drastic changes – a tragedy for his family and the party and his country. Tuesday afternoon we had tributes to him and by far the best came from Jeremy Thorpe in a most moving speech. His wife had been recently killed in a car accident and this was his first appearance in Parliament since. He told me afterwards that he felt this was the moment to come back – he delightfully said that at moments such as this the House of Commons reacts as a family.

On Wednesday I went to Caroline Thorpe's[69] Memorial Service at Westminster Abbey - packed - address by Archbishop of Canterbury and violin solo by Yehudi Menuhin who played Caroline's and Jeremy's favourite Bach concerto. Most moving, again.

Then we went on to debate arms to S. Africa – lots of emotion again from Labour. Alec made a bad speech and was muddled and over-tired. But the day was saved by an excellent wind-up speech from Robin Balneil who dealt entirely with the defence aspect and he had the Labour Party absolutely silent! The Commonwealth (black) are being very stupid about it but we have to stand up for British interests now and again and this is one case. Thursday was a mixed day, too. City in the morning, lunch with the Board of Securicor and

---

[65] Patrick Maitland, 17th Earl of Lauderdale (1911-2008), Conservative MP for Lanark, 1951-59. Chairman of House of Lords Select Committee on EEC Scrutiny, 1974-9.

[66] Sir Arthur Douglas Dodds-Parker (1909-2006), Conservative MP for Banbury, 1945-59; Cheltenham, 1964-74. Marten succeeded Dodds-Parker as MP for Banbury in 1959.

[67] A reference to Dodds-Parker's 4,125 majority in 1955, his last election in the Banbury seat.

[68] Iain Macleod (1913-1970), Conservative MP for Enfield West, 1950-70. Editor, *Spectator*, 1963-5. Chancellor of the Exchequer, 1970.

[69] Caroline Thorpe, née Alpass (1938-70), wife of Liberal party leader Jeremy Thorpe. She died in a car accident 10 days after the 1970 general election.

an invitation to go on the Board (which I gratefully accepted!). Then to the House – PM's questions and a series of statements on dock strike, etc, - Tony Barber had just started to make a statement on the Common Market negotiation when an object was thrown from the gallery – it rolled under the seat of the leader of the Opposition (he wasn't there) and I was sitting on the front bench below the gangway ready for a supplementary question to Tony – I thought it was a thunder flash but it didn't go bang but omitted white smoke! Then another landed by the mace and rolled to Tony and someone said it was C.S. gas and we walked out eyes running and coughing! The Whip on duty, not knowing the procedure, knew he had to do something so took a deep breath and said "I beg that this House do now adjourn" and was promptly sick. I went to the tea room and several people (jokingly) said "Neil, this is taking your anti-Common Market too far!" It was an Irishman demonstrating events in N. Ireland! It took 2 hours to clear and then we proceeded. Friday I did an hour's TV programme on the Common Market in a programme called "the Great Debate" with Duncan Sandys[70] and Dick Taverne[71] for the pros and Douglas Jay and me for the antis with an invited audience – a good idea but too short to be really worthwhile. In the evening a wine and cheese party at Chipping Norton and then the recess started 24 July – 27 Oct. and a good thing, too!

20.10.70

On 19 Oct. there was a meeting of the F&GP[72] called by the Chairman to discuss my Common Market attitude – full turnout except for one and they unanimously disapproved of the action and attitude of the President and Chairman! Game set and match to me! But the Chairman did reveal some very curious views on how he thought an MP should do what he is told. The committee was clearly <u>very</u>

---

[70] Duncan Sandys, Baron Duncan-Sandys (1908-1987), Conservative MP for Norwood, 1935-45; Streatham, 1950-74. Son-in-law of Sir Winston Churchill. A fervent pro-European, he formed the 'United Europe Committee' in 1947.

[71] Dick Taverne, Baron Taverne (1928-), Labour MP for Lincoln, 1962-1973; Democratic Labour MP for Lincoln, 1973-4. In 1972 Taverne was deselected by his constituency Labour party for his pro-EEC views. He triggered a by-election in his constituency, winning it with 58% of the vote. He lost his seat in the October 1974 general election to Margaret Jackson, who would become Margaret Beckett, future Labour deputy leader and Cabinet Minister.

[72] Finance and General Purposes Committee.

disapproving of him and the President. I really feel it is going to be extremely difficult to carry on working with him. Anyhow, it is an example of how with right on your side it is right to stand up for what you believe in – had I conceded, I would have been giving into pressures, a thing no MP should ever do because once you do it, where does it end?

1.11.70

Parliament reassembled on Tuesday 27 when the new Chancellor Tony Barber announced his package deal of cuts to Govt. expenditure, reshuffling investment grants to allowances, and generally moving towards making industry and people stand on their own feet more – also 6d off income tax! It went well with the Conservatives and Labour were furious because it took away so many of the Socialist props for cosseting all and sundry. It went over quite well in the country. In the evening drinks at the French Embassy and then dinner at the Turf Club with Sir Charles Mott-Radclyffe[73] – he gave a splendid dinner party for his old chums to celebrate his retirement from Parliament – those there included Lords Butler (Rab)[74], Hailes[75], Colerain[76], Brook[77],

---

[73] Sir Charles Mott-Radclyffe (1911-1992), Conservative MP for Windsor, 1942-1970.
[74] Richard Austen 'Rab' Butler, Baron Butler (1902-82), Conservative MP for Saffron Walden, 1929-65. Chancellor of the Exchequer, 1951-55. Leader of the House of Commons, 1955-61. Home Secretary, 1957-62. Foreign Secretary, 1963-4. He was feted as a possible Prime Minister but his heart was not in the fight.
[75] Patrick Buchan-Hepburn, 1st Baron Hailes (1901-1974), Conservative MP for East Toxteth, 1921-50; Beckenham, 1950-57. Governor General of the West Indies, 1958-62.
[76] Richard Law, 1st Baron Coleraine (1901-1980), Conservative MP for Kingston upon Hull South West, 1931-45; Kensington South, 20 November 1945-1950; Haltemprice, 1950-4. Author of works arguing against the increasing role of the state in politics, see *Return from Utopia* (1950) and *For Conservatives Only* (1970).
[77] Henry Brooke, Baron Brooke of Cumnor (1903-84), Conservative MP for Lewisham West, 1938-45; Hampstead, 1950-66. Home Secretary, 1962-4.

Thorneycroft[78], Selwyn Lloyd, John Peyton[79], Tufton Beamish[80], Phil Goodhart[81], Anstruther Grey (Lord?)[82], Spencer Summers[83], Dodds Parker, Jasper More[84], Steve Hastings[85], Bill Deedes[86], a wonderful mixture but what was the common theme? I know that Charles and I got on well because we had laughed about politics! Wednesday debated Parliamentary Constituencies and that went through.

Thursday, Geoffrey Rippon[87], now doing the Common Market negotiation, made a statement on the Common Market negotiations. He was very bullish about success and rather irritated the House. He gives the appearance of giving too much away in advance and this will need watching. Friday up to Birmingham to do TV "Midlands Members" then back to London on Saturday to speak at a CPC Conference on the Common Market. Bless them, they let me make the opening speech and I was able to spike a lot of the usual pro-CM examples in advance.

---

[78] Peter Thorneycroft, Lord Thorneycroft (1909-94), Conservative MP for Stafford, 1938-45; Monmouth, 1945-66. Thorneycroft was Chancellor under Macmillan and resigned in protest at an increase of £50m spending in 1958.

[79] John Peyton, Baron Peyton of Yeovil (1919-2006), Conservative MP for Yeovil, 1951-83. Peyton stood against Mrs Thatcher in the second round of the Conservative leadership election in 1975, gaining 11 votes.

[80] Sir Tufton Beamish, Baron Chelwood (1917-1989), Conservative MP for Lewes, 1945-74. Beamish was a member of the Monnet Action Committee for United States of Europe, 1971-6.

[81] Sir Philip Goodhart (1925-2015), Conservative MP for Beckenham, 1957-92. Held a constituency referendum on EEC entry in 1971.

[82] William Anstruther-Gray, Baron Kilmany (1905-1985), Scottish Unionist MP for North Lanarkshire, 1931-45; Berwick and East Lothian, 1951-66. Ennobled, 1966.

[83] Sir Spencer Summers (1902-1976), Conservative MP for Northampton, 1940-5; Aylesbury, 1950-70.

[84] Sir Jasper More (1907-1987), Conservative MP for Ludlow, 1960-79. Resigned as a government whip in 1971 over EEC membership.

[85] Sir Stephen Hastings (1921-2005), Conservative MP for Mid Bedfordshire, 1960-83.

[86] William 'Bill' Deedes, Baron Deedes (1913-2007), Conservative MP for Ashford, 1950-74. Editor, *Daily Telegraph*, 1974-85.

[87] Aubrey Geoffrey Rippon, Baron Rippon (1924-97), Conservative MP for Norwich South, 1955-64; Hexham, 1966-87. After the reshuffle caused by the death of Iain Macleod, Rippon was promoted as Chancellor of the Duchy of Lancaster responsible for EEC entry negotiations.

8.11.70

A very busy week – masses of constituency correspondence and parliamentary work to get through – working until 2a.m. most nights. Wednesday and Thursday we had a debate on the Chancellor's statement. The Labour Party still very angry and tried every trick in the trade to wreck the debate – massive shouting and heckling (really disgraceful) and an accusation by a new left wing Labour MP that the Govt. was "fixing" Hansard by altering what the Chancellor had said. Subsequently it had been found to be completely bogus! The next day he apologised – he is part of Willy Hamilton's team of wreckers[88] - and a nasty lot they are, too – he apparently trains them!

Saturday, Armistice Day parade at Banbury on Sunday and then drive to Hereford to speak at Brockhampton Court at a Birmingham Y.C. w/end Conference. Here I deployed the argument that by joining in the CM it meant ultimately ending up in a United States of Europe where Britain would become a province – this went well and got a fair press.

15.11.70

Monday we had a debate on Rhodesia and the continuance of sanctions – the point being that if we are to negotiate a settlement with Smith[89] we don't want to give away this card beforehand. Labour said we should also say that sanctions would continue if no settlement is reached – Alec D-H said we would not go into negotiation on the assumption that negotiations would not succeed! 25 Tories voted against, but Labour supported Cons. Govt. Tuesday lunch with Lord Campbell about the Common Market and made tentative arrangements to visit Mauritius, Australia and N. Zealand after Xmas. Thursday elected to Anglo-American Committee – met Rippon at F.O. Committee to hear about negotiations. He really was rather pompous and evasive and he will get a bad name if he goes on like this. I imagine that, altho' he tries to give the impression that things are going well, there are some formidable obstacles and I am still hopeful,

---

[88] The MP who made the accusation *was* Willie Hamilton, Labour MP for Fife West. Hansard, Commons Debates, 4 November 1970, Vol. 805, Col. 1105.

[89] Ian Douglas Smith (1919-2007), Prime Minister of Rhodesia, 1964-79. Declared unilateral independence in 1965. Since then there had been a bitter row in parliament, and the Conservative party, over sanctions implemented by Harold Wilson. Marten was not a supporter of Smith.

in spite of de Gaulle's death, that the French will say no[90]. Friday wine/cheese party at the Ballards and then on to the Executive at Woodstock. No troubles there and I was pretty firm about the Common Market! On Saturday I went to Banbury to meet representatives of the Chamber who were distributing sugar as a warning against the Commonwealth Sugar Agreement being thrown overboard by joining the CM – glad to see the Chamber getting in the act!

22.11.70

Spoke at Warwick University on Monday evening – on Common Market again! OK but the University was filthy and the students pretty grotty! Tuesday lunch with the Canadian High Commissioner – a nice but rather dull man. Wednesday spoke at London University on Foreign Affairs and in the afternoon we had the first meeting of the action group of all-party MPs of the anti-CM – this is a coordinating committee to discuss tactics and is chaired by Robin Turton Father of the House and has 6 Cons. and 6 Lab. M.P.s; Derek Walker-Smith, John Farr[91] (for agriculture) Harmar Nicholls[92], Ronald Bell[93] (legal), self. Lab. has Douglas Jay, Peter Shore[94], John Silkin[95], Alf Morris and others. Thursday a dullish debate on Defence. Friday spoke on CM at Rugby and Saturday again on CM at Malvern (West Midlands C.P.C.) – a lot of anti CM-speaking – but it _must_ be done. The latest Poll (O.R.C.) gives 64% against entry and 29% for. We must continue these meetings all over the country because, with the exception of the _D._

---

[90] French President Charles de Gaulle vetoed British membership of the EEC in 1963 and 1967.
[91] Sir John Farr (1922-97), Conservative MP for Harborough, 1959-92.
[92] Sir Harmar Nicholls, Baron Harmar-Nicholls (1912-2000), Conservative MP for Peterborough, 1950-74.
[93] Sir Ronald Bell (1914-1982), Conservative MP for Newport, May 1945-June 1945; South Buckinghamshire, 1950-74; Beaconsfield, 1974-82. Anti-marketeer who would face deselection in 1972 because of his anti-EEC views. Bell's death in 1982 caused a by-election in which the Labour candidate was one Tony Blair.
[94] Peter Shore, Baron Shore of Stepney (1924-2001), Labour MP for Stepney, 1964-74; Stepney and Poplar, 1974-83; Bethnal Green and Stepney, 1983-97. Secretary of State for Economic Affairs, 1967-9. Secretary of State for Trade, 1974-6; Environment, 1976-9. Contested Labour leadership in 1980 and 1983, coming last in both.
[95] John Silkin (1923-87), Labour MP for Deptford, 1963-74; Lewisham Deptford, 1974-87. Contested Labour deputy leadership, 1981, coming third.

Express, all papers are either passionately for or neutral and so are the T.V. companies. It is certainly true, in spite of all that, the pros are failing to make headway. The next operation is to make constituents write to their MPs – this will give the wobblers something to think about!

On Sunday we went to drinks with the Courages at Edgecote before lunch to meet the Queen Mother. She was her superb self looking wonderfully young and charming. We spoke about the time she came to Witney by helicopter and landed on the newly cut grass and the rotors of the helicopter covered us all in grass cuttings! Then we got onto politics and she said she doesn't like the CM project – she put it well and said the British people did not want to go in by instinct. She was remarkably interested in politics and spoke quite frankly about it.

29.11.70

Monday we debated the additional aid to Rolls Royce – Labour looked rather silly as they were responsible for the form of contract which gave rise to part of the trouble. Mr Marshall, Dep-PM of New Zealand came to talk to us about CM – very good explaining how CM would affect NZ agriculture. Wednesday farewell to Kuwait Ambassador at Claridges followed by Services dinner; and Thursday did a BBC broadcast in the morning and then we had the debate on Industrial Relations in the afternoon. It was to take note of the Consultative Document. Robert Carr[96] opened extremely well but when the Solicitor General[97] wound up he was treated to a continual series of interventions, cat-calls and interruptions – he simply was not allowed to speak one sentence at a time – disgraceful behaviour which does no good to Parliament. Quiet w/end – needed!

---

[96] Robert Carr, Baron Carr of Hadley (1916-2012), Conservative MP for Mitcham, 1950-74; Carshalton, 1974-76. Secretary of State for Employment, 1970-2; Leader of the House of Commons, 1972; Home Secretary, 1972-4.
[97] Sir Geoffrey Howe, Baron Howe of Aberavon (1926-2015), Conservative MP for Bebbington, 1964-66; Reigate, 1970-4; East Surrey, 1974-92. Solicitor General, 1970-2; Minister of State for Consumer Affairs, 1972-4. Howe was central to the controversial legislation of the Heath administration, the Industrial Relations Act and the Prices and Incomes policies, the latter branded the Heath 'U-turn'. He was a reforming Chancellor from 1979-83, but fell out with Mrs Thatcher as Foreign Secretary thereafter. His resignation in 1990 precipitated the fall of Mrs Thatcher.

6.12.70

Spoke on Monday, in a rather silly debate on a private motion by Alf Morris, saying that "the Conservatives did care about inflation"! It gave me a good opportunity to have a go at Alf with whom, altho' he is Labour, I have worked on many things – disabled, anti-CM. etc. Good thing to be seen to oppose him now and again! In the evening there was a debate on the dismissal of Lord Hall[98] as head of G.P.O. – he was <u>most</u> inefficient and Chris Chattaway[99] sacked him – Lab. reacted with a censure motion in the heat of the moment and when it came to the debate they had no case to make and fell flat on their face. Chris was <u>excellent</u>. Otherwise it was a dull week with fairly formal stuff – Air Corporations Bill, Coal Bill etc. – lots of meetings on CM where things seem to be going well for us, the latest Gallup Poll gave 66% against and 16% for joining CM! One of the best yet and it shows that in spite of all the pro-propaganda, there has been a slight shift to us. Also a week of lunches, cocktail parties and dinners. Lunched with British Airport Authority and sat next to Aubrey Jones[100] who is quitting the old Prices and Incomes Board. He said he was very pro-CM but being in touch with the heads of all Depts. in Whitehall, he only knows of one head of Dept. who thought we would get in! Also there was Sir George Edwards[101] of British Aircraft Corporation whose pet project the BAE 3-11 had just been turned down for Govt. funds – anything available had gone to Rolls Royce the previous week – so BAE may buy the Lockheed 10-11 - and if Lockheed goes bust this will be a grave embarrassment and to Rolls too who make the engine for Lockheed.

13.12.70

This week started well with an electricity black-out. The electricity workers had put in a wage claim for some 30% - the Electricity Council

---

[98] William Hall, 2nd Viscount Hall (1913-85), Chairman of the Post Office, 1969-70. Hall's *Times* obituary (27 June 1985, p. 10) claims his dismissal was political, that Hall would resist privatising parts of the post office.

[99] Sir Christopher Chattaway (1931-2014), Conservative MP for Lewisham North, 1959-66; Chichester, 1969-74. Minister of Post and Telecommunications, 1970-2.

[100] Aubrey Jones (1911-2003), Conservative MP for Birmingham Hall Green, 1950-65. Chairman, Prices and Incomes Board, 1965-70.

[101] Sir George Edwards (1908-2003), industrialist and aircraft designer. Chairman, British Aircraft Corporation, 1962-75.

put in an offer of 10% that was rejected. So the workers decided to go slow: not strike, because they are not allowed to. Loads were reduced and we had regional blackouts for 2 or 3 hours a day at a time. In the Commons MPs had candles to read the aide papers and as the afternoon wore on it got very gloomy, so some oil lamps were produced which improved things a little – one was put in the aisle beside where I was sitting – the tall and haughty Hugh Fraser failed to see it and knocked it over! It began to burn and David James[102] (Dorset) picked it up and took it out – it was a good sight to see him rushing out with a flaming oil lamp and he brought the House down when still holding it he stopped at the Bar, turned to the Speaker, bowed and then continued on his way only to appear a few seconds later calmly walking in with another lamp! The go slow continued all week, against a background of mounting public anger, many letters saying "stand firm". The Government did everything in its power to get the Elec. Council to stand firm – but in the end it is for the Council to decide. The workers did not give in but on the Saturday the Government took Emergency Powers – this should make the workers think. They refused to go to arbitration.

Geoffrey Rippon made a statement on the Common Market and the antis and the pros – both interrupted him – he really was vague. The Speaker, Horace King, announced his decision to retire at the end of the year – altho' he had been a good Speaker he was obviously getting weary of it all – it must be an awful strain. The Government announced that they and the Shadow Cabinet had decided on Selwyn-Lloyd to succeed adding that nevertheless it was a "House of Commons matter"! Apparently the option was John Boyd-Carpenter[103] or Selwyn and they invited the Shadow Cab. to make their choice. The Shadow Cab. opted for Selwyn by 8-4, primarily, I'm told, because they believe he won't last too long, that he will be "easy" and when they get back they can nominate Fred Peart[104]! All the wrong reasons – in addition to that Selwyn has been a controversial politician with Suez and nurses pay pause[105]. Then all hell broke loose

---

[102] David James (1919-1986), Conservative MP for Brighton Kemptown, 1959-64; North Dorset, 1970-9.
[103] John Boyd-Carpenter, Baron Boyd-Carpenter (1908-1998), Conservative MP for Kingston upon Thames, 1945-72.
[104] Fred Peart, Baron Peart (1914-1988), Labour MP for Workington, 1945-76.
[105] He was Foreign Secretary during the Suez crisis in 1956 and Chancellor from 1960-62 during which time he instituted an unpopular pay pause in the public sector.

because neither party had consulted the back-benchers! We were all very umbraged and the more so because many thought that John could be the better and firmer Speaker, he is more coherent, is married (and Speaker is a lonely job). So we started a pro-John lobby rolling on a bi-partisan basis – Sir Brandon Rhys-Williams[106] leading it up – the Government must <u>not</u> behave like this. Sir Harry Legge-Bourke Chairman of the 1922 was very pro-Selwyn and did not behave very well in failing to call a meeting of the Executive when he first heard about it.

The workload is getting fairly heavy – masses of correspondence and many many meetings on CM – I find myself working until 2am most mornings and up at 7.15 – but I feel mightily sleepy by Friday!

20.12.70

Monday and Tuesday we debated the new Industrial Relations Bill on 2nd reading – it went far more peacefully than most expected – I imagine H. Wilson has told his party to behave properly! On Tuesday we had a meeting of the CM Safeguards Committee and invited Geoffrey Rippon to come! He was severely quizzed and totally failed to give any convincing arguments! More people seem to be having doubts. I got a letter in *The Times* about the vote on the CM and brought in the point that Ted Heath had said in Paris (5/5/70) that "it would not be in the interest of the Community that its enlargement should take place except with the full hearted consent of the Parliaments and peoples of the new member countries". The question is how does the Government judge if it has the full hearted consent of the peoples? Without a referendum it would be difficult – so I suggested a referendum first and then a vote in the House, thereby leaving the final decision to Parliament! This is a line I am now plugging and it seems to be gaining in strength. Debated the CM at the Royal Commonwealth Society with Dick Taverne – an enjoyable and sensible occasion. Saw the New Zealand, Canadian, and Mauritius High Commissioners about the CM in private meetings.

Meantime the row over the Speaker rumbles on. Increasing backbench dissatisfaction at the way it has been handled. But all the tactics are being employed to get Selwyn into the chair. The case the

---

[106] Sir Brandon Rhys-Williams (1927-88), Conservative MP for Kensington South, 1968-74; Kensington, 1974-88.

Govt. raise seems to centre on not having a split, not backing anyone and that dear old loyal hard-working Selwyn 'should have a pension'. Hardly a word on the really important question of who would be the best Speaker of the House at this time. Every time the Govt. is criticised for the way it handled it, it falls back on the argument that it is following precedent! It is a shabby performance and they know it. Harry Legge-Bourke was really off-side at the 1922 Committee. He summed it up that it was the feeling of the meeting that the Govt. nominee should be supported – not so! He made an awful emotional appeal to loyalty etc! The "very honourable steady knights of the shires" can be very un-honourable when they want to be!

A minor flash back to this time last year – when I sent H Wilson a card for his 30th wedding anniversary. I met him outside the loo in the voting lobby – he stopped and reminded me of it and said if I was in the Swan at Minster Lovell I was to have a good bottle of Burgundy on him and send him the bill!

24.1.71

On 1st Jan. I took off for a trip around the world. Flew to Sydney Australia in one go – 36 hours by Quantas via New York, San Francisco, Honolulu, Fiji. Arrived to face a large press interview at the airport at 7.30 a.m.! Got in many points about the CM, sugar and the Australian farmers and got a good press. Next day meeting with the Colonial Sugar Refiners and lunch. Alf Morris (Lab), his brother Charles[107] (Lab) and William Clark[108] were there, too. Next day to Canberra to meet the head of their Board of Trade to hear about the Government's views on sugar, dairy produce, and fruit if we should join the EEC without proper safeguards. It is clearly going to be hard on them as such a high percentage of their exports come to UK.

Flew next day Thursday 7th to Auckland NZ where was met by Minister of Housing, Rea, and Tim and Peter Nevins. Press Conferences again at airport, broadcast on radio, another on T.V. and endless Press Conferences! I put the NZ's in the picture on the CM – not what they had been lead [sic] to believe! Visited meat freezing factories, dairy plants, and sheep farms. It is clear that the sheep farmers will suffer greatly as they send 90% of their lamb exports to

---

[107] Charles Morris (1926-2012), Labour MP for Manchester Openshaw, 1963-83.
[108] Sir William Clark, Baron Clark of Kempston (1917-2004), Conservative MP for Nottingham South 1959-66; East Surrey, 1970-74; Croydon South, 1974-92.

U.K. - and the tariff barriers will hit them badly. People, by the thousands, will suffer. Spent the night with Tim Nevins at his farm, good dinner! And then went on to meet a group of farmers and spent the evening talking to them. They <u>hated</u> the idea of joining CM because partly of their business and partly because of their belief that it would ultimately sever their links with the UK and the Crown – they feel this <u>so</u> strongly. Next day on to New Plymouth by car where I was met by Sir Roy Jackson[109] the Speaker of NZ Parliament. Was taken around dairy factories, had meetings with farmers, journalists etc. and went on and on for <u>hours</u>. Then a dinner given by the Speaker and some much-needed sleep. Next day visited a rhododendron garden up in the hills – beautiful site and on to lunch with a farmer who had a lot of friends to meet me and tell me their anxieties. Flew to Wellington with David Thompson[110], NZ Minister of Defence, and met Alf Morris who had come down from Australia. Monday (11) meetings with the Dairy Board, Meat Board, Foreign Office, Federated Farmers, lunch in Parliament, dinner with Sir Arthur Galsworthy[111] our High Commissioner. Next day, flew to Sidney [sic] – sat with Sir Keith Holyoake[112], NZ Prime Minister, and disabused him of some of his ideas on CM. Free afternoon so went to the Test Match and saw England beating Australia! What a noise they make with the beer can chorus on the hill! But completely uninhibited and that was a pleasure. Next day flew on to Mauritius, overnight and landed in the lovely warmth. Was whisked off to meet the acting PM Mr. Ringdoo[113] and our High Commissioner and lunch with Chamber of Commerce – a lovely island, Indians, Creols, Tamils, Hindus, Moslems and French. Sugar forms 90% of their exports so any cut back would have a desperate effect upon unemployment and would lead to political battles with the Maoist parties making a strong bid for power. Had tea with the Governor General, Sir Len Williams[114] ex Sec. Gen. of Lab. Party – splendid, just like the last century. Indian servants, tea on the

---

[109] Sir Roy Jack (1914-1977), Speaker of the New Zealand House of Representatives, 1967-72 and 1976-7.
[110] David Thomson (1915-1999), New Zealand Minister of Defence, 1966-72.
[111] Sir Arthur Galsworthy (1916-1986), UK High Commissioner to New Zealand, 1970-3; UK Ambassador to Ireland, 1973-6.
[112] Sir Keith Holyoake (1904-83), Prime Minister of New Zealand 1957, 1960-72. Governor-General of New Zealand, 1977-80.
[113] Sir Veerasamy Ringadoo (1920-2000), Governor General of Mauritius, 1986-92. 1st President of Mauritius, 1992.
[114] Sir Len Williams (1904-72), Governor General of Mauritius, 1968-72.

terrace, sponge cake and stayed at a lovely hotel by the sea, <u>glorious</u> swimming, spent all Saturday, until my Lufthansa plane took off at 6pm, on the beach. Flew back via Dar-el-Salam, Nairobi, Entebbe, Cairo, Frankfurt.

Arrived back to the usual stack of work! But it was really worthwhile as it gave me the facts I wanted for my anti-CM campaign. Straight into the Industrial Relations Bill and an all-night sitting and then a 2-day debate on CM through which I sat and was not called! Pity as I had a lot to say! But it was an <u>excellent</u> debate particularly speeches by Douglas Jay, Peter Shore, Derek Walker-Smith and Enoch Powell. In the debate itself we won <u>hands</u> down – the pros, including Tufton Beamish, were really <u>pathetic</u>.

31.1.71

Several people on the Conservative side have left the pro-camp as a result of the debate – most of them have not become anti – but they have moved away from the definite pro camp – we do have one or two more recruits to the antis – the grey area in the middle is large and fluid. The pros are depressed and getting a bit nasty! – an interesting sign. The battle is certainly hotting up – the pros are spending a six-figure sum on their propaganda effort! We have little money, a few thousand only so we must use every channel of communication to the public. I have this week written letters to the *Daily Telegraph*, *Economist*, written an article for *The Times* and the *Spectator* and a French broadcast. I have 2 T.V. appearances coming up and a lecture at Chatham House. It is taking up most of my time. Jim Callaghan[115] had a private gossip with me and told me that while he had never been a violent pro he was not going to alter his position until the terms are known – my bet is that he will do so then. Bumped into Harold Wilson and he told me he had just dictated a paragraph about me in his book – I thought it must be about the P.Q. and/or the New Year's Eve postcard! Spent a good time with Alec D-H in the smoking room talking about the Commonwealth Prime Ministers Conference – he was most amusing. Next day spent an hour with Ted Heath (as a member of the Executive of the 1922) and he too was full of very funny

---

[115] James Callaghan, Baron Callaghan (1912-2005), Labour MP for Cardiff South, 1945-50; Cardiff South East, 1950-83; Cardiff South and Penarth, 1983-7. Held all four great offices of state: Chancellor, 1964-7; Home Secretary, 1967-70; Foreign Secretary, 1974-6; Prime Minister, 1976-9.

stories. Anyhow the PM came out of it really well and the Govt. is actually now on a better footing – the air has been cleared, I hope.

Much of the week was spent on the Industrial Relations Bill under heavy opposition attack. First the Guillotine Motion, getting to bed at 5am! Tuesday 2am, Wed. 3am, Thursday 5am – quite a week. The final farce came on Thursday when the Guillotine fell up to Clause 20 and only 10 Clauses had been discussed. So at midnight Lab. decided to vote against all the remaining clauses and we solemnly, on that day, had 28 divisions and between 12 midnight and 5am we voted 20 times! No debate allowed, just voting. Then some Lab. members sang the Red Flag! Quite a week – a bit silly but perhaps understandable on their side.

7.2.71

Thursday Rippon made a vacuous statement in the House on the CM negotiations and irritated everyone by avoiding saying much about the failure to get near agreement on the initial contributions to the Community Budget, we are miles apart on this altho' of course it is the final permanent level of contribution which really matters, probably £500m a yr. Then there was the shattering announcement that Rolls Royce had gone bust and that the Govt. was taking over the aero engine part i.e. 'nationalising' – quite right: my view is that if private enterprise cannot take it over then the Govt. had to – it supplies 208 airlines and 85 Air Forces with engines and could not be allowed to die. But it looks as though, if the Americans and Lockheed do not help, the RB211 will go down the drain. Went on ½ hr T.V. programme with Eamon Andrews[116] on that subject and the Common Market.

14.2.71

The week was once again dominated by Rolls Royce and Industrial Relations. Some misgivings in Cons. Party about our handling of RR case – we have virtually said Lockheed can whistle for their money and this is bad for Britain's standing in commercial dealings. Also many want a fixed date by when the Govt. must come to Parliament to ask for continuing powers. It seems as tho' the Govt. is moving into rough waters! Tuesday Common Market (anti) dinner – went well but

---

[116] Eamonn Andrews (1922-87), TV presenter.

a few of the old ones (Burden[117] particularly!) were a bit stupid. Thursday did two broadcasts in French, one on Belgian radio and one on French Canadian T.V. An active anti-CM week in Parliament one way or another!

21.2.71

Monday Consolidated Fund and free for a change. Did T.V. with Norman St. John Stevas[118] on the Common Market – 1922 Committee Party for the lobby in the evening. When I walked in Boyd of the *Guardian* congratulated me on winning the battle of the CM! He reckoned that we now had enough to block it in Parliament – Robert Carvel[119] of the *Evening Standard* did the same and so did 2 others – it seems clear that the top lobby correspondents believe we won't get in! Tues/Wed. spent on the Industrial Relations Bill – 4am bed! Thursday lunch to discuss sugar and the CM and a riotous censure motion on prices and unemployment. Unemployment is at above 700,000 and prices are shooting up – the political commentators urge us to have a compulsory prices and incomes policy – I hope the Govt. won't yield to any such pressure. It looks as tho' wage claims are dampening down – this is the only way – but the workers are creating the unemployment by their wage demands – the firms simply cannot employ so many people and have little profit left for investment.

28.2.71

Monday was a short debate on the Post Office strike – it still goes on and no one seems to worry very much – the local postmen must be very fed up with it. Tuesday and Wednesday were the last days of the Industrial Relations Bill Committee Stage – 4am bed on Wednesday! We marched 8 miles through the division lobbies on it!

Launched my anti-CM motion (Private Members Ballot) on Wed. eve with a Press Conference and it went quite well – was in *The Times*, *inter alia*, first edition but struck out of subsequent editions! Dined with Peter Emery[120] to meet Senator from USA – one of the other

---

[117] Sir Frederick Burden (1905-87), Conservative MP for Gillingham, 1950-83.
[118] Norman St. John Stevas, Lord St. John of Fawsley (1929-2012), Conservative MP for Chelmsford, 1964-87. Leader of the House of Commons, 1979-81.
[119] Robert Carvel (1919-1990), journalist.
[120] Sir Peter Emery (1926-2004), Conservative MP for Reading, 1959-66; Honiton, 1967-97; East Devon, 1997-2001.

guests was Geoffrey Rippon, he was aggressive and started by asking how my "Communist friends" were! He must be hard put to descend to that level! Friday met young French party in Commons and explained U.K. attitude to EEC – shook some of them. Executive Committee of Association in the evening at Burford – harmless. Dined on Saturday evening at All Souls with Douglas Jay – had an entertaining time over the port sitting between Jo Grimond[121] and Douglas – too much port, tho!

7.3.71

Defence debate on Monday and Tuesday – statement on Mid East and whether we would stay there – I think Alec D-H has probably got the best he can out of it although it doesn't satisfy the right wing. However, Alec gave the impression that he would be able to achieve something but of course negotiations are confidential! The 'left' of the Party (including oddly on this occasion Enoch Powell) want complete withdrawal from the Gulf – this I think is wrong because it will leave a vacuum which the Russians will fill – our forces will be small and largely for training purposes but can be reinforced and this will be the deterrent. We shall see how it works out. Tuesday I delivered myself a lecture at the Royal Institute of International Affairs on the case against joining the Common Market – spoke for 50 minutes with Lord Gladwyn[122] in the front row! I think it went well! Sir Fred Catherwood, Chairman of N.E.D.C.[123], was my chairman – he gave me a lift on the way back and said he too was against joining the CM! A powerful ally[124].

---

[121] Jo Grimond, Baron Grimond (1913-1993), Liberal MP for Orkney and Shetland, 1950-83. Leader of the Liberal Party, 1956-67.
[122] Lord Gladwyn Jebb, Baron Gladwyn (1900-1996), acting Secretary General of the United Nations 1945-46.
[123] National Economic Development Council, also known as 'Neddy'.
[124] Sir Fred Catherwood (1925-2014), Director General of the National Economic Development Council, 1962-71. Conservative member of the European Parliament for Cambridgeshire, 1979-84; Cambridge and Bedfordshire North; 1984-94. Catherwood's *Times* obituary (4 December 2014, p. 72) states he was a 'passionate' supporter of Britain's membership of the EEC.

21.3.71

Industrial Relations Bill Mon., Tues. and Wednesday – tedious but it ended each night at about midnight. Tuesday escaped for an hour and went to a pub to welcome C.P.A. delegation for the current conference. Spent ¾ hour in the smoking room on Tuesday evening with Jack Ashley (Labour) who is stone deaf but who can now lipread – he rather sweetly wanted to consult me to see if I thought he was being too rude to the PM at question time.[125] His trouble is that he cannot hear reactions of the House to his supplementaries so I agreed that if I was in my place when he was on his feet I would try and indicate to him how it was going!

Rippon had his next meeting in Brussels with CM Ministers on Tuesday – headlines in the papers were "Common Market negotiations at their lowest ebb" – pleasing news to me! Apparently Geoffrey only had 90 minutes with them and made no progress. The Six[126] Ministers, meeting the day and night before, failed to agree on New Zealand agricultural exports, Commonwealth sugar and the British contributions to the Community Funds during the transitional period. No progress at all! The French obviously want to spin the negotiations out because we want them finished early by June/July – death by slow strangulation? Then after the meeting, on the following day, the French announced they wanted to settle the sterling problem before entry – this is a major problem. The question I ask at this stage is whether the French are merely being difficult in order to extract the maximum out of the negotiations for France or whether they do not want us in and are merely trying to make things so difficult and protracted that we give up. Certainly the public won't stand for much more of this and we cannot really give way. So, as for today, it looks as though we won't get in. Sweden decided this week to say no to entry, primarily for reasons of neutrality, foreign policy unity and monetary union. Norway's Govt. broke up (coalition) and the

---

[125] Ashley had asked the Prime Minister when he would make a national broadcast on the Government's record. The quip in question was a sarcastic jibe that 'the programme "Dad's Army" would be in serious danger of losing its audience'. Hansard, Commons Debates, 16 March 1971, Vol. 813, Col. 1185.

[126] Germany, France, Belgium, Italy, the Netherlands, and Luxembourg were known as 'The Six', as in the six founding members of the EEC.

Socialists have taken over leaving Mr Borten[127] the now ex-PM of the Centre party (who is anti) to lead a campaign against entry.

28.3.71

On Monday we had F.O. questions and set upon Geoffrey again! All we seemed to get were non-answers because he had nothing to say. I feel sorry for him in a way – but if he was more forthright about things he would get better treatment. Tuesday was the last day of the report stage of the Industrial Relations Bill and Labour staged a stupid demonstration. When the guillotine came down, they decided to vote on all outstanding clauses. Voting started at midnight and went on until noon Wednesday! We had some 65 divisions and, all in all, I reckoned we walked 5 miles. But it passed quite agreeably and the discipline amongst the Conservatives was excellent but not so Labour – our majority went from 30 to over 100 at times! My knees ached a bit at the end because there wasn't much sitting down - and certainly no sleep. But we must review the procedure whereby this farce doesn't happen again. So having entered the House at 12 noon Tuesday I left it again 12.30 afternoon Wednesday! Back at 2.30 for questions and a meeting with some U.S.A. journalists from Brussels and then back to the flat for 2 hrs sleep before returning for the final 3rd reading vote at midnight. And so it went to the Lords.

An odd thing happened during the 'sponsored walk' – Michael Clark Hutchison[128] and I saw in the early edition of the *Daily Mirror* (at 3am) the news that the Government was publishing some fact-sheets on the Common Market and distributing them free via the Post Office. We took it up with Willy Whitelaw[129], Leader of the House, who was reported as being responsible and asked him if it was true. He flew into a rage, snatched the press cutting from me, tore it in half and hurled it on the floor – trembling mightily and gripping his fingers like a man possessed, he shouted "I will not have my

---

[127] Per Borten (1913-2005), Centre Party Leader and Prime Minister of Norway, 1965-71.
[128] Michael Clark Hutchison (1914-1993), Conservative MP for Edinburgh South, 1957-1979. Anti-Common Market.
[129] William Whitelaw, Viscount Whitelaw (1918-99), Conservative MP for Penrith, 1955-83. Leader of the House of Commons 1970-1972. Held many senior positions in government: Leader of the House of Commons, 1970-2; Secretary of State for Northern Ireland, 1972-3; Employment, 1973-4; Home Secretary, 1979-83; Deputy Prime Minister, 1983-88. Created Viscount Whitelaw, 1983.

colleagues believing Mirror reporters rather than me" – whereupon I slowly picked up the paper and explained I was merely asking if it was true. He then calmed down and said he knew something of it and would enquire. Later that evening Tony Royle[130] (F.O.) told me it was true but that the pamphlets were "objective"!! They weren't of course. The previous week Willy W. had done the same to me about another matter over the Common Market – completely lost his temper because in the Expenditure Sub-Committee on Education I had asked the Treasury for a paper on the effect on our available resources if we did enter the CM on the terms we proposed. This apparently caused an uproar in the Treasury and Willy was upset because he said he was responsible for starting the Expenditure Committee and I had caused him embarrassment! My doubt is that a man who can go almost berserk twice in a week like that is hardly fit for high office – delightful a person he is. However, it made for an entertaining break in the all night walk!

Thursday I went to visit the EEC HQ at Brussels with Robin Turton, Peter Shore and John Silkin. We had a good series of meetings with the heads of depts. and this confirmed (a) they did not expect and could not justify the growth rate which we are told would be dynamic (b) they were all set for a Federal system of a United States of Europe (c) they wanted us in to help put things right particularly vis-à-vis the French (d) they all said the Common Agricultural Policy was a nuisance. The day before there had been a battle in Brussels with the farmers – two killed and 140 in hospital – over farm prices – compare this with our Price Review! At lunch I was able to argue informally with them and showed them the opinion polls moving steadily against entry in particular the last one this week which gave 66% against entry and only 22% in favour. Back from Brussels at 10pm and dined with Smedvigs at the Dorchester.

Friday Joan and I went to Jersey where I was to speak at the dinner of the Chamber of Commerce. Lovely w/end, nice people, Peter Baker looked after us and we spent a lot of time at his home by the sea. I made my speech and spoke against the CM – this went well because Jersey is against joining – they are a tax haven and low income tax and they attract many people and firms this way. If we join, they will have to harmonise their tax to the CM V.A.T. at the level set by CM – this will clobber them. I told them I would watch their interests.

---

[130] Anthony Royle, Baron Royle (1927-2001), Conservative MP for Richmond, 1959-83. Minister of State at the Foreign Office, 1970-4.

Reverting to the CM and Willy Whitelaw, as part of his pacification, he asked me to his room for a drink during which he said he knew the PM had offered me a job and that I had turned it down and he admired me for this and regretted it but hoped it would come right in the end. The PM, during a vote, was behind me and I was moving slowly – he tapped me on the shoulder and said "Come on, go faster Mr Europe"! I replied "I am going as fast as our negotiations"! He was good humoured about it – which is v. nice.

4.4.71

Budget on Tuesday, excellent performance by Tony Barber - a nice sense of humility; such a change from the arrogant Roy Jenkins. He cut £546m in taxation which added to the October cuts was a total of £951m. He honoured many election pledges and was enormously popular with the Tory Party he got a standing ovation, first time ever, I believe for a Chancellor in modern times. Pensions were raised and Bank Rate cut on Thursday. He has put £345 [mn] in cash resources into industry. All this should restore confidence. It was well received in the City. Dined with Dame Joan Vickers[131] in the evening with Commonwealth MPs. Wednesday had a meeting in the F.O. with Alec D-H – a general chat with the F.O. Committee. Lunched with Australian sugar people and went to debate the CM at Maidstone with David Crouch[132] (pro) - good meeting 250 – mostly anti-CM Stayed night with John Wells[133]. Thursday spoke at Bicester at a dinner – spoke on Budget and Friday spoke to Oxfordshire Monday Club on CM in Oxford.

25.4.71

Reassembled. F.O. questions and we had a good one on CM. Dined with Sir Keith Holyoake, N.Z Prime Minister, at L'Escargot in Soho – he was in good Commonwealth heart, and we talked a lot about the CM. Tuesday Securicor Board meeting. Sat between Lord Brooke and

---

[131] Dame Joan Vickers (1907-1994), National Liberal MP for Plymouth Devonport 1955 beating Michael Foot by 100 votes. She contested Devonport as Conservative in 1964. Held the seat until defeated by David Owen in February 1974. Created Baroness Vickers of Devonport in 1975.
[132] Sir David Crouch (1919-1998), Conservative MP for Canterbury, 1966-87.
[133] Sir John Wells (1925-2017), Conservative MP for Maidstone, 1959-87.

Marquis of Willingdon[134] at lunch and they were about to start their stint on Industrial Relations Bill! They thought it might go on for a long time – they have no guillotine in the Lords! Thursday spoke at annual lunch of Norwegian Chamber of Commerce at Savoy – spoke on CM and said that political implications should be brought into negotiation – am now running this line. Friday evening spoke at Cons. Cwth Council meeting on alternatives to CM – went well.

2.5.71

Monday lunched at Chatham House at a meeting for Mr Bury[135], Australian Foreign Minister. He was extremely dull – professor type! Wed. did German T.V. on CM and got across some good points. In the evening debated CM at S. Kensington but it was too rushed as I had to leave to vote. We had a good anti-CM meeting of MPs and discussed tactics for the meeting of 1922 Committee – it should be good!

Unemployment has risen to 800,000 – not good – but it is largely due to low growth and squeezed profits and high wages settlements. Firms have had to sack people who are surplus to streamline costs as they cannot afford to pay them the higher wages. One day the penny will drop. However, sad as it is for a man to be unemployed, they are not too badly off these days. When the Budget works through, and confidence mounts, investment in industry will go ahead and jobs will return. We shall see!

On the CM, which takes up so _much_ of my time now, I hear on the grapevine that the Cabinet is getting less enthusiastic and is getting very vexed at the procrastination of the Six. Rippon is getting himself out on a limb. The unpopularity is good and the Govt. must take this into account. Also 1972 will be a year of major legislation for the Cons. Party prior to the election and to add the CM legislation will be unbearable on Parliament. So all hangs, or almost, on the next meeting May 11-13 in Brussels.

9.5.71

On Tuesday had a meeting with some Conservatives from constituencies who wanted to firm up a Conservative anti-Common

---

[134] Inigo Freeman-Thomas, 2nd Marquess of Willingdon (1898-1979), Liberal party whip in the House of Lords, 1948-9; Chief whip, 1949-50.
[135] Leslie Bury (1913-1986), Australian Minister for Foreign Affairs, 1971.

Market Constituency Group – we thought we would wait until after the May meeting at Brussels. Wednesday was the 1922 lunch and Prime Minister at the Savoy. At drinks beforehand he joked with me about our anti-CM campaign and we talked about his new boat. At lunch I sat at the top table between Lord St Aldwyn (Lords Chief Whip) and Peter Thomas[136] (party chairman) because I am on the Executive. During his customary 20-minute speech he mentioned most things – but not the CM – there was a lot of comment about this but I think it was because he knows the negotiations might break down and he knows too it is a divisive subject so why mention it! The same afternoon, under the shadow of the Deutschmark-Dollar crisis, we had Willy Brandt, German Chancellor, speaking in the Grand Committee room. He was good. With a weakening dollar money was pouring into Germany so they have closed their Banks. Under the EEC there is supposed to be a coordinated monetary policy on exchange rates because of the agricultural policy. Germany should re-value or float the mark – France wants her to slap on foreign exchange controls etc. – but I cannot see this happening. If there is disagreement it will lead to a glorious row in the CM. CM Finance Ministers will meet on Saturday and on Monday the German banks will have to re-open. Also on Monday CM Foreign Ministers meet to prepare their replies to our proposals for entry and on Tuesday Rippon meets them for the crucial meeting – what a setting!

On Thursday the 1922 Committee debated the CM – mostly on the tactics. It was quite a fair meeting with both sides taking part – I would say it showed just under ½ against, ¼ for and the rest neutral.

Friday was my AGM at Blenheim Palace. Lots of dreary admin then I spoke on Govt. policy over wages and inflation, etc., and general policy after which I went on to my tours of Canada, Australia, NZ, Mauritius and my visits to Brussels rounding it off with the anti-CM theme! My Chairman Friswell was <u>not</u> pleased – no matter.

16.5.71

The Germans <u>did</u> float the DM[137] – French anger! The big thing of the week was Rippon's negotiations in Brussels – there was a tremendous puff by the Establishment and the Press to launch it - and after the

---

[136] Peter Thomas, Baron Thomas (1920-2008), Conservative MP for Conway, 1951-66; Hendon South, 1970-87. Conservative party Chairman, 1970-2. Welsh Secretary, 1970-4
[137] Deutschmark.

second tedious day we heard about a great "breakthrough" over Commonwealth sugar – the Press hailed it as a great event - officials said "we are in"! But when we read about the details it was pretty clear that, far from getting the "bankable assurances" he demanded for specific quotas after the end of the CSA[138] in 1974, all he got was a statement from them that the enlarged community would "have at least" to safeguard the interests of those developing countries where economies depended heavily on the export of primary products and notably sugar. This was back into square one and meant nothing at all. If he carries on like this, he will cease to be trusted so far as his judgement is concerned. We created hell in the Press and in Parliament and on radio and T.V. and the penny dropped – interestingly, the subsequent week-end press shared this view and took him to task. He promised to consult the sugar producing countries – they won't agree – so he will have to go back to Brussels and negotiate, I suppose. Even the pro-marketeers like de Freitas and David James were shocked. The next stage is Ted going to meet Pompidou[139] on 20/21 May – if he comes back with nothing about New Zealand, over which public feeling is very sharp, it might well be the beginning of the end of the negotiations.

Tuesday I saw the Indian High Commissioner for 1 hour over the E. Pakistan problem – he was very worried lest the awful economic situation there should lead to an anarchist take over – he said Britain and UN should get together over this. Friday we flew to Aberdeen to speak at a meeting on the CM. Sir Tufton Beamish was saying why we should go in and I why not and then there was a debate and a vote – the antis won. Just previously in the Scottish Party Conf. they had voted in favour of going in – this shows the loyalty to Alec! Back to Aberdeen and plane to London – Alec D-H was on the plane, too, and I told him of our debate – he seemed amused. Undoubtedly the CM is coming to the boil and anxieties in Parliament are increasing.

24.5.71

Monday Rippon answering questions on CM and in particular on the so called 'breakthrough' on sugar – it transpired that the form of agreement was in no way acceptable to Parliament – Geoffrey got a real roasting and the PM was there to see it. He must sense the

---

[138] Commonwealth Sugar Agreement.
[139] Georges Pompidou (1911-74), President of France, 1969-74.

difficulties of getting through any agreement which is not up to scratch. Tuesday did a T.V. programme with Eamon Andrews on the sovereignty issue of joining CM. Also did French T.V. and BBC radio with Maurice Edelman[140] on CM. A very busy week. Tuesday evening went to see Marshall[141], dep. PM of New Zealand (together with Robin Turton and Derek Walker-Smith) to tell him he had no need to concede anything on NZ dairy products as he had the country and Parliament behind him and if he did concede the NZ opposition would defeat him at the next election. We were not convinced that he had a very stiff backbone on this and that he had been given "the treatment" by Rippon.

Wednesday down to Wilton Park Surrey to lecture 30 Europeans on why we should not go into CM – this shook some of them and did them good! In the afternoon Joan made a splendid speech at the Conservative Women's Conference saying that if PM took us into CM against will of people it would split the Tory Party – this hit the headlines and was frowned upon by the Whips! But it certainly stirred it up and fired a warning shot across his bows. In the evening as a member of the 1922 Exec. we entertained the Area Chairmen to dinner – again a vibrant discussion about the CM! Appeal to loyalty to Ted! How out of touch they are if they think that matters over the CM issue! All the week now is on CM. PM went to Paris to meet Pompidou for Summit. A rosy communique and the Press is glowing – but the test will come on 7 June and 22 June when Rippon has to negotiate the details, we await PM's statement on Monday – he will get a grilling! Friday NFU[142] day on horticulture very anti-CM. Then 3 village green meetings – CM (anti) all the time ending up with a brains trust with Dame Pat Hornsby-Smith[143] – again mostly on the CM and all anti.

30.5.71

PM made his statement on Monday – there were expectations of a standing ovation – but there wasn't one! He answered quite well but

---

[140] Maurice Edelman (1911-75), Labour MP for Coventry West, 1945-50; Coventry North, 1950-74; Coventry North West, 1974-5.
[141] Sir Jack Marshall (1912-88), deputy Prime Minister of New Zealand, 1960-72; Prime Minister, 1972.
[142] National Farmers' Union.
[143] Dame Patricia Hornsby-Smith, Baroness Hornsby-Smith (1914-85), Conservative MP for Chislehurst, 1950-66 and 1970-74.

made one big mistake – he was pressed to say that he wouldn't bounce the country into the CM by having a definite vote on the question in July. He said he wanted to keep his options open – this was a mistake – he should have said he would leave plenty of time for consultations. I asked him about federalism and he replied that he and Pompidou agreed that decisions would be made by the Council of Ministers and denied an effective European Parliament and Government. I simply do not believe this is realistic – it is the soft sell. Lunched Tuesday with the Butter Packers' Association who said that unless CM regulations were amended we could not mix our butter as we do now! Met High Commissioners of the sugar producing countries on Tuesday evening – they all said that Rippon's assurances were not good enough – quite right – they assemble next week with their Ministers and tell him so – I hope he will have to renegotiate the so called 'breakthrough' agreement. Debated at Hendon North with Norman St. John Stevas on CM and won the vote. Did a BBC programme with Roy Hattersley[144] on Thursday and then home after lunch for the "Whit recess" – one week and a damned busy one at that.

We lost the bye-election at Bromsgrove.[145] Our candidate said beforehand that the issues were CM, prices and unemployment in that order. We did not win Itchen Southampton either[146] and the candidate said beforehand 'If I loose [sic] votes it will be on the CM' – he did! So it is clear to me, at least, that the CM is an issue and the Conservatives are not holding support. I believe it is dislike of the feeling of being bounced into it and from this the loss of confidence in Ted. On one or two things he seems to be back pedalling, i.e., that we need the "full hearted consent of Parliament and peoples" now means only parliament; and again when I reminded him of his statement that if we joined the British would be the first to press for Parliamentary control of the CM now means only control by the Council of Foreign Ministers! I admit it's a bit hard to be held to every statement you make but it does begin to accumulate that the 'honest Ted' we sold to our constituents isn't quite this chap. If he obstinately forces us into the CM many feel that if it is against the wishes of the people we shall

---

[144] Roy Hattersley, Baron Hattersley (1932-), Labour MP for Birmingham Sparkbrook, 1964-97. Labour party deputy leader, 1983-92.

[145] The Conservative majority at Bromsgrove in 1970 was 10,874. Labour won the by-election in 1971 with a majority of 1,868.

[146] By-election caused by the retirement of the Speaker, Horace King. Labour won the by-election with a majority of 9,675, with 22,575 votes to the Conservative who polled 12,900.

loose [sic] the next election for certain - and then the daggers will plunge deep and cut off his head. I believe the only choice for him now is to accept that the terms are not right and use the next opportunity to say so - and he would be very popular – or is he too obstinate? We must discuss at the 1922. There is growing trouble in the Party – it will become very bitter if it goes on.

On Friday, Bloxham School Council, then drive to Matlock in Derbyshire to debate CM with Jim Scott-Hopkins[147]. It was in the town hall and about 120 people present – all went well but the audience was so very anti that the Chairman did not call for a vote to save the embarrassment to Jim, the local MP, who is pro! Spent a very pleasant evening with him afterwards at his home in Chatsworth Park gossiping until 2.20 am. He felt that if we don't go in Ted will have to resign – maybe. What about Reggie Maudling[148]?

From Matlock drove down to Oxford to interview Peter Oppenheimer[149] about the economics for the ITV film – then did a broadcast on BBC on the money flowing into the European Movement.

6.6.71

Wednesday went to Brussels for filming in front of EEC building for my ITV film. Thursday met parents about school bus and in evening spoke at St. Catherine's College Oxford on CM. Friday Bloxham for Founderstide where Sir George Edwards spoke and then to Bicester where the Con. Party invited us as guests with a view to the new seat! Sat. coffee morning in Club at Banbury, then to London to speak at big anti-CM Rally at Central Hall with Michael Foot, Derek Walker-Smith and Sir Arthur Bryant in the Chair – very well attended by 3,000 and good T.V. coverage and radio and I did French T.V. afterwards – a really successful rally that got things going.

---

[147] Sir James Scott-Hopkins (1921-95), Conservative MP for North Cornwall, 1959-66; West Derbyshire, 1967-79. Conservative MEP for Hereford and Worcester, 1979-94. Leader of the Conservatives in the European Parliament, 1979-82.
[148] Reginald Maudling (1917-79), Conservative MP for Barnet, 1950-74; Chipping Barnet, 1974-9. Chancellor of the Exchequer, 1962-4. Home Secretary, 1970-2. He became embroiled in the Poulson affair, so named after the businessman John Poulson.
[149] Peter Oppenheimer (1938-), academic and economist. Fellow of Christ Church College, University of Oxford.

13.6.71

Tuesday Parliament reassembled after a very short and busy recess – spent most of Tues., Wed. and Thursday at ITV station making my film on why we should not join the CM – it was a fascinating exercise of insight into how TV works (Thames, I gather, are particularly good) - their demand for accuracy was encouraging. The timing down to absolute seconds was also fascinating but slightly irritating as so much had to be cut out. On Thursday I went on TV. 24 hours about CM and Friday to Deauville for the "weekend sportif" we lost the tennis but had an <u>excellent</u> time and much chat about the CM. TV shadowed us.

20.6.71

Panorama with an invited audience on Monday and Tony Royle, Shirley Williams[150] and Peter Shore – it was reckoned the antis won the day. Tuesday eve. Speaker's dinner for Canadian MPs. Wed. spoke at Chelsea on CM and Thursday was my film on ITV – I believe it went well. Geoffrey Johnson-Smith[151] an expert on TV and MP for E. Grinstead said it was "the most professional thing he had seen of that type". The CM still underlies our every action – the Party is getting into a mess and I quietly fear for its future.

27.6.71

Rippon's statement was on Thursday 24th. On Mon. 21st we had F.O. PQs and Alec was answering on CM and did not do very well - at a party that night he said to me, laughingly – "never again will I do CM PQs on my own!" Tues 22nd lunched at *Spectator* – odd lot! Friday spoke at Rugby CPC[152] on CM with John Wilkinson[153] – very good

---

[150] Shirley Williams, Baroness Williams (1930-2021), Labour MP for Hitchin, 1964-74; Hertford and Stevenage, 1974-9. Social Democratic MP for Crosby, 1981-3. Secretary of State for Education, 1976-9. Founder member of the Social Democratic party, 1981. Made Baroness Williams of Crosby, 1993.

[151] Sir Geoffrey Johnson Smith (1924-2010), Conservative MP for Holborn and St. Pancras South, 1959-64; East Grinstead, 1965-83; Wealden, 1983-2001. TV presenter and journalist.

[152] Conservative Political Centre.

[153] John Wilkinson (1940-2014), Conservative MP for Bradford West, 1970-4; Ruislip Northwood, 1979-2005. Initially a pro-marketeer, Wilkinson's views changed and he became a eurosceptic. He was one of the 7 Conservative MPs to

debate and he did well – but it was overwhelmingly anti. Saturday a glorious row broke out. I was to attend Banbury branch Conservative Fete and got a letter from the Agent[154] saying that the Banbury Town Central Committee had decreed that I should confine my remarks to thanks only – I decided not to speak and the Press asked why so I told them – pow! Up it went – MP gagged etc.! Maybe it will clear the air.[155]

4.7.71

Monday Geoffrey Rippon made his final statement on the negotiations – got a reasonable reception and was more polite (too much so for some!) to the House. He brought back 'terms' for NZ and our contribution to the budget – terms perhaps better than we expected (thanks to anti-CM activities). But underlying was a suspicion that all was not being told – time will tell, as details become more available. The fight is now on and we must mainly concentrate on the political implications as I have always said. Tuesday, Securicor Board meetings and Sr. Colombo[156] Italian PM spoke to us in Committee on CM – smooth and not impressive as he was too vague. Meetings with Gerald Nabarro[157], Enoch Powell, Derek Walker-Smith, Angus Maude and self to plan an anti CM meeting at Brighton for the Conference in October. Then another meeting that evening to launch our anti-CM Conservative organisation in constituencies[158] – went well and Roger Moate[159] took chair v. well.

11.7.71

Finance Bill report stage Mon., Tues. and Wed. – I moved an amendment to relieve disabled passengers from paying for car licences

---

lose the whip in 1994 by refusing to vote with the government on the EC Finance Bill. Richard Body joined them in sympathy.

[154] Harry Webb.

[155] It did not clear the air. This was to be the start of the long-running dispute between Neil Marten and his constituency Association.

[156] Emilio Colombo (1920-2013), Italian Prime Minister, 1970-2.

[157] Sir Gerald Nabarro (1913-73), Conservative MP for Kidderminster, 1950-64; South Worcestershire, 1966-73. Anti-marketeer.

[158] This was the Conservative Anti-Common Market Information Service (CACMIS), formed in June 1971.

[159] Sir Roger Moate (1938-2019), Conservative MP for Faversham, 1970-97. Moate chaired CACMIS.

£25 and an estimated total £25,000. My opening speech was to quote extensively from Maurice Macmillan's[160] speech when he moved the same clause two years ago from opposition – a dirty trick, but it worked. About 20 other people spoke in support and no one in favour [of the government]. The Royal Garden Party was on and the front benches had agreed no divisions until 7 pm – but that didn't concern me and I threatened to call a division when the Govt. would have been defeated – so the Chancellor was called and he gave in and he accepted the new Clause. Quite a triumph and I got plenty of praise (thanks to the Queen!). I was told that this was the first time since Winston Churchill had been Chancellor in the early 20's that the Govt. had given away in the House across the despatch box. The then junior minister, Mr Samuel, was sacked the next day and made Lord Mancroft[161]! Common Market White Paper the next day - and a buzz of T.V. and I did 24 Hours with Rippon, Lever[162] and Shore. Not a good White Paper, omitting the cost, omitting the loss in Cwth. Prefs.[163], making too many propaganda points and, in the end, I believe it will rebound against the European case and we shall see.

Thursday we discussed the issue of a free vote or a vote of confidence in the 1922 – as normal inconclusive! Saturday Blenheim Palace British Legion Parade 50th Anniversary – beautiful day and the Duke opened it. Had a meeting in the evening with my Chairman Friswell and we reached a better understanding on how to disagree!

18.7.71

Tuesday 1922 Executive met PM – rather useless discussion on CM, economy and Ireland – pleasant but not notable. Tues. eve went on BBC radio on what was called a "CM Marathon' with Reggie Maudling, Dennis Healey, Harold Lever, Barbara Castle[164]. It lasted 2

---

[160] Maurice Macmillan, Viscount Ovenden (1921-1984), Conservative MP for Halifax, 1955-64; Farnham, 1966-83; South West Surrey, 1983-4. Son of Harold Macmillan. Chief Secretary to the Treasury, 1970-2.

[161] Arthur Samuel (1872-1942), Unionist MP for Farnham, 1918-37. Financial Secretary to the Treasury, 1927-9.

[162] Harold Lever, Baron Lever of Manchester (1914-1995), Labour MP for Manchester Exchange, 1945-50; Manchester Cheetham, 1950-74; Manchester Central, 1974-79.

[163] Commonwealth trade preferences.

[164] Barbara Castle, Baroness Castle (1910-2002), Labour MP for Blackburn, 1945-79. Secretary of State for Employment, 1968-70; Social Services, 1974-6. Labour MEP for Greater Manchester North, 1979-84; Greater Manchester West, 1984-9.

½ hours with listeners phoning in with questions – good fun and I gather the listeners enjoyed it. Wednesday was our wedding anniversary and Joan dined at the House to celebrate. Thursday debated CM at Putney and won. Friday spoke on Anguilla Bill to give semi colonial status to Anguilla and separating from St. Kitts – this is what should have happened 3 years ago. Then back home to 3 village green meetings and finally supper with Dr and Mrs Jules who had invited about 60 people to hear my views on CM – they had done this because they were so furious with the local Conservatives for trying to gag me and twist my arms – v. nice of them. Sat. eve. Deddington Cons. barbecue and Sunday Drinks at Arkwrights in Swalcliffe and Dr Hudson in Banbury in evening. All chat about CM – it really is getting the most boring subject.

25.7.71

Monday we had a 'teach-in' on Anti-CM in Grand Committee Room. Sir John Winnifrith, Peter Oppenheimer, Peter Shore, a fisheries man – quite a good show. Ski Club reception in Lords to raise money for Olympic team. Spoke at Belgravia YCs on CM in evening. Tuesday did German Radio in morning on CM, lunched with Robin Oakley[165] (Crossbencher) – very agreeable type! Then debated CM at Chiswick in evening – they are having a referendum[166]. Wednesday played tennis against Lloyds (we won) and then gave them lunch in the Lords. CM debate (4 days) started in the House[167] – I was called 4th after the 3 party leaders and have asked to speak the following day. However, it seemed to go all right and got a fair write up in *Times*[168]. Sat through Thursday's debate and then had a quiet w/end with no engagements.

---

[165] Robin Oakley (1941-), journalist. Crossbencher columnist in the *Sunday Express*. BBC political editor, 1992-2000.
[166] Keep Britain Out was running an all-postal vote referendum in Brentford and Chiswick. On 26 July the result was declared, the turnout was 22%, with 5,439 against joining and 2,613 in favour.
[167] On 22 July, the European Movement took out a full page avert in *The Times* (p. 5). It listed celebrities and politicians advocating British, Danish, Norwegian, and Irish accession to the EEC. Names included footballer Jimmy Greaves, Sir Alec Guinness, Eric Morecambe, Laurence Olivier, Peter Ustinov, Henry Cooper, and Jilly Cooper.
[168] Marten warned that Tory MPs were being told to reject their election addresses and told the House that 'arm wringing' was beginning to be used by party managers (*The Times*, 22 July 1971, p. 8.).

I am trying to take the party politics out of the CM debate – it seems to be working – but we shall have to wait and see.

1.8.71

The CM debate ended as it started – pedestrian. Dennis Healey wound up and Reggie Maudling for us – they were both unenthusiastic! Tues. night debated CM at Oxford Business School with Dick Taverne – good fun.

Wed. back to Industrial Relations Bill (Lords Amendments). In the evening went to see Chairman of Party Peter Thomas and Chief Whip Francis Pym about arm-twisting over CM – Derek Walker-Smith and Robin Turton, too – it was an amusing session, DWS was at his most legal/pompous best – we asked him [Pym] to say publicly that he deplored arm-twisting but he wouldn't – anyhow it was a good shot across the bows. Thursday Ted H. came to 1922 and gave a speech – a technocrat – not inspiring. It seems to me that now Labour has voted in Nat. Exec. to oppose entry into CM it has become and will become more so a Party political affair – if only Ted had said a free vote at the beginning he might have been saved – but if he has to rely upon Labour votes he will be entirely a prisoner of Lab. during the consequential legislation – he really has stuck his neck out and could well be defeated now - and would have to resign.

8.8.71

Parliament teetered to an end this week. Industrial Relations all the week and rose on Thursday 5th. But CM seemed to dominate all behind the scenes. Two constituents came to see me and tried to persuade me to abstain! Our group seems to retain its determination to vote against. Plans for recess are roughly to prepare to revive opposition in mid-Sept. and in the meantime to carry on the campaign in the Press and by writing pamphlets. We had a congenial party for the antis and potential antis to show strength and stiffen the backbones of the wobblers. Thursday led a delegation to Minister of Loc. Govt. Graham Page[169] with Banbury Boro' Council about development of Grimsbury area. Then had ITV director Ian Martin and David Elstein

---

[169] Sir Graham Page (1911-81), Conservative MP for Crosby, 1953-81. Minister of State for Local Government, 1970-4.

to lunch - and so home to face the music on the CM in the constituency! We'll see.

26.8.71

And I did, too! Quite the most entertaining thing since I have been the MP for Banbury. In the early part of July my Agent said we should have a meeting of the Executive to discuss the report of the Finance and General Purposes Committee on arrangements for the constituency debate on the CM. The notice for the meeting went out on 19 July (5 days after the Chairman and President had been to see the Chairman of the Party, Peter Thomas, at Central Office!). The notice said "I am sure there is no need to stress the vital importance of this meeting". I smelt a rat and expected a row in some shape or form about my opposition to CM. But I let it rest on the basis that I was in the clear. My reason for feeling in the clear was that (1) I voted against applying to join in 1967 (2) I made my position absolutely clear at the AGM in early 1970 (with acclaim) (3) I was proposed for adoption by my Chairman Friswell in the full knowledge of my opposition to CM and out of 350 present there were no objections (4) at my meetings during the election I always said, when asked, that I would vote against it unless persuaded by argument that I was wrong and (5) I put it firmly in my election address that I was opposed to entry and (6) (see Oct '70 diary) the F&GP had backed me solidly against the President and Chairman. So everyone who voted for me (37,712) was on notice of my views. I really do feel in the clear. But, in the last few weeks, I have had a number of letters probably about 12 from the 'gentry' mostly couched in the same terms, that while they realised I was against it they would feel betrayed if I voted against it and asking me to vote for the CM – I find it really <u>revolting</u> that people who hold themselves out as the pillars of upright behaviour should behave in such a way, i.e., asking me to vote in a way which would mean me telling an enormous lie! It is clear to me from the pattern of the writers that probably John Schuster the Assoc. President had been persuading his chums to write to me - Friswell, too.

Then one day before the Executive fixed for Thursday 12 Aug, my Agent dropped in unannounced at home and gave me various papers including one, a sealed envelope, containing a notice to include on the Agenda of that meeting a resolution unanimously presented to the Executive by the F&GP from a meeting they had held on Monday 9 Aug. – to which I had not been invited. The resolution was:

"That this Executive Committee of the Banbury Division of the Oxfordshire Conservative Assoc. expresses its confidence in the Prime Minister and the Government in their domestic and foreign policies. We support the decision to join the EEC as an integral part of the Government's long term policies."

The rest of the Executive had been given the motion the day before and I was the last to be told! One day's notice of what was no more than a thinly disguised vote of censure on me after 12 years as the MP. I was rightly much annoyed by this. At least the Agent or Chairman could have let me know earlier – but it shows that they are prepared to play every dirty little trick in the book to do me down – just because I am sticking to my election pledge. The real trouble is that (I think) the Party has got into a panic about the vote on 28 Oct. They foolishly have given the impression of saying they are going to make it a vote of confidence and then Labour came out against it, and they must now depend on Labour dissident support to avoid defeat, assuming that 30 Tories will vote against it. They know they have got themselves in a difficult position and are now probably trying desperately to get Associations and Agents to get their MPs to change their minds - hope of OBEs or promotion?!! Anyhow it all seems to stem back to that meeting on 14 July with Peter Thomas, who, of course, fervently denies it!

The Executive duly met in Woodstock Town Hall on 12 Aug. at 7.30pm. There were all the usual faces, many of them not on the Executive at all but there as "alternates", a casual arrangement which has worked unnoticed in the past but now was being clearly exploited to put in friends of the President. Friswell in the Chair acting like a dictator. I was told I couldn't vote only being "an invited member" – a good start. Then Schuster made a speech proposing the motion which can only be described as fanatical in which he said that "the only thing which can now stop entry is the defeat of the Government and that the vote could be a close-run thing". Then, from the floor, it was proposed by Commander Jenkins that the motion be referred back because we were to have 5 debates and why pass the motion before the debates – quite right – I tried to speak to that but Friswell would not allow me! Then took place some of the wettest contributions from the floor as to why we should join the CM – really so stupid as to be useless – it was sad to see some of the local people who are regarded as one's friends and who a few months ago had been cheering me on in opposition to the CM now ratting on me and saying we must go in, merely because they fear the Govt. will be defeated – what a <u>gutless</u> lot. I was invited to wind up and expected to speak for some time, altho' I had been allotted 10 mins (without notice from the Chairman). After about 18 mins I was told to end before I had really got going. So I concluded by saying anyhow the resolution was bad because it said that entry into the CM was an integral part of Conservative Policy – I quoted the Manifesto which said we would only go in if the terms (eg. for N. Zealand) were right. If we had not got terms we would not have gone in and would have steamed on to success. However, they were in no mood to reason having been conditioned to vote for it regardless of the arguments. So the motion was passed by 49 to 10. After which we discussed the debates to be held and I won my point about them being public. I then said a few words in reply to Wilfred Fox who said that altho' he didn't agree with my CM views he thought I was a jolly good MP and had my confidence – no one opposed that! I thanked him and said a word about the integrity of MPs and announced that I would not seek adoption for Mid Oxon, the new seat, but would continue to sit in my present one. According to Area, this is merely a "minor boundary adjustment" and no re-adoption is necessary until the next election – I wonder very much if they will try and pull a fast one! Rumour has it that they will.

After that meeting, which frankly disgusted me and depressed me because of the behaviour of the President, Chairman, F&GP and many of one's friends, we adjourned to the 'Bear' where Stanley Knight and Richard Ratchille (CPC Chairman) were in a fury about it all and the row went on in a curious love hate relationship and beer! Sun. evening we drove home.

Next move was a Press Conference by Schuster and Friswell when they gave it to the Press on Monday. I heard about this so had one <u>immediately</u> after in the White Lion and trumped their remarks. And so it all got in the Press and Lois Hey of the Charlbury Branch was superb in denouncing it to the Press as a dictatorship and Stanley Knight of Kidlington was good too. Then it got into the nationals and it really made the Association look odd. It has done no good – only harm. So I must watch events locally now very closely – I feel they are up to no good and some want to get me out. What seems to have narked some people is my TV appearances! Can you believe it? I can believe anything after this. So, off to the mountains of Norway for 10 days - and I suppose they will be stirring it up behind my back in my absence.

10.10.71

On the plane to Norway the man in front of me was reading the *"Guardian"* and right across the back page was an article entitled "Conservatives at Banbury Cross"! A very amusing account of the row which couldn't have done "them" any good and certainly made their faces red. The local press had letters in my support and generally people have been very kind in supporting me for my stand and calling the Executive all sorts of names. So I sense that I have the public behind me except for the "landed gentry" friends of Schuster and the Banbury Lester group.

Back from the mountains to the debates. On 13 Sep. at Beckenham versus Bill Rodgers[170] (Lab.) in Phil Goodhart's constituency – he is having a referendum on the subject[171]. On 16 Sep. in Worthing versus Peter Blaker[172] where not unnaturally they were largely anti. 21 Sept. at Orpington versus Bill Deedes – clearly very anti. Then Parliament was recalled for 2 days debate on the Irish situation[173]. No real sight of any defection from our cause except plausibly Geraint Morgan[174] under pressure. 24 Sept. spoke at Harvard Advanced Business Course on CM and same evening at Witney versus Pat Hornsby-Smith. 27 Sep. spoke at Savoy Hotel at lunch for HA businessmen and in evening at Sidcup versus Pat Hornsby-Smith again – pretty anti. 29 Sep. at Chipping Norton versus

---

[170] William 'Bill' Rodgers, Baron Rodgers (1928-), Labour MP for Stockton-on-Tees, 1962-81. Social Democratic MP for Stockton-on-Tees, 1981-3. Founder member of the SDP. Secretary of State for Transport, 1976-9.

[171] The Beckenham result was a marginal victory for the 'Yes' camp, and the only one they took real interest in, sending activists to canvass. Goodhart said his vote would be bound by the result. On a turnout of 12% (it was an in-person vote), the Yes side won with 3,757 votes to 3,587.

[172] Peter Blaker, Baron Blaker (1922-2009), Conservative MP for Blackpool South, 1964-92.

[173] In August Operation Demetrius led to the internment of 342 men in Northern Ireland, all of them Catholic. This unleashed a wave of rioting in Catholic communities against the policy.

[174] William Geraint Morgan (1920-95), National Liberal and then Conservative MP for Denbigh, 1959-83.

Selwyn Gummer[175]. 30 Sep. at Kidlington versus Christopher Ward[176] (ex MP) where the pros objected to a vote! (- incidentally at Chipping Norton a vote <u>was</u> taken and it went 60% anti – 40% pro). 1 Oct. at Banbury with Bill Deedes and finally 4 Oct. at Carterton with Michael Heseltine[177]. By the end of it I was thoroughly bored and I feel the country is too.

The last hurdle was the inaugural meeting of the new Association on 7 Oct. There was some rumour that, when creating the new Association with its new rules, there might be a cry for re-adoption – happily it went smoothly and no one tried any funny tricks – actually it was only classified as a minor boundary alteration so adoption does not come until the next election. By then the rumpus may be over and the Association will unite to hold the seat – at least I hope so! - and I will have honoured my election pledge.

Opinion in the great debate is certainly moving against entry. In a marathon TV programme with 1000 invited audience from various parts of the country they took a poll before they started and it was 35% pro and 40% anti – after the programme the same people were asked to vote again and it was still 35% pro and the anti went up to 52%! The last Gallup was 47-35, NOP 46-36, Harris 44-35, ORC 50-34, *Fin. Times* 52-36. So the swing back is on – thanks to the Great Debate – we all thought this would happen. And so to the Party Conference – rigged in advance!

17.10.71

Lot of anti-CM activity at Brighton. We had a shop near the Conference stuffed with anti-CM literature: it was a meeting point and gave antis heart. We distributed literature galore. Enoch Powell gave a good speech at the debate – altho' the vote was 2000+ to 300+ in

---

[175] John Selwyn Gummer, Baron Deben (1939-), Conservative MP for Lewisham West, 1970-4; Eye, 1979-83; Suffolk Coastal, 1983-2010. Held various offices in the Thatcher and Major administrations: Conservative party chairman, 1983-5; Paymaster General, 1984-5; Minister of Agriculture, 1989-93; Secretary of State for the Environment, 1993-7.

[176] Christopher Ward (1942-), Conservative MP for Swindon, 1969-70.

[177] Michael Heseltine, Lord Heseltine (1933-), Conservative MP for Tavistock, 1966-74; Henley, 1974-2001. Held various high offices in Thatcher and Major administrations. Secretary of state for Defence, 1983-6; Environment, 1990-2; Trade and Industry, 1992-5; Deputy Prime Minister 1995-7. Contested Conservative leadership in 1990, losing to Mrs Thatcher and then to John Major.

favour[178]. But in the evening we had a meeting in Brighton attended by 400 where they voted 300-33 against! But everyone was delighted with the meeting and it encouraged the antis that the cause was far from lost. We are getting more support. Colin Mitchell[179], William Clarke [sic], Peter Fry[180] have joined us – all the referenda show 2-1 against – I gather from Enoch that the Party is really worried.

24.10.71

Too true! At 11.15 Monday I went to see deputy Chief Whip Humphrey Atkins[181] and told him my calculations was 32 to vote against – minimum, plus some bonus points making it up to possibly 40 and no knowledge of abstentions. He reluctantly admitted he thought I was right. I have always kept Humphrey informed, in agreement with our group. Over the w/end the *Sunday Times* published a similar list, Jasper More, a Whip and Vice Chamberlain of Household, resigned because he opposes entry into CM on political grounds, as I do. Blow me! Monday evening the Govt. decided to give Conservatives a free vote. This was clearly a panic move when they realised that the threat of a 3-line whip, which had enabled Associations to try and twist the arms of anti-market MPs, had totally failed to make more than 2 or 3 cave in – good on the courage of anti-MPs. People don't think much of those who caved in. This was all very embarrassing for my Executive who had been saying I was wrong to vote against a (3 line) and on a vote of confidence. They must look red in the face because their entire case against me has been pulled away from under their feet.

Tuesday we had a meeting of our group and it was resolute about voting against – we reckoned we had forced the Government into a free vote and that we are playing a war of nerves and therefore, on the consequent legislation, the position was to stick together and give no indication of our tactics and even to give the impression that we would all be voting against it – in fact I expect only about 20 to do so regularly altho' the lyric is to continue opposition. That would be

---

[178] Actual vote was 2,474 for entry, 324 against.
[179] Lt. Col. Colin Mitchell (1925-96), Conservative MP for Aberdeenshire West, 1970-4.
[180] Sir Peter Fry (1931-2015), Conservative MP for Wellingborough, 1969-97.
[181] Humphrey Atkins, Baron Colnbrook (1922-96), Conservative MP for Merton and Morden, 1955-70; Spelthorne, 1970-87. Deputy chief whip, 1970-2. Opposition chief whip, 1974-9. Secretary of State for Northern Ireland, 1979-81.

enough, if Labour oppose it, to block the Govt. Labour have decided to have a 3 line against, how many will vote for entry – how many? No one knows but it seems to settle down to either 50 Lab. against and few abstentions or 20 and a lot of abstention – will it be full-hearted support? Thursday eve. came the result of my referendum in my <u>new</u> constituency 65.6% against, 32.6% in favour, 1.8% spoilt – total votes cast, 6,008 i.e., 3956 for, 1965 against, 87 spoilt.[182] That's one in the eye for my executive! It was done on the basis of every 10th household on the electoral register was invited to say if he wanted his MP to vote in favour or against and prepaid reply envelope opened by Dep-Mayor Woodstock. Relieved!

So now all the polls are showing over 50% against and the referenda too are up to the 60%-70% against. The debate started on Thursday and I opened on point of order about Guernsey and Jersey wanting to come and be heard at the bar of the House. The Speaker said it was not for him! Alec D-H was v. poor but some of the speeches particularly Nabarro were good. Pro-speakers are unconvincing.

31.10.71

The debate continued Mon-Thursday – an excellent week not so much of debate but of speeches of declaration of attitudes. Strangely, although one is fed up to the teeth with debating it outside, within the House it is entirely different and I found it hard to leave the Chamber. To me fell the role of chief organiser of our anti-CM group and although we started the week with 35 we got 39 into the lobby against. I was particularly glad to see Toby Jessell[183], Carol Mather[184], Jim Kilfedder[185], Stanley McMaster[186], Rafton Pounder[187], Jasper More, Geraint Morgan in the lobby – they were my doubtfuls and by nursing them they came in. However, I don't expect them all to continue

---

[182] Interesting that Marten described for and against as being for and against his position on CM entry, and not the proposal itself.
[183] Toby Jessel (1934-2018), Conservative MP for Twickenham, 1970-97. On 2 September 1971 it was reported in *The Times* diary (p. 12) that Jessel was under pressure from his constituency association, like Marten, to change his vote on the EEC.
[184] Sir David Carol Mather (1919-2006), Conservative MP for Esher.
[185] Sir James Kilfedder (1928-95), Ulster Unionist MP for Belfast West, 1964-6; North Down, 1970-7. Independent Unionist MP for North Down, 1977-80. Ulster Popular Unionist MP for North Down, 1980-95.
[186] Stanley McMaster (1926-92), Ulster Unionist MP for Belfast East 1959-74.
[187] Rafton Pounder (1933-91), Ulster Unionist MP for Belfast South, 1963-74.

opposition – I expect only about 20 to do so. The vote was 356 in favour 244 against a majority of 112. 69 Lab voted against 3-line whip and in favour, 39 Cons. on a free vote voted against. The evening before the forecast was 40 Lab. to vote against and 15 to abstain but on the morning of the vote they apparently decided to vote *en bloc* against because of safety in numbers! But this is only the beginning of the story. The pressure will not start on us. My own view is that the Govt. will find it very difficult because Labour will not support Cons. on procedural motions and they have clearly said that if Cons. start doing Cons. things about Rents, Rhodesia etc. they will not support them! Back then to us!

14.11.71

On Sat 30th Oct. Joan and I went to the Virgin Islands as the guest of Torolf Smedvig who was opening his Yacht Club/Hotel Marina on Peter Island. Back to UK by jumbo jet and arrived in flat midday Monday for the vote that evening on the Queen's Speech. Mainly spent the week catching up on correspondence and events. Common Market wise, the Govt. hasn't made up its mind yet about the legislation so we are mostly keeping our options open – it will be quite a tactical game! The fishing negotiations are still unsettled and Norway and Denmark have second thoughts about joining – I feel events may possibly move in such a way that it may be seen in our best interest not to join – so we really want to spin out the legislation as long as we can – for example, the economy of the Six is flat, CM farmers are demanding higher prices and this will affect the cost of food, Italian elections and so on.

21.11.71

Housing Bill on Monday and Local Govt. Bill Tues. and Wed. Rows over N. Ireland and the Compton Report which cleared the Army of cruelty in interrogating IRA. Elections for Committees all went. I was re-elected to the Executive of the 1922 – surprise-surprise i.e. CM! The legislation is pouring out and it is going to be a heavy session. Friday spoke at Oxford Tech on future of Parliamentary Democracy – then Executive of constituency in the evening. At the meeting I reminded them of the previous one (where they were so beastly) and that they had said the vote on the CM would be a vote of confidence and could be a narrow thing and they were wrong on both counts. I said how difficult it was for people outside parliament to make judgements on votes etc. and then went on to say that I wouldn't comment on the consequential legislation as it hadn't been drafted yet. Further, as the vote on 28 Oct. was a vote on the principle and that it was a free vote it was unthinkable that the consequential legislation should be anything other than a free vote. I also said that Govts. don't resign on defeats on legislation so to say that I might bring the Govt. down was a fantasy. I then appealed to the Association to relax and not to damage the Cons. cause anymore. It went over well, and I <u>hope</u> peace is restored.

28.11.71

Monday lunch at the *Spectator* – not v. interesting. Tuesday Securicor Board meeting. Unemployment lobby by Trades Unionists and the customary punch-up outside St. Stephens entrance. Dinner at Café Royal to hear Mr Eberle[188] Pres. Nixon's Trade Adviser – he tore into the CM and pleaded for free trade over the widest possible area! Wednesday statement on Rhodesia which went over well with the Conservative Party. Alec explained that he felt at least that he had broken the log jam and that it was a reasonable settlement – if not accepted, it would mean the drift to S. Africa and apartheid. The setting up of a Commission of Acceptability is the best thing because the Rhodesian people will be consulted about it. The drafting of the Treaty of Accession is running into difficulties in that the Six are now disagreeing over the interpretation of the terms agreed with Rippon!

5.12.71

Monday debated Ireland again and the Labour Party voted against us on the grounds that they wanted to end internment – this would take the sting out of the Army's campaign to put down the IRA. Lunched with the Zambians who didn't like the Rhodesian settlement – naturally! Meeting of the 1922 Exec. to discuss the new rules for the adoption of candidates and re-adoption of MPs – this is an attempt to centralise control of the Party and it virtually means that MPs may have to have primaries before every election. There will be a row over this. On Wednesday the Rhodesian settlement was debated and there were no defections from the Conservatives – I believe it was because

---

[188] William Eberle (1923-2008), US Trade Representative, 1971-4.

we saw it as the last chance to prevent Rhodesia going the S. African way of apartheid – Alec D-H said the proposals had moved the logjam and that in the end the proposals would have to be approved by a Commission of Acceptability. Much will depend on the way the Commission works when it seeks the opinion of the Rhodesian people – who will it see? What political activity will be allowed during its visit? Some see the settlement as a 'sell-out' – that's going too far, but I see many ends which are not tied up and equally many points which have been fluffed. Foreign opinion will not like it. Sadly, I felt it right to vote with the Government – I don't trust the White Rhodesians in the long run.

Rippon returned from Brussels and made a statement on the CM negotiations over fishing – there was no agreement – he has virtually said he won't give in and the Six have said they won't either! The French seem to be sticking their toes in for what must be political reasons – they seem to be saying that if we join the Club the rules couldn't be bent for the applicants – that is fine. Also a row over the definition of British citizenship – this is the sort of real problem we shall meet on the consequential legislation if it ever arrives. I gather Ministers are really worried by the French attitude, particularly as Schuman left the meeting at Brussels to return to Paris to fulfil engagements there!

In the evening a dinner was given at the Reform Club in my honour for my anti-CM work – very kind of everyone. Host was Christopher Frere-Smith, and the MPs present were Dick Body[189], John Sutcliffe[190], Teddy Taylor[191], Stanley McMaster, Jim Molyneaux[192], Derek Walker-Smith, Gerald Nabarro, Roger Moate, John Farr, Ronald

---

[189] Sir Richard Body (1927-2018), Conservative MP for Billericay, 1955-9; Holland with Boston 1966-97; Boston and Skegness, 1997-2001. Resigned the Conservative whip in sympathy with Eurosceptics who voted against the EC Finance Bill in 1994. Joined the UK Independence party in 2004.

[190] John Sutcliffe (1931-), Conservative MP for Middlesbrough West, 1970-4.

[191] Sir Edward 'Teddy' Taylor (1937-2017), Conservative MP for Glasgow Cathcart, 1964-79; Southend East, 1980-97; Rochford and Southend East, 1997-2005. Taylor resigned from the Government to vote against the principle of joining the EEC in 1971. However, he voted for the enabling legislation in 1972. Co-founder of Conservative European Reform Group, 1980. Lost the whip in 1994 by voting against the EC Finance Bill.

[192] James Molyneaux, Baron Molyneaux (1920-2015), Ulster Unionist MP for South Antrim, 1970-83; Lagan Valley, 1983-97. Leader of the Ulster Unionist party, 1979-95.

Russell[193], Eric Bullus[194], John Biffen[195], David Mudd[196] and non MPs Bruce Campbell QC[197], Charles Beatty QC, Dennis Cox and Tony Newton-James, we dined <u>extremely</u> well and then discussed the CM consequentials etc.

Friday Conservative Ball at Chipping Norton and my birthday!

12.12.71

Thursday a meeting of KBO[198] at Grand Committee Room – packed 250 people – we briefed them on the continuing struggle – I spoke with Derek Walker-Smith and John Silkin. Rippon has given in on fishing and it should cause a rumpus in the House – the fishery MPs are not in the mood to be hoodwinked.

19.12.71

On Monday Rippon made a statement on fish – derision on the Labour benches but most of the Conservative fishing MPs seem to accept it – the query is that having got a 10 yr. period (a derogation) for continuing limits, what happens at the end? Rippon says a review and surely if we didn't agree with the 'review' we veto it and then it all goes back to square one, i.e., open fishing in all waters of EEC, i.e., there is no long-term security. It was interesting that the Norwegian Ambassador who came to our Anglo-Norge Committee on Wed. said the Norwegians did not share Rippon's interpretation, they were politely saying he wasn't telling the truth. This will all have to be

---

[193] Sir Ronald Russell (1904-74), Conservative MP for Wembley South, 1950-74.
[194] Sir Eric Bullus (1906-2001), Conservative MP for Wembley North, 1950-74.
[195] William John Biffen, Baron Biffen (1930-2007), Conservative MP for Oswestry, 1961-83; North Shropshire, 1983-97. Held various offices in the Thatcher administration: Chief Secretary to the Treasury, 1979-81; Secretary of State for Trade, 1981-2; Leader of the House of Commons, 1982-7. Recorded the second highest number of votes against EEC accession legislation. Enoch Powell recorded the highest number of votes against the legislation.
[196] David Mudd (1933-2020), Conservative MP for Falmouth and Camborne, 1970-92. Surprisingly Mudd stood for parliament as an independent in 2005 in his old constituency, taking only 2% of the vote.
[197] Bruce Campbell QC (1916-1990), barrister and Conservative MP for Oldham West, 1968-70.
[198] Keep Britain Out.

thrashed out during the legislation debates – as for Cwth. sugar and NZ.

Friday, saw the Danish Parliament had voted on Common Market (only provisionally a progress report vote) and they failed to get their 5/6 vote.

26.12.71

Monday we debated MP pay increases on a free vote – no vote against it! Tuesday we did the Queen's pay again to a fairly thin house – 47 (?) voted against it but for a variety of administrative reasons – not all Republicans! Wednesday we adjourned for Xmas and Thursday I did my rounds of the hospitals at Chipping Norton and Banbury. The *Banbury Guardian* had a nasty leader about me implying I had been neglecting Banbury – I hope I sorted out the Editor who was very apologetic on the 'phone'! Christmas at home with the family only – very warm, even the lilac trees and the wall flowers are budding! A little snow just after Xmas but it didn't settle.

During the recess I put a lot of work in the constituency foregoing my usual skiing holiday in order to repair some of the CM damage. Visited the social security office, labour exchange, and had a fine old row with the Oxford Water Board over the change over from spring to mains water at Chadlington. Plenty of this on radio, TV and newspapers ending up with the first lead in the *Daily Telegraph*! Not a very restful recess!

23.1.72

Parliament reassembled on Mon. 17 Jan. and the first item for us was the debate on the CM on Thursday 20th where Labour had put down a motion saying that the Treaty of Accession should not be signed until it had been published and considered by the House. This really was quite sensible and it was in line with something I had put to Rippon in Nov. However, to be credible Labour should have thought of this before and it was patently clear that they only did it as a political gimmick to embarrass Ted H. and to provide an opportunity for Labour pro and anti to unite. It was in the event a silly debate and the Cons. leadership put down an amendment, which was what the vote was about and on which we voted, merely saying that the Treaty of Accession would not become operative until ratified and approving the laying before the House of the text of the Treaty and the proposals for the legislation. 4 antis voted against and the rest of us just abstained – the Govt. majority on this amendment was 21 and the substantive vote as amended 20 – we, the abstained, sat in a bloc and for 6 mins had the power to defeat the Govt. on the eve of the signing of the Treaty of Accession – but we didn't – it would have looked too expedient for words!

30.1.72

Monday debate on unemployment which has now topped the 1 million mark. Tuesday an emergency debate on Rhodesia which flopped – it was started off by the riots in Rhodesia to do with the Pearce Commission[199]. Otherwise a dull week. The CM legislation was introduced – merely 12 clauses! Labour was very upset and perhaps they can unite against 2nd reading and then it should really be a close run thing.

6.2.72

A dull lot of debates this week[200]. Unemployment again on Monday (it is now over 1mn!), electricity on Tuesday, Industrial Relations on Wednesday, and the Tote Bill on Thursday. Tuesday was memorable for the day Bernadette Devlin[201] pulled Reggie Maudling's hair[202]. There had been a march in Londonderry on Sunday and the IRA had used it as a cover to beat it up and in the ensuing fracas 13 were killed – the Parachute Regt. was involved and they are hated by the IRA. All hell broke loose and on Tuesday Bernadette Devlin was determined to make a show. As she was not called by the Speaker she was furious and darted across the Chamber and flung herself at Reggie on the front bench and pull[ed] his hair and slapped his face. She was set upon by

---

[199] Riots had broken out in Harare, Fort Victoria, and Umtali. The government announced that 15 people had died in the disturbances.
[200] It could hardly be described as dull, the furore over unemployment passing 1 million and Bloody Sunday set the government up for a year of difficult crises.
[201] Bernadette Devlin (1946-), Unity MP for Mid Ulster, 1969-February 74.
[202] On 30 January 1972 British soldiers fired upon and killed 13 people during a protest march in Londonderry. In the government's statement on the shooting the next day, Devlin is reported to have hit Maudling and pulled his hair, having accused him of lying when he said that the Parachute Regiment had been fired at first.

Whips and then Delargy[203] attacked the Whips and there was a punch up – B.D. was taken out by Bob Mellish[204] opposition Chief Whip, sobbing! End of story. But the question was whether the Speaker was right to play it cool or whether he should have named her and suspended her. Anyhow next day he gave a lecture on discipline in the House and said we should have no more unseemly scenes! Next day the British Embassy in Dublin was burned down by the mobs and Lynch seems to be getting worried in case the IRA take over in Eire. Anyhow, it is an awful state of affairs – how does it fit in with the Common Market?!

Friday spoke at Bristol University – 2¼ hour drive each way and a really awful meeting – about 50 but it was wrecked by the anarchist group who simply came to disrupt it and to air questions about Ireland when I was talking about the Common Market legislation – am coming to the conclusion that it is not worth speaking at universities anymore.

Saturday evening Enoch Powell came to Banbury to speak at a Monday Club dinner at the Whately Hotel – I replied for the guests in a light hearted speech. Then Enoch made a blockbuster of a speech saying that now Pakistan had left the Commonwealth, the Paks [sic] here who were not British subjects should go home! Not up my street at all!! A bit embarrassing[205].

13.2.72

Coal strike goes from bad to worse with pickets getting tough – it was debated on Tuesday in reasonable calm but it is certainly brewing up for a major fight. Wednesday another dinner given by Frere-Smith at the Reform Club for the anti-CM group, good dinner and great *amitie*. The 2nd reading is next week and it could be a close thing for the Govt. They are worried! Labour will mostly vote against on the excuse that

---

[203] Hugh Delargy (1908-76), Labour MP for Manchester Platting, 1945-50; Thurrock, 1950-76.

[204] Bob Mellish, Lord Mellish (1913-1998), Labour MP for Rotherhithe, 1946-50; Bermondsey, 1950-82. Opposition chief whip, 1970-4. In 1982 Mellish resigned his seat in protest at the left-ward drift of his constituency Labour party. The subsequent by-election saw Simon Hughes of the Liberal party beat Peter Tatchell, the Labour candidate.

[205] In later diary entries Marten becomes a close ally of Powell, primarily due to the Common Market, but this entry is a reminder that Marten did not wholly embrace Powell's views on immigration.

the Bill is too small! This should shed the image of "integrity" of Jenkins and Co. If all Labour vote against we could probably muster about 20 to vote against. Govt. is saying it will resign if defeated. It is stupid of the Whips to say this because it is highly unlikely with unemployment over 1 million (and likely to be more with the strike), N. Ireland, a national coal strike – it would be an act of the utmost irresponsibility to do so at a time like this - and this is our moment of power to block it without causing a General Election. It is a fascinating combination of circumstances. By next week, we shall know.

The Association Executive met on Friday evening and I spoke about CM – they were gunning for a fight but as before – it never came. I was threatened by the Chairman Friswell that if I brought the Govt. down or "embarrassed them" the Executive would act!! I will take no notice.

Friday lunch – spoke at Industrial Life office lunch – boring speech! But all the other 3 speakers paid a compliment to my "integrity" over the CM.

20.2.72

That was some week! The 3 day debate on the European Communities Bill took place on Tues., Wed., Thursday. I spoke on Wednesday mainly about honouring pledges – see Hansard (16.2.72). It was a <u>filthy</u> week. Ted Heath assumed the role of Chief Whip and had in anti-CM MPs to tell them individually that he and the Govt. would resign if he didn't get the 2nd reading Bill! Quite astonishing in the midst of a national Coal strike (with Emergency powers), N. Ireland, massive unemployment, Rhodesia, etc. – I said in my speech that it would be an act of the utmost irresponsibility and would only be seen as the Govt. running away from its responsibilities. I had nice letters of congratulations from colleagues – a valuable part of our Parliament. The Chief Whip had an hour with me not exactly trying to persuade me but discussing it! The pressures were enormous – every Minister we met said the Govt. would resign. The debate was not very thrilling except the wind up speeches on Thursday night. Ted H. said in the last few moments that if the 2nd Reading was rejected "my colleagues and I are unanimous that, in this situation, this Parliament could not sensibly continue". That was the threat, not a very noble ending – many of my constituents called it 'Blackmail'. But in spite of that 15

Cons. antis voted against the Bill[206], all the Lab. pros deserted the Govt., 4 abstained of Cons. antis and 5 of Lab. pros – Libs divided 5-1 – net result 309-301, majority 8!! A major snub for Heath and the Govt. But he will press on. He was in fact saved by the 5 Libs voting for the Bill. During the count the Govt. benches looked very glum even white and almost green. <u>Intense</u> excitement – it looked for a moment that they were beaten. After the vote, big scenes of resign etc. and counter demos. Jeremy Thorp [sic] was manhandled by Lab. as if to drag him across the floor of the House to the Cons. side, he having saved the Cons. Govt. As I went through the lobby the one behind me was Bill Rodgers, a very nice sincere pro-Market ex Minister of Lab. Govt. He had tears down his face and he covered his face as he voted – I have never seen anything so dreadful in my 13 years in Parliament. Politics in the gutter. The whole of the CM has dragged Parliament down. I am very sad. On the w/end many congratulations from locals for standing to my principles. No comment from my Chairman!

---

[206] They were Conservatives and Unionist MPs from Northern Ireland: Ronald Bell, John Biffen, Richard Body, Anthony Fell (Con, Great Yarmouth), Michael Clark Hutchison, John Jennings (Con, Burton), John Maginnis (Unionist, Armagh), Neil Marten, Roger Moate, James Molyneaux, David Mudd, Gerald Nabarro, Enoch Powell, Robin Turton, and Derek Walker-Smith. Angus Maude, Harmar Nicholls, Ronald Russell, and James Kilfedder abstained.

Part Two:
The Fall of Ted Heath

27.2.72

Monday started with a debate on disablement during the course of which Sir Keith Joseph[207], Min of Soc. Sec, announced new rules for disabled drivers and in the process paid a kind tribute to me and my work for the disabled. In the evening we had a meeting of the 1970 Group[208] and discussed the following day's debate on the Money Resolution for the European Communities Bill – we mostly agreed to abstain. Later the next day the debate took place and the Govt. had a majority of 30 – it shouldn't matter because we can debate the subject again on Clause 2. Had the abstainers voted against the majority would have been 14. Enoch Powell made a brilliant speech denting the Govt's. case quite a bit. Joan went to Burford AGM in my place and I came under attack with a motion deploring my vote – she defended me so well that they withdrew the motion and all was peace and quiet – it seems that if the case is explained they accept it – my trouble is that I cannot be at the AGMs which are midweek. So the knives are put in by Friswell and Webb. Thursday spoke at Maidstone lunch on the CM legislation and it went well. Spent weekend quietly at home fortified by the w/end papers headlines of "Tories split" etc. and a leader in the *Banbury Guardian* entitled "What do they want – a man or a mouse"!! This played right into my hands.

5.3.72

Further saga on the CM this week: on Tuesday, when we were due to start the Committee stage on the floor of the House, the amendments selected for Clause 1 were tiddlers and only announced at 1pm for debate the same day. Michael Foot quite rightly and brilliantly

---

[207] Sir Keith Joseph, Baron Joseph (1918-1994), Conservative MP for Leeds North East, 1956-87. Held senior office in Heath and Thatcher administrations: Secretary of State for Health and Social Services, 1970-4; Industry, 1979-81; Education and Science, 1981-6. Regarded as the intellectual godfather of what became Thatcherism. Expected to challenge Heath for the Conservative leadership in 1975, but an ill-delivered speech in Birmingham on 19 October 1974, which was interpreted as having eugenicist tones, derailed his campaign.

[208] Conservative dining club established by Sir Derek Walker-Smith to organise opposition to the EEC.

queried the selection as being too restrictive when the Govt. had given assurances that all things were debatable on the Committee stage. Grant Ferris[209], Chairman of Ways and Means, ruled that amendments designed to vary the terms of the Treaties are not in order. If that was so, then all the details we had understood could be debated, no longer were. This was a question of major constitutional importance.

A fascinating debate took place and in the end, the Lab. opposition announced it would put down a motion of censure the next day in the Chair (a technical one) – that being so there was no point in going on with the Committee stage as we didn't know the outcome of the Chairman's decision on the result of the motion of censure. It was a superb parliamentary performance by Michael Foot and the "antis" gained the first round in the battle by knocking two days off the time for the Bill. Next day the motion of censure was defeated, so presumably the amendments will not be widened. After the 10 O'clock vote on that motion the Govt. (rather stupidly, I thought) decided to proceed to the Committee stage but this was resisted in a fascinating display of points of order until 7am. The Committee then moved on to the first amendment for 5 mins. and the House adjourned.

The Conservatives are in danger of giving the impression of steamrollering the Bill through – many backbenchers are simply wholly prepared to jettison Parly. procedure to get their ends – it is nauseating – cries of 'Reichstag' are heard! This sort of thing combined with the obvious arm twisting in constituencies will do us no good – also the failure to get "full hearted consent" is a breach of an election pledge. The whole question of the CM is showing Conservatives up in a most <u>sickening</u> light.

12.3.72

Monday started with a vote of censure on the Govt. for its handling of the EEC legislation – I voted for the Govt. for a change! Tuesday lunched with the Portuguese Foreign Minister – they are worried about the effect of their UK trade in textiles, tomatoe [sic] puree and cork if we join the EEC. Tues. afternoon Committee stage proper on

---

[209] Robert Grant-Ferris, Baron Harvington (1907-97), Conservative MP for St. Pancras North, 1937-45; Nantwich, 1955-74. Deputy Speaker of the House of Commons, 1970-4. In debates relating to finance and where the whole House of Commons sits as a committee, the Speaker vacates the chair for the chairman of 'ways and means', usually the deputy Speaker.

the EEC Bill – a fascinating debate and really worthwhile – highlighting the loss of sovereignty – I believe this will get through to the public in the end – polls are swinging our way again! Wednesday same again. Thursday a debate about Wales and it seemed like a half-hol.! Joan and I lunched with Pam and Enoch Powell – it was fascinating, domestically and conversationally.

19.3.72

On Tues. and Wed. we continued with the European Communities Bill – again an excellent debate going into the very fundamentals of the whole question of Parliamentary control and the surrender of sovereignty. The pity of it is that the pro-marketeers are conspicuous by their absence – if only they were able to hear the debate I am convinced many of them would begin to have second thoughts – but they are either obsessed with it or are just lobby fodder. The basic theme of the week has been that we should write into the Bill that, on important treaties, we should legislate rather than pass them merely by an affirmative resolution – i.e., properly debate them and amend if necessary. This would particularly apply to such things as defence, economic and monetary union. We had the Govt. majority down to 11 at one stage.

The big joke of the week was President Pompidou on Thursday, two days before meeting Ted Heath at Chequers, announced that France would have a referendum on the enlargement of the Communities! This fits in splendidly with my amendment to the Bill which calls for a consultative referendum! Went on the BBC to speak about it – it certainly has embarrassed the Govt. altho' I expect the French will say yes in the end. However it strengthens my case a lot.

26.3.72

This week started with a debate on Ireland and then we had the budget all week. A 'give away' budget £1,200m in all[210]. That is £300 million tax cuts in 2 yrs. as opposed to Labour's £3,000m increases! Plenty of tax changes on the way including VAT and negative income tax – on the whole it got a good reception at first but many thought it would be

---

[210] Known as either the 'dash for growth' budget or the 'Barber boom' budget that precipitated massive inflation in the mid-1970s.

inflationary without doing enough to get the economy going again. The stock exchange went up then down and was lower than when the budget was announced. In the budget Tony Barber announced a return to investment grants – great laughter by Labour[211]. The next day John Davies[212] announced a return to another form of IRC (which we abolished)[213] and got a standing ovation from Labour! General depression on the Conservative side because we are going back on our election promises - and we are returning to socialist doctrines in a panic.

Friday morning was the long-awaited announcement on N. Ireland – the Govt. to take control of everything from Westminster, Stormont suspended, internment to be eased and (big joke) plebiscites i.e., referenda! on the border issue. The N. Irish MPs regard it as a sell out and about 5 of them will now return to the anti-CM lobby – others like Biggs-Davison[214] were furious as they saw it as a surrender to the IRA forces – at least a partial surrender. Ian Paisley said N. Ireland should be totally integrated into the UK – he is probably right. I believe we should close the border and make Irish foreigners and disbar them from voting in our elections – perhaps it is a bit too early for that. Anyhow, the Govt. policy is a big gamble and we shall just have to see how it turns out. Willy Whitelaw was made Secy. State N. Ireland and in tributes to his leadership he was clearly v. moved to tears.

2.4.72

Budget wind up on Monday while the anger over N. Ireland smoulders – massive meeting of Home Affairs Committee. Willie Whitelaw came and spoke – while there was a lot of sympathy for him,

---

[211] See entry for 1 November 1971, in Barber's first budget investment grants had been abolished and instead turned into allowances.

[212] John Davies (1916-1979), Director General, Confederation of British Industry, 1965-9. Conservative MP for Knutsford, 1970-8. Held various offices in the Heath administration and Thatcher shadow cabinet: Secretary of State for Industry, 1970-2; Chancellor of the Duchy of Lancaster, 1972-4. Shadow Foreign Secretary, 1976-8. Died of a brain tumour, 1979.

[213] The Industrial Reorganisation Corporation, established in 1966, sought to merge industry and make it more competitive. The Heath government announced its abolition in 1970, only to reintroduce it in 1972, another U-turn.

[214] Sir John Biggs-Davison (1918-88), Conservative MP for Chigwell, 1955-74; Epping Forest, 1974-88. Biggs-Davison was a Catholic, right-winger and devout pro-European.

he seemed to me to be appealing to "loyalty" of the Party *a la* Guards officers rather than making a case – I am not convinced he is the right person for the job. What I think worries the Party is (a) letting down PM Faulkner[215] and the Stormont (b) letting down our nice N. Irish Unionist members (c) the draconian powers to be assumed by S/S N. Ireland and (d) the constitutional question and (e) will anything be achieved?

Tuesday we debated the 2nd Reading of the Bill and there was a majority of over 450 as Labour supported it – 18 voted against including some Conservatives and over 30 Cons. (including self) abstained. A very odd situation. There was a lot of cross-current at work including Common Marketing. Next day, Wednesday, came the Committee stage and it went all night until 11.30am Thursday thus loosing [sic] the Easter Adjournment debates! However the Govt. got its Bill and 7 out of 8 N. Irish Unionists declared they would no longer automatically support the Govt – they did not resign the Whip so that they could attend our Party Committees! In terms of the Common Market this probably means more recruits for our side – about 3 more I guess, totalling 5. Already there are signs of some of the old antis coming back into the fold. It is a very interesting example of how a Govt. can, drip by drip, build up a head of resentment within its own Party and almost imperceptibly the MPs who are displeased find a camaraderie and tend to support each other in their causes[216]. We have the CM, lame ducks[217], N. Ireland, Rhodesia, all upsetting some and then in the Budget the reconstituted IRC and investment grants coming back – the Govt. is clearly on the defensive and is reacting by turning everything on its head! In the general state of disillusionment lies our best hope of defeating the CM. It is also a good example of how it is folly to steam ahead on a policy such as CM where the country is divided relying on the support of the opposition – in this case the PM knows there were 39 Cons. against and we only have a

---

[215] Brian Faulkner, Baron Faulkner (1921-77), Prime Minister of Northern Ireland, 1971-2. Under direct rule, announced in March 1972, the Northern Ireland parliament was prorogued and powers assumed by the Secretary of State for Northern Ireland.

[216] Marten here explains, almost word for word, Airey Neave's strategy to elect Mrs Thatcher Conservative leader in 1975. Neave encouraged his colleagues to give Heath a fright, playing off the unpopularity of the Conservative leader.

[217] The government had pledged not to bale out 'lame duck' businesses and industries. It would U-turn on this too with its Industry Act, and arguably already had with Rolls Royce and Upper Clyde Shipbuilders.

majority of 26. I have an amendment to the EC Bill calling for a consultative advisory referendum – if Labour supports it (and it looks as though they will) we could well win it because there are enough disaffected people to support it. This could be a turn up for the books! And now a short Easter recess of one week.

16.4.72

Back to Parliament on 10 April to be greeted by the resignation of Roy Jenkins, Harold Lever and George Thompson[218] [sic] and other smaller fry from the Labour front bench because of my referendum amendment which the Lab. party will be supporting! Extraordinary how a small, mild amendment can have such a traumatic effect – I believe they were stupid to have resigned on this and not on 2nd reading or Clause 2. Some wags are now saying I should withdraw my amendment thus leaving them looking very silly! That was the event of the week in Parliament: I was popular with all Conservatives and popular with a lot of Labour MPs for having got rid of Jenkins! Fluid politics! Nora and Torolf were over from Norway so plenty of wining and dining. Thursday 2 radio programmes and Friday eve. my AGM expected trouble – none came. I spoke on the CM votes etc. and I think everyone accepted it, although not all agreeing – many said how right I was to stick to my principles – I was heartened – a poll came out saying 79% of my constituents thought I was right, 75% Conservative thought so and 46% would vote Cons. at next election, but if we didn't join CM 16% more would do so! So it was game set and I hope match with the Association. I gather they want to let it rest.

23.4.72

A week, as usual, almost devoted to the CM! Tuesday was my amendment on the referendum – it was taken with an amendment of Labour's calling for an election before entry – but the two were voted on separately. The debate was a very good one, high quality and quite a few MPs said it was historic because it is one which will be referred to in the years ahead. I spoke after the opposition opening speaker (Peter Shore) for 4 mins and had a good hearing – the House was, I

---

[218] George Thomson, Baron Thomson (1921-2008), Labour MP for Dundee East, 1952-73. Secretary of State for Commonwealth Affairs, 1967-8. European Commissioner, 1973-7.

think, genuinely interested and the public certainly wanted it debated. However it got mixed up with Labour resignation speeches and the Conservatives had a 3-line whip and what with Labour pro-marketeers abstaining it was defeated by a majority of 49 – a pity! Next day I spoke on the EFTA amendment that we should not join [the CM] unless they got a square deal. Wednesday PM spoke at 1922 lunch and appealed to anti-CM Cons. to stop their resistance – then, at a press briefing after, this was announced – a poor way to treat a private meeting. The next vote was only a Govt. majority of 8!!

30.4.72

Tuesday and Wednesday CM Bill – it goes on and on with fury mounting with the pros because they are kept up late! A guillotine was obviously on the way. I made 4 speeches in the 2 days having made 2 the previous week. But we are getting nowhere – Govt. agreeing to no amendments. On Thursday the guillotine was announced – what now – Michael Foot made the best point – i.e., how can PM claim to have full-hearted consent of Parliament if he has to use the guillotine to get the Bill! All the days seem one way or another to be on the CM these days - Willy Whitelaw came to the 1922 Committee to explain Ireland – he got a fairly good reception! Compromise on the way, I smell.

7.5.72

Tuesday the Govt. introduced the guillotine motion on the EC Bill – usual row but this time there was a genuine feeling not confined to the antis – that it was premature – I got in a short speech at the end of the debate – the Govt. majority was 11. The next day we debated on the first day of the guillotine and it all seemed different and fairly pointless – we got the Govt. majority down to 4[219], and 8 on divisions – this shook them!

---

[219] Not as resounding a victory for the anti-marketeers as it may appear. The government majority was so low because pro-marketeers arrived back late from a party hosted by Duncan Sandys. It was the smallest majority in all divisions on entry to the EEC due to traffic and poor time keeping rather than persuasion.

Now we must plan carefully to have a division on a minor matter at dinner time to catch them out[220] because we must try and get <u>one</u> amendment at least to get report stage. Enoch P., John Biffen and I are working on this. Now there will be a pause on the EC Bill for a week or two to allow the Finance Bill to get on its way. Local elections – Cons. lost many seats - and control of Banbury.

14.5.72

Tues., Wed. and Thursday were Finance Bill Committee Stage – mainly dealing with the introduction of VAT. This enabled us to get on with catching up on the CM, largely reviewing the voting record of antis and deciding to put the pressure on certain ones via constituency supporters. I doubt if it will have any effect – mainly because the country now seems to have accepted our entry and got bored with the subject. The Eire referendum went massively in favour and the Italian Elections were not so polarised as to produce a Communist or Fascist government. So, the hurdles to our entry are getting lower and lower! The only hope now is either we defeat it on 3rd reading or that something catastrophic happens outside. The Labour Party might pass a conference resolution to come out again! This could prove awkward. Rail strike on – off – on – off and now been referred to a ballot of employees.

21.5.72

Another quiet week with Mon., Tue. and Wed. on Finance Bill Committee Stage on floor of House on VAT! This enabled me to get on with catching up on everything and taking it a little easy. No major excitements – Ireland does not improve and the Protestants seem to be taking a harder line.

28.5.72

Monday 2nd Reading of Industry Bill – a complete reversal of Conservative policy – no more determination to avoid propping up lame ducks. It seems we will be helping any failing industry almost

---

[220] Marten obviously heard what happened with Duncan Sandys party and tried his own hand at scuppering the Bill. It only needed amending once for it to be void. The Bill had to pass unamended.

anywhere in the country – all in aid of unemployment. But it has shaken some Cons. MPs and of course it had the support of the Labour Party and their derision at John Davies the Minister of Trade and Industry. Tuesday Alec D-H announced the result of the Pearce Commission on Rhodesia, i.e., that the Rhodesian people as a whole do not accept the proposed settlement. The policy now seems to be to let matters stew for some time in the hope that an initiative will come from Rhodesia itself – meantime sanctions continue. Wed. we had another day on the European Communities Bill by shere [sic] argument we won the day but the Govt had a majority of 5 on one of the votes because the Liberals voted for an amendment.

11.6.72

Parliament reassembled on Mon. 5 June with 2 days on the Housing Finance Scotland Bill and one day on EEC Bill. We had a great meeting at the House on Wednesday afterward by CACMIS[221] – about 200 people from all over the country assembled in Committee Room 14 on the first anniversary of our formation. Enoch Powell gave a stirring speech to the troops – we then had a question hour which I replied to and Enoch spoke again and then I wound up thanking Roger Moate who took the chair quite excellently – a great guy!

Thursday's debate on EEC was about Clause 2(3) the financial provisions – again our amendment made good sense and we won the argument but the Govt. won the division by 6 votes. One day we shall win! Enoch spoke well and I spoke, too, on the role of the expenditure committee going to Europe to examine expenditure of our monies paid over to the Community.

18.6.72

Spent Monday mostly trying to rally support for opposition to Clause 2 vote on Wednesday. Nabarro and Bullus have agreed to vote with us again and all the Irish (left, right and centre) will be with us. EEC debate Tuesday and Wednesday took up all the time. Spoke on Wednesday, with mutterings from pro-Conservatives about being a wicked speech because I said that the real motive behind our entry was that we are basically an imperialist power and we would seek to 'colonise' the CM if we joined, spread the English language, keep up

---

[221] Conservative Anti Common Market Information Service.

links with USA – in fact everything to get under the skin of Pompidou! The vote took place in high tension at 7.30pm and the Govt. had a majority of 8 again – very distressing because it was due to 12 (probably 9) abstentions by Labour 'pros' – there will be a blistering row in the [Labour] Party over that. It was a pity because it would have been a real blow to the Govt. We must now keep it up and see if we cannot get an amendment through and so get a report stage.

28.6.72

Another 3 days Tues., Wed., Thurs. on the European Communities Bill – it's getting a bit difficult because it means being in the Chamber from 3.30-11 and preparing speeches and whipping etc. – everything else has to be fitted in. We press on but even with majorities of 4 we never win even an amendment because the Labour pros "regulate" the final few votes by abstention.

Went to N. Ireland on Friday and Sat. – fascinating – it was the final few days before the ceasefire announced by the IRA. I went with Derek Walker-Smith and Norman Tebbit[222] – D. W-S did not seem well. We helpcopted from Aldersgrove to GHQ and had a session with Gen. Tuzo[223] GOC[224]. From there we visited various military outposts on Shankhill Road etc. – it certainly was warlike! But the troops were in great fettle. The damage from explosions was awful because it was so crude and pointless. The terrorism of people by the IRA was odious. The big question was whether the IRA were genuine or whether they were using this as an excuse to negotiate and retrain and in the meantime to see what sort of a bargain settlement they could get out of the British. The Protestant UDA[225] were deeply suspicious of the deal with the IRA because they felt there <u>must</u> be strings to the deal and they didn't know what they were. Either way it seems the IRA were on a good wicket. It could end up with the UDA having no-go areas and the IRA retuning to no-go areas with the

---

[222] Norman Tebbit, Lord Tebbit (1931-), Conservative MP for Epping, 1970-4; Chingford, 1974-94. Created Lord Tebbit of Chingford, 1992. Secretary of State for Employment, 1981-3. Conservative Party Chairman, 1985-7.

[223] General Sir Harry Tuzo (1917-98), General Officer Commanding and Director of Operations in Northern Ireland, 1971-3. Commander-in-Chief British Army of the Rhine, 1973-6. NATO Deputy Supreme Allied Commander, Europe, 1976-9.

[224] General Officer Commanding

[225] Ulster Defence Association, founded 1971. Protestant paramilitary organisation.

troops in between. We visited the two girls who had their legs blown off in an explosion – two sisters – awful! – they were Catholics, too. Saturday we went to Londonderry and to the Bogside, the worst no-go area – very much war-time atmosphere – snipers abound and explosions – 3 soldiers killed that night when their vehicle was blown up on the road. The military said they had knowledge of an Algerian and a Korean who were with the IRA in the Bogside advising on urban guerrilla tactics. A sad destruction of a lovely town.

2.7.72

Tues. and Wed. on EEC Bill again – the debate is now less exciting as it is getting to the duller part. Govt. majorities between 7 and 15 – not good. The £ was floated the previous week and it seems to be working out at a 6% devaluation – what a curious thing to have to do having agreed the previous month to narrow the bank of currency fluctuation to join with the EEC in a step towards monetary union – it really makes a practical nonsense of the Common Market – the French must be v. unhappy – will they say 'No' again?

9.7.72

Monday F.O. questions and a lot of dud answers on the CM. Anti-CM dinner with James Towler[226]. Tues. and Wed. final stages of the EC Committee. I went to Norway on Tuesday for a board meeting in Stavanger of Securicor (Norway) – curious way Securicor have of working: they were trying to run Bergen, Stavanger and Oslo from London yet having a Norwegian chairman without any managers! Returned on Wednesday to vote on EEC. Position in Norway is that they are 44-37 against going in – if they didn't then probably Denmark won't and that of course will alter all the balance of contributions and voting. On Wednesday Pompidou sacked Chaban-Delmas[227], the French Prime Minister and replaced him with an arch-Gaullist Prime Minister[228] – a good (or anyhow better) man for M. Pompidou has decreed that we must return to a fixed exchange rate before we enter

---

[226] James Towler (1932-98), railway passenger representative and businessman. Chairman, Transport Users Consultative Committee for Yorkshire, 1979-85. Anti-Common Market activist.
[227] Jacques Chaban-Delmas (1915-2000), Prime Minister of France, 1969-72.
[228] Pierre Messmer (1916-2007), Prime Minister of France, 1972-74.

the CM – not much appreciated in the UK! It just could be that he is working up to another 'Non' – but I am always optimistic.

16.7.72

Thursday was third reading of EEC Bill and the Buckingham Palace Garden Party. Went with Joan and Mary Louise – lovely day – too many people. We were presented to the Queen and after small talk she got on to the Common Market! She referred to the important division tonight and I said the Govt will have a majority of 15 (- actually 17!). She asked me why I was against it and I said it would end the Commonwealth – she, of course, was very tactful but I believe I read in her eyes (always v. expressive) that she did not like the idea. I only wish I had been able to suggest giving her a private briefing on it!

And so back to the last vote on CM in the Commons – got into the Chamber at 5.30 and tried to get in a speech – but was not called. It really is a scandal to have only 1 day on 3rd reading and that on a Thursday with statements etc. – only 6 hours including 4 front bench, a maiden speech and plenty of Privy Councillors [sic]! Anyhow it was a curiously poor debate, no one rising to great heights - and the voting was 301-284, i.e., 17 majority. The majority was obtained by Liberal support and Labour abstentions – we had 16 Cons. voting against and 4 abstaining. So it was a curious victory once again because 13 Labour abstained. So now it is ended in the Commons. The scene shifts, not to the Lords who will let it through without much ado, but to Norway and Denmark and their referenda and to the marginally more Gaullist government in France. The whole CM seems to be creaking at the seams and the large countries are all in some sort of trouble and so are the currencies. So there is still hope!

30.7.72

Monday Foreign Office questions and a debate on the industrial situation. The gaoled strikers were released[229] and the House of Lords

---

[229] On 21 July 1972 five shop stewards from the Trade and General Workers' Union (TGWU) were imprisoned in violation of the Industrial Relations Act after they refused a court order prohibiting picketing. This ruling came from the Industrial Relations Court (IRC) that the Act had created. The ruling led to mass walkouts and within a week the Court of Appeal overturned the IRC. It was interpreted as a fatal blow to the authority of the Industrial Relations Act.

reversed the decision about the unions not paying fines and held them responsible for the action of the shop stewards. No sooner had the dockers been released when they called a national dock strike for the end of the week!

On Tues. and Wed. the Lords debated the CM – I listened to some of it and many of the arguments were really dated, the sort of thing we heard 2 years ago and now very worn out. The Earl of Lauderdale is keen to get an amendment to the Bill because he said a surprising number of peers were disgusted at the way it was forced through the House of Commons.

Wednesday a.m. tennis against the City Livery Club at Hurlingham which we won handsomely. Then back to lead a delegation to Baroness Sharp who is investigating the case of the disabled divers – she is obviously a tough nut! After that a meeting with the Prime Minister of the 1922 Executive – he gave me the impression of being bored with us! Probably was! He took a different line on N. Ireland from Willy Whitelaw and seemed to be saying that the IRA could never be beaten and that in the end we shall have to do a deal with them! Willy on the other hand seems to have been "brought to his senses" by the awful explosions last week-end and 4000 more troops have been sent to N. Ireland and he seems at last to be starting to clear the "no-go" areas.

I find this difference intriguing – PM gave the same sort of impression at the 1922 Committee when he came for his end of term talk. He seemed to be on the defensive and gave a poor performance for him. Some talk in the w/end press about who would succeed him – he has certainly gone downhill in his Party's esteem largely through turning his policies on their heels. If he now gives in over the Industrial Relations Act he will be in danger. He showed not a flicker of humour at the 1922. He referred to the importance of Summit [sic] Conference[230] in Oct. as the agreed land-mark and he referred to the referendum for N. Ireland as a 'constitutional innovation'!! If we can have a constitutional innovation for N. Ireland why not one on the CM!! Dick Body went to France to see Couve de Murville[231] about Britain's entry into CM and found him v. interested in our views – Enoch Powell hoped to get over to France for some pre-Summitt [sic] speeches.

---

[230] EEC Summit
[231] Maurice Couve de Murville (1907-1999), Prime Minister of France, 1968-9.

6.8.72

The dock strike started last w/end and on Thursday there was a Royal Proclamation for a state of emergency to cope with things if they get too bad during the recess. It is difficult to know what the Government is going to do – it will be the last straw if they give in. One feels the absence of the solid and reliable Reggie Maudling who resigned last week as Home Secretary because of disclosures (probably unfounded) in the bankruptcy of Mr Poulson. Ted is getting a bit lonely at the top without Iain Macleod and Reggie.

13.8.72 [also for September 1972]

Monday started with a lunch in Chancery Lane which I organised via Jane Armstrong[232] of Toronto Star, a helpful anti-CM lobby correspondent. It was for Nicolas Chatelaine[233] and London reps of *le Figaro* to meet Enoch Powell in order to get him and his views on CM publicity on the Common Market. It seemed to work and they said they would fix up a forum for him – so far so good – let's hope Couve de Murville does the same for him. Alf Morris and I went to Norway and Douglas Jay/Peter Shore Dick Body/Roger Moate to Denmark. Two other anti-CM meetings that day, the Study Group and CACMIS. Both decided to continue the struggle – CACMIS until the end of the year anyhow.

It has been a rough but fascinating session. A massive amount of legislation, hotly contested, dominated by the CM affair. Colleagues very nice about opposition – but I feel it has been somewhat dishonestly bulldozed through Parliament. The Tory Party is mumbling about the PM, the economy could go well from now on, but we are in rough water and the country is divided. The dock strike continues and is a key to the future.

Against this background we flew to Majorca on Tuesday 15 Aug. where our kindly family doctor Wilfred Hudson has lent us his charming villa at Carla d'Or. Back at home the days were dominated by the Olympic Games at Munich – work was almost impossible if there was a TV set anywhere near! Then the tragic excitement of the Arab terrorists breaking into the Israeli living quarters and holding 9 hostages (having killed 2) demanding as a price for their release the

---

[232] Jane Armstrong (1915-1999), Canadian journalist and war correspondent.
[233] Nicolas Chatelain (1913-1976), journalist, *le Figaro*.

release of 200 Arabs being held by the Israelis. This was all televised live and was very dramatic. In the end all were killed after the Germans had made a fair measure of it. Three terrorists were captured and held by the Germans – reprisals can be expected and terrorism will increase. Inflation roars ahead in the UK, Uganda Asians will be coming in - letters from constituents criticise Ted Heath for weakness.

8-11 Sept. I spent in Norway with Alf Morris observing their consultative referendum. Having proposed one myself in the EEC debate it was v. interesting to observe. While there the opinion polls forecast 60% no and 40% yes! This has fascinating implications because Denmark will follow suit and if so it will alter the whole balance of the original negotiations – we shall see! The TUC has also voted against CM and if these 2 countries do so also it should influence the Labour Party at their conference to do so - and all this could collectively make Pompidou have doubts at the Summit meeting (if it takes place).

On 23 (Monday) Sept., having debated the CM at Bristol with David Hunt[234] YC Nat. Chairman (v. impressive chap) for the Police Federation, I returned to London to await the result of the Norwegian referendum – it was as exciting as a general election and the results were very volatile until 1am. In the event Norway voted 'NO' – 54% to 46% on a 75% turn out. This gave a great boost to the antis here and I was on the radio calling for a referendum here, article in *Evening Standard*, letters to Press etc. Peter Shore and Dick Body and D Jay went off to Denmark to stiffen them – we have suddenly developed a closer liaison with antis in Scandinavia which perhaps we should have done before. Enoch Powell went to Brussels to say Britain doesn't want to go in! The next objective is to get the Labour Party to pass a harsh CM resolution at their Conference and then Pompidou may well have second thoughts – all is not over yet! It was a busy week culminating in a tennis match at Wimbledon against the French Parliament which we lost 5-4 – lots of prizes and a very pleasant 2 days. We now await Denmark's referendum!

And Denmark voted on 2 Oct. 'Yes' – great pity; but the Danish Govt. had used every trick to get this result including closing the foreign exchange market because of a threat of a 20% devaluation if they said No!

---

[234] David Hunt, Lord Hunt of Wirral (1942-), Conservative MP for Wirral, 1976-97. Marten was right to be impressed, Hunt served several junior and senior ministerial posts in the Thatcher and Major administrations, including Secretary of State for Wales, 1990-93; Employment, 1993-94.

Then the Labour Party Conference edged a stage nearer saying 'No' by passing more than one resolution but the general and fair impression seemed to be that they said they would renegotiate and put the results to a referendum. It was not clear what would happen if the CM said they would not renegotiate but I imagine that as things develop (or fail to develop) between now and the next general election this will become clearer. The Cons. Party motion on the CM was completely wet, so it meant that even I could vote for it! I spoke to the motion merely calling for a referendum – Alec turned it down flat. Amusing incident – the proposer of the motion said we should have a Minister for Europe – I said in my speech that one person who would not have that job was me! Alec, in reply, said I should not be so sure – stranger things had happened before![235]

22.10.72

Parliament reassembled on 17 Oct. for 2 weeks prior to prorogation. First day back was again a debate on CM Summitt [sic] meeting. I spoke on the referendum and how the facts of the vote on 28 Oct. '71 had all changed and the real time to decide the issue was now. No reply! A silly debate really. On Thursday we debated whether Parliament should be televised – everyone very excited about it – I went on TV beforehand and said my piece and then had to wind up for the Conservative anti-TV lot – had good sport in my speech and the House turned down the proposal by a majority of 26 – I hope that is the end of it. The Summitt [sic] Conference went on and there were rows but nothing serious enough to stop our entry. I really cannot see anything to stop us now – unless the French do something odd at the last moment. Anyhow, there are still 2 months – but not a lot of hope.

29.10.72

PM made his statement on Monday about the results of the Summit Conference. The Press had blown it up as a great triumph for Ted – but Parliament let the gas out of that balloon! There were great claims about Regional Policy having been fixed – but, in essence, the vital question of how much we would get out of it was never even

---

[235] In 1979 Marten was appointed a Minister of State at the Foreign Office responsible for Overseas Development. Not quite Minister for Europe but, even then, Marten would have been surprised to have been told he would see out his parliamentary career in the Foreign Office.

mentioned! And without that it is meaningless. Great play about moving to political union by 1980 – but no definition of what it meant! Net impression was that it was a fair amount of waffle. Talks of pegging the £ in connection with our entry set off a substantial fall in Sterling – two factors added to it (1) a German report that we would peg at £2.25 and not £2.40 and (2) our inflationary situation and the talks at No. 10 between Govt., CBI and TUC which do not look like succeeding. Will the Conservatives then have to impose a Statutory Prices and Incomes Policy? We have always preached that it would not work!

5.11.72

The "drama" (was it real?) of the inflationary talks with CBI and TUC continued all the week with the £ going up and down accordingly. The Queen opened Parliament on Tuesday 31 Oct. – I had to go to the dentist – but, as for the speech from the Throne, I didn't miss much – it contained little we didn't already know. PM spoke on the address about the Downing St. talks and then came to the 1922 Committee to explain it all again – he was quite good. The debate on the address went on all week without attracting much excitement. Lunched on Thursday at GLC about education – Margaret Thatcher[236] spoke well.

Meantime, the No. 10 talks have broken down and so PM is due to announce his policy on Monday – all reports say there will be a prices and incomes freeze for six months or so – but what then? This is just what we criticised about Labour, and we castigated them heavily at the last General Election for the absurdity of it all and the fact that the inflation was due to the dam which burst once the compulsion had ended. Rough time coming.

12.11.72

On Monday the PM announced his 'package' – freeze on everything for 90 days (with an option for 60 more) while the Govt. works out its policy! Surely it should have done so before! No apology no sackings – in fact it seems that the Govt. claims that it was elected to do just this! So it seems we have adopted just the policies of the Socialists. As Robin Maxwell-Hyslop[237] said in the previous 1922 Committee 'the

---

[236] Margaret Thatcher, Baroness Thatcher (1925-2013), Prime Minister, 1979-90.
[237] Sir Robin Maxwell-Hyslop (1931-2010), Conservative MP for Tiverton, 1960-92.

PM should sack himself'! It was a wretched week. I abstained on the 2nd Reading of the Bill to freeze prices because I could not get an assurance that we would revert to our policy on which we were elected once the 90 days was over – I thought it wise that someone should fire a warning shot across the bows of the Govt. to remind them to come back.

Thursday we had the Rhodesian sanctions order again renewed after Alec D-H had said there was just a chance of a settlement with Ian Smith. But this must be the last time. All together a bad week. Harry Legge-Bourke announced he was not seeking re-election for the 1922 Committee Chairmanship (he appears to have cancer) – I am being urged to stand but I don't think I will as it is quite a tie and restricts freedom of action! Lunched on Thursday at Chatham House to meet Renato Ruggiero[238], Mansholt's[239] chief adviser for the Common Market – I asked him about the amount of regional aid he is thinking of and apparently it is $50m a year for the 9 – peanuts – so much for the triumph of the Summit!

19.11.72

Continual suggestions that I should stand as Chairman of 1922 Committee but I decided not to as it was too close to the anti-CM furore to be decent – as the polling time drew near I began to regret it as the Party clearly wanted someone of an independent mind who would be guaranteed to stand up to PM – they had 8 options! Paul Bryan, Fitzroy MacLean[240], James Ramsden[241], Derek Walker-Smith, David Renton[242], Ian Lloyd[243] (!), John Hall[244] and Edward Du

---

[238] Renato Ruggiero (1930-2013) Director General, World Trade Organisation 1995-9.
[239] Sicco Mansholt (1908-1995), President of the European Commission, 1972-3.
[240] Brigadier Sir Fitzroy Maclean (1911-1996), Conservative MP for Lancaster, 1941-59; Unionist MP Bute and Northern Ayrshire, 1959-74.
[241] James Ramsden (1923-2020), Conservative MP for Harrogate, 1954-74.
[242] David Renton, Baron Renton (1908-2007), National Liberal and then Conservative MP for Huntingdonshire, 1945-79. In 1968 Renton was one of the three remaining National Liberals who switched affiliation to the Conservative party. Created Lord Renton, 1979.
[243] Sir Ian Lloyd (1921-2006), Conservative MP for Portsmouth Langstone, 1964-74; Havant and Waterloo, 1974-83; Havant, 1983-92. Knighted, 1986.
[244] Sir John Hall (1911-1978), Conservative MP for Wycombe, 1952-78. Knighted, 1973.

Cann[245]. The first five were clearly Establishment types and no one really wanted them. John Hall was vice-Chairman and deserved it altho' he is a 'grey' figure, not rebellious, and not well-known. In the end, after a 2nd ballot, when all but the top 3 (Bryan, Hall and du C) were eliminated, we elected du Cann. I believe he was chosen because he is regarded as an independent somewhat anti-Heath man – yet his opening remarks on taking the chair was "I am a supporter of the PM and the Govt." – was he elected under false pretences!? We shall see - I feel he says these things for reasons of diplomacy and tactics but underneath I just don't believe it. It is interesting because he is not a House of Commons man – he's never there – so it must have been for that reason[246]. Now he must attend.

We have started a motion on heavy lorries. I drafted one and got Angus Maude to launch it (so it was not obviously anti-CM) and we quietly got 100 names and many Conservatives. CPRE[247] will write to all MPs to sign. Then I hope Labour will have a ½ supply day and a vote on it instructing John Peyton (Min of TPO[248]) not to agree at Brussels. This will establish the sovereignty of Parliament! Also we are having a similar go on Cwth. immigration. Things are looking up.

26.11.72

The event of the week, overshadowing all else, was the defeat of the Government by 35 votes on the new immigration rules. These rules, in pursuance of the Immigration Act 1971, give a precedence to CM nationals over Commonwealth nationals in certain respects, particularly employment. A huge row blew up in *Daily Express* who got it all technically wrong but nevertheless got the feeling of the people right. This made some MPs wake up! For the first time they realised what the CM means. There was a big meeting of the Home Affairs Committee and Robert Carr was very good but failed to

---

[245] Sir Edward du Cann (1924-2017), Conservative MP for Taunton, 1956-87. Economic Secretry to the Treasury, 1962-3. Conservative party Chairman, 1965-67. Chairman of the 1922 Committee, 1972-84. Du Cann's election to the chairmanship of the 1922 Committee was a warning to Heath that the backbenches were unhappy. Du Cann and Heath hated one another.

[246] Du Cann had substantial outside interests. The 1922 Executive would later meet at the Milk Street offices of Keyser Ullman, where Du Cann was the bank's chairman.

[247] Campaign for the Protection of Rural England.

[248] He was minister of Transport Industries.

convince us and indeed, as subsequently at dinner with him, failed to grasp our feelings. The same when he opened the debate and when Alec D-H replied. In the end, some 60 Conservatives either abstained or voted against the Govt. and they were defeated to the great cheers and celebration of everyone. Ted looked v. sick (naturally). He will now have to hoist in that he simply cannot ride roughshod over his Party. The Whips calculated that we would lose by 30 – so Ted must have known and he tried his bullying tactics again and this time the Party said enough. This could be somewhat of a milestone in Ted's position and we hope to rub it in again on Wednesday over heavy lorries[249]. This could be an interesting long term development. As a result of this the Govt. will open up conversations with Cwth. countries to get an agreed immigration policy on the basis perhaps of reciprocity of rights. I voted against the Government - and as a result was sacked from the board of Securicor!! On Friday the CBI came out against narrow exchange rates (snake in the tunnel)[250] as they said it would lead to deflationary policies etc. – we told them this 2 years ago! Slowly but almost too late the British are waking up.

3.12.72

Another good week. Labour picked up on our motion on heavy lorries as we hoped and had a ½ supply day. By then 92 Tories had signed it saying they did not want any heavier lorries. So to avoid risking another defeat the Govt. accepted Labour's motion!! By doing so they also accepted, according to Rippon's 2nd Reading speech on EEC Bill, that it was a matter of national interest requiring unanimous agreement (see my speech). As the French are keen to raise the limits, they will be furious. The debate amounted to an instruction to our Minister to agree to no increase – they now have no power to do so! That being so, the French will either try to rush through a regulation on 18 Dec. (next meeting in EEC on subject) and so it will be a directly applicable law in this country on 1st Jan. (in which case we will have

---

[249] Harmonisation of transport policies meant British roads had to accommodate larger 11-ton axle lorries from the continent. The motion instigated by Marten and Maude was heard at the end of November and without a division agreed that 'This House, mindful of the environment, is against bigger and heavier lorries', Hansard, Commons Debates, 29 November 1972, Vol. 847, Cols. 511-60.

[250] The 'snake in the tunnel' was the term used by EEC countries attributed to the policy of currency harmonisation to keep their currency values within a margin of 2.25% of the Dollar.

caused a direct confrontation over sovereignty) or it will be postponed until after we join on 1st Jan. when our Minister will be forced to use the veto! Either way a row will brew up. Next week Labour try and get a postponement of VAT! Gradually the chickens will come home to roost and those who voted <u>for</u> EEC will carry the can and enable Labour to say at next election that it's all so unpopular that if you vote Labour they will take you out - and so we lose. All instruments of ratification have to be deposited by 31 Dec. – so far only UK and Denmark have done so. Belgium and Holland have no Government so may not be able to do so – Eire is in doubt – France may be withholding until we peg the £ - so there is hope yet! Went to see Max Aitken[251] on Wednesday and told him (apropos of our victory over Govt. immigration) that when press and MPs and public work together we can win – he took the point!

10.12.72

On the whole a quiet week debating *inter alia* VAT postponement and the Consolidated Fund. I was able to raise at the 1922 Executive the question of the state of the Party. I referred to the reversal of our election pledges and the difficulty we would have at the next election over this, to creep to socialism, the need for the Govt. to take its party with it on policies and finally the loyalty question where the priorities were Queen, country, democracy, Party and its principles and its leaders in that order. I went on to say that the backbenchers and the Exec. had in the past been too weak to the PM when they met him and had let the Govt. get away with things and our loyalty should be to Party and principles and to see that the Govt. stuck to them. General agreement and we would continue next week.

Bye-election at Sutton and Cheam and Uxbridge. The Liberals won Sutton and Cheam by turning our Gen. Elec. majority of 12,696 into a Lib majority of 7,417! A 32% swing! The anti-CM candidate did not do well and only got 1,332 votes. Labour did very badly dropping from 11,261 to 2,973 votes! At Uxbridge where we should logically have lost we won by 1,128 down from 3,646. Labour came second and Libs third. There were 4 other odd candidates the National Front

---

[251] Sir Maxwell Aitken, 2nd Baronet (1910-1985), son of Lord Beaverbrook. Fighter pilot. Conservative MP for Holborn, 1945-50. Disclaimed his title three days after the death of his father in 1964.

polling 2,920! This is worrying – it is presumably an anti-immigration vote.

17.12.72

An easy week – the Govt. seems to be wanting to repair its fences with its overworked backbenchers! On my Expenditure Committee we interviewed Lord Goodman[252] about expenditure on 'Fanfare for Europe' – quite amusing and it was an example of getting at expenditure before the event and then subsequently alter it. 1922 Exec. continued its discussion on the 'state of the party' and everyone seemed worried at the direction in which we are moving – Bernard Brain[253] [sic] said he even wondered to which party we belong! We are all dining with PM on Tuesday at No. 10.

24.12.72

A quiet week in Parliament which rose on Friday 22nd. Monday lunched with Ravi Tickoo[254], owner of the largest tanker in the world 470,000 tons, Kashmiri by birth but <u>very</u> fly. Dined with Granada at final of four dinners to do with a book on Parliament[255]. Tuesday the Executive of the 1922 dined with the PM at No. 10 – I believe this was the first time ever for the Executive to dine at No. 10. It was a very pleasant affair, good food and drink. After dinner we sat around over the port for the usual 1922 discussion with the PM. He started off by giving what he called a survey of his strategy. It can be summed up by likening it to a talk from the President of the Board of Trade! He was full of figures of steel, coal and oil production, contemptuous of industry, City and Trades Unions, and I thought very complacent and out of touch. This must be because he is surrounded by yes men. He seemed unaware of the feeling in the country. I was asked to speak next by Edward du Cann and I returned to the theme about broken

---

[252] Arnold Goodman, Baron Goodman (1913-95), Chairman, Arts Council, 1965-72. Goodman led a committee to organise cultural celebrations marking British entry to the EEC, including the 'Fanfare for Europe'.

[253] Sir Bernard Braine, Baron Braine (1914-2000), Conservative MP for Billericay, 1950-55; South East Essex, 1955-83; Castle Point, 1983-92. Knighted, 1972. Ennobled, 1992.

[254] A Kashmiri shipping magnate.

[255] Anthony King, *British Members of Parliament* (London: Macmillan Press Ltd., 1974).

election pledges and how if both major parties did this our political system would disintegrate. That didn't go down too well because he cannot bring himself to admit it. The conversation then roamed through what happens after the freeze, immigration of more Asians, law and order, Civil Service, Ireland and so on. But the PM was not impressive – no political uplift at all – all nuts and bolts.

21.1.73

Schuster and Friswell got at me again wanting me to sign a statement to be read out at all Branch AGMs that I was a loyalist to Ted and his policies! I have jabbed at this – I don't like individuals being idolised – it is the Party to which one is loyal, its principles and the manifesto policies. If the leader becomes virtually socialist does one join him in his Socialism as a Conservative or does one remain a Conservative? The way things are going now the 2nd Phase of the anti-inflation policy is more socialist than the Socialists![256] The Party really is in a mess – a huge balance of payments deficit looming up, the need to fix the £ for the Common Market, industrial troubles looming up because of the control on wages, VAT coming in. All in all, the Govt. seems to have let things slide too long without checking the money supply and inflation – has gone back on most of its economic policies and all the cartoons now show Ted sucking a pipe in a Gannex mack (*a la* Wilson).

Meanwhile, Ted came to Banbury to see an Italian Orchestra perform in 'Fanfare for Europe' – he got booed etc. as he went in by the anti-CM people! I helped at the launching of Uwe Kitizinger's[257] book on Europe and CM at Dorchester – made a short speech which went well.

28.1.73

Parliament reassembled on Mon 22 Jan. The previous week PM had held a press conference at Lancaster House to announce Phase II. He is accused of insulting Parliament by not announcing Phase II to Parliament – he could certainly have recalled Parliament a few days

---

[256] Established the Pay Board and Price Commission to oversee a statutory prices and incomes policy. A pay limit of £1 was implemented plus 4% of the average weekly pay bill.

[257] Uwe Kitzinger (1928-2023), academic and adviser to the European Commission, 1973-75. The book Marten references is *Diplomacy and Persuasion: How Britain Joined the Common Market* (London: Thames and Hudson, 1973).

earlier or delayed the announcement until we reassembled – he gives the image of trying to behave like Pompidou in a Presidential way. And again, he consults the CBI, TUC and the Retailers – but completely failed to consult with the Parliamentary Party. He really is behaving very oddly! And when Phase II came in we found in the Bill that the Prices and Incomes Board and Commission, an outside body, has the right to issue stop orders on pay and prices without Parliament having a say: surely these orders must be referred to Parliament for confirmation. The mood of the Party is such that everyone dislikes it, there is much quibbling but everyone is supporting the Government because it has got itself into a mess – I feel reasonably sure the policy will fail - and then Ted will be in dire trouble. The Parliamentary Party is in a mood of waiting and seeing – by the way Ted has behaved he has not got much sympathy left in store.

4.2.73

On Monday we had the counter-inflation Bill debate. The Libs supported it and Lab. opposed it so the majorities were in the 30s – only one voted against, Enoch Powell! The general mood of the Party is that they dislike this form of state control socialism, it is dangerous because if Lab. got back we cannot oppose its continuation and that it will anyhow end up in a mess. Ted, by his Presidential approach, has certainly pinned the policy firmly to himself. If it fails he will be in dire trouble – Enoch could then come more out on top.

The more one examines the policy the more incredible it seems – intervention at every turn – it <u>must</u> have been dreamed up by the Civil Servants – but why the Cabinet approved it I simply cannot comprehend. It may have some marginal effect but will bring dreadful distortions in the end and cannot be healthy. Great outcry in the Finance Committee, even the supreme "loyalist" Sir Harry d'Avigdor Goldsmid[258], attacked the Govt for its crazy policies on Govt. expenditure, with which everyone agreed, but called for support nonetheless! I really am beginning to despair of this Govt.

Looking back it all started in early '72. The Govt. panicked over unemployment and reversed its lame duck policy. Then they gave in to the miners' strike and then the railwaymen. They increased

---

[258] Major Sir Harry d'Avigdor Goldsmid (1909-1976), Conservative MP for Walsall South, 1955-74.

and increased public expenditure, failed to reduce the rate of increase of the money supply, tried to get the growth rate up to 5% based on consumer expenditure which sucked in imports and caused the balance of payments to deteriorate, net result the floating £ declined by 10% (devaluation) which added to inflation; and joining the CM will do the same and VAT due on 1 April, too. It seems that everything it does with one hand it cancels out with the other. I think the backbenchers must insist that in the next phase in the autumn we return to Conservative policies – otherwise the Party will be in dire difficulties.

11.2.73

The Water Reorganisation Bill on Monday, censure motion on housing on Tuesday and the Public Expenditure debate on Wednesday. The Govt. came in for a lot of criticism for increased Govt. expenditure from such people as Harry d'Avigdor Goldsmid and Ed du Cann, Chairman and ex-Chairman of Expenditure Committee respectively. This increased expenditure must <u>surely</u> be inflationary when we are trying to stop inflation! Maplin Airport Bill on Thursday, again demanding vast resources and expenditure – the party not happy about it. Why the Govt. goes crashing on like this is hard to understand.

18.2.73

Monday did a broadcast to comment on Harold Wilson's 10th anniversary of his accession to the leadership of his Party! Was chosen because of my PQs to him[259]. In the evening dined with Sir Michael Wright at the Norwegian Club – excellent dinner to discuss CM – also there were Douglas Jay, Peter Shore, Eric Deakins[260], Robin Williams[261], Christopher Frere-Smith and Dick Body – it ended up in a bit of Ted bashing but it was interesting to hear the Labour MPs discuss their internal problems on the Market.
    We talked about starting up an anti-Federalist Movement to counter the pro-Federalist movement of the European Movement.

---

[259] Marten asked Wilson the most parliamentary questions when he was Prime Minister, 1964-70.
[260] Eric Deakins (1932-), Labour MP for Walthamstow West, 1970-74; Walthamstow, 1974-87.
[261] Sir Robin Williams (1928-2013), anti-marketeer donor.

This requires thought – best to get some pro-Market MPs to launch it. Tuesday lunched with Australian High Commissioner who has just arrived – really rather deadly and crude – an ex-Labour politician[262]. Dined with Hal Campbell about sugar – he told me a most alarming story about how the Govt. was cheating over subsidies to the refiners when under Common Market rules we should not be subsidising at all. It is bound to come out sometime.

More and more rumours of the Civil Service and the City losing confidence in Ted. Apparently he just overrides his ministers and dictates to them. The City is angry with him over his policy. If this really is developing (and if the Counter Inflation fails) he will be in real trouble – then at an election what is the option – Ted or Harold – will the nation want either – or will they call for someone else? Could there be a coalition in a crisis excluding both?

Just for the record, on 30 Jan. my Association F&GP decided to place on the Agenda of the next Executive the question of the adoption of a candidate. On 7 Feb. I was told by Agent Webb that there was not much to be discussed at the Executive mainly quotas; yet all the time he knew because he had been at the F&GP and kept it from me. Then on 7 Feb. I was asked to propose the 'Council' at the Chipping Norton Mayors dinner so, in view of foregoing, I accepted. On 9 Feb. I was informed it was to be put on the agenda. Very suspicious! Also AGM, usually in April, fixed for June. Are they mobilising against me? I think so but Chairman Friswell says they are not. Who can one believe? This is started so they say by the small clique in Banbury under Geoff Lester[263] – but he is the front man, I think, for Schuster and Friswell. Will see how it goes – major bust up if they decide to 'open the list' to other candidates.

25.2.73

After 10 o'clock division Exec of 1922 met to discuss present situation – general consensus that Govt. having made its policy must stand firm. General criticism of Govt. U-turns etc!! Enoch Powell back from visit to USA and says people are getting so disillusioned with Govt. that many are questioning whether they need Govt.!! We see the

---

[262] John Armstrong (1908-77), Senator for New South Wales, 1938-62. High Commissioner to the UK, 1973-74.
[263] Mayor of Banbury, 1962.

beginnings of that here in the general fed-up-ness of people with the two main political parties.

4.3.73

Monday spoke at Bow Group on Select Committees then dined with anti-CM people at Reform Club to discuss formation of anti-Dear Food Campaign! All the old rebels there – quite like old times – but enjoyable as it was the feet were in the air! Tues. and Wed. we debated the Counter Inflation Bill – although Labour had a 3-line many were away at the 3 bye-elections, so the Govt. had majorities in the 60s – no good rebelling in these circumstances, particularly as my Constituency Executive were meeting on Friday to consider my readoption! In the event the rebels didn't really rebel – they abstained – but most people concluded that the Bill and the policy is a nonsense and would not work and would end in shambles by the autumn with Ted in a bind!

Lunched on Wed. with Sir Michael Wright and Sir George Bolton[264] to discuss the general situation – they want Enoch Powell for leader – we are to organise a conference in late Sept. on Free Trade! On Friday evening I proposed the toast of the Borough at the Chipping Norton Mayor's Banquet while my Executive decided whether to recommend me for re-adoption! They did but only 2 voted against me – Pat Colegrave and Waine from the new part of Bicester. Collapse of effective opposition! AGM in June and after that I will go on the offensive.

Thursday night Dick Taverne was returned for Lincoln by a majority up from 4,000 to 13,000 on the sole issue of the right of an MP to use his judgement and not be dictated to by his local Party caucus. This was _terrific_ and reinforced my case as I had threatened to stand if not re-adopted for voting against the CM[265]! This result must have helped in my re-adoption. It was an important result for Parliament and the whole principle involved. Note – Cons. did very badly in all 3 by-elections Lincoln, Dundee, Chester le Street – do the polls _really_ support our freeze policy?

---

[264] Sir George Bolton (1900-82), banker. UK executive director, International Monetary Fund, 1946-52.
[265] For the full story to this see Tim Aker, 'Re-assessing the Conservative Anti-EEC Rebellion, 1971-2', *Parliamentary History*, Vol. 42 (3), pp. 391-408.

11.3.73

Prices and Pay Code debate on Monday – this is the guideline document for the Prices and Incomes Boards – the more one considers it the more dotty it seems! Tuesday the Budget – Tony Barber was very tired – he had been in the middle of the latest currency crisis of the dollar. He did not get a standing ovation this time except from a few – it was a neutral budget which will be hard to recall in a few months time except that the Govt. budget deficit was £4,400m to be raised from the public – too much and this <u>could</u> lead to trouble later. Meanwhile the currency crisis goes on – attempts are being made for a joint float with the EEC countries – this is viewed as a step towards monetary union – it is stupid and will harm us in the end.

Wednesday went to N. Ireland to observe the referendum – v. well organised. Flew RAF. Stayed at Stormont Hotel, dined Lord Windlesham[266] Wed. night, visited polling stations in Belfast, Armagh, Porterdown and they were all very well run and I had no complaints. But one Labour MP, Duffy[267], was firing complaints everywhere helping the Catholics to say that it was rigged. The great majority of Catholics abstained but the result was v. good for us and there was about a 60% turnout with only 5% against.[268] Where a district was mixed Protestant Catholic the Cats. voted – but in particularly Cat. areas the intimidation was such that they didn't vote. Now for the White Paper in a few weeks' time and then the local elections. Lunched with Willy Whitelaw on Friday and then flew home. Meantime the IRA caused 2 explosions in London and badly damaged the Old Bailey with 200 casualties and two other bombs were defused one just 150 yards from our flat! They will probably do it again when the White Paper is published. On w/end Dickie Sharples[269] now Governor of Bermuda, was assassinated in the grounds of Government House – cruel blow.

---

[266] David Hennessy, 3rd Baron Windlesham (1932-2010), Conservative peer and academic. Minister of State for Northern Ireland, 1972-3.

[267] Sir Patrick Duffy (1920-), Labour MP for Colne Valley, 1963-66; Sheffield Attercliffe, 1970-92. As of 2024 he was Britain's oldest surviving former MP.

[268] On a 58% turnout, 98.2% voted to remain part of the UK and 1.08% voted to join with the Republic of Ireland.

[269] On 10 March 1973 Sir Richard Sharples and Captain Hugh Sayers were shot and killed in the grounds of the Governor's residence, Government House. The assailants, Larry Tacklyn and Erskine Burrows, were caught, tried, and hanged in 1977, the last people to be executed under British rule.

18.3.73

White Paper on N. Ireland due out some time soon and security precautions are being stepped up for a further demo of bombing – Parliament is wide open to attack unless we tighten up the checking system[270].

25.3.73

Defence debates this week – really very dull and fairly non-contentious. Lunched at Dorchester on Tuesday as guest of Time-Life[271] – only other guest was Roy Jenkins; he displayed an interesting lack of understanding on detail of the Common Market but on the whole was quite bullish about the economy. Thursday lunched at the *Spectator* but it was short and we didn't get very far. General atmosphere is improving because unemployment is coming down in leaps and bounds and growth is strong and the strikes are temporarily petering out. But it may be quiet before the storm.

Willy Whitelaw presented his White Paper on N. Ireland on Tuesday (without any bombs!) and it was a sensible paper except for the fact that it did not increase the number of N. Irish MPs at Westminster. This was in my view a mistake but I gather Labour would not have this because it might increase the number of Cons. MPs and the Cons. feared it might get in more wild and independent MPs. I suggested to Willy that he should agree to put in the Boundary Commission and play it long and this would I believe make it acceptable to the loyalists. As might be expected the N. Irish reacted all over the place in the oddest way!

1.4.73

The main fun and games this week has been Joe Godber's efforts in Brussels to resist any increase in farm prices. He is playing, rightly, for a freeze. I put down a motion supporting him and saying that the House of Commons will not accept any increases. Now Labour has picked this up and is having a half day supply on it – should be interesting! The point I want to establish is that Parliament must

---

[270] A frightening prediction. In 1979 Airey Neave was killed in a car bomb explosion driving out of the Palace of Westminster car park.
[271] Book and media publishers.

express its sovereign power and that this will be our instruction to Godber and he must then use the veto. The Govt. has always claimed that it cannot do anything to control the price of food because we cannot control overseas prices – now, here is a chance when for once they <u>can</u> exercise some control – if they don't they will look very silly.

8.4.73

Tuesday a debate on EEC food prices prior to the settlement by EEC Council of Ministers – I spoke taking the view that it was contrary to the Govt's. policy of counter-inflation to agree to any increases in food prices and if they did not use their veto they could never again claim that the rise in food prices was due to overseas factors outside their control. I abstained because the Government's amendment avoided the rise which in effect was an attempt to establish the sovereignty of Parliament before the event and to give instructions to our Minister. The Govt. won! They are intent on not binding our Ministers before negotiations.

15.4.73

A dull parliamentary week enlivened only by the sale of EEC butter to the Russians – they have ½m tons of surplus butter from which EEC consumers must pay £837 a ton – the Russians bought 200,000 tons @ £144 a ton!! Wide open for all sorts of snide remarks and we made hay of it. The public understand this – the EEC is increasingly looking the absurdity it is. Local Election for new CCs on Thursday – Labour took control of GLC and other major urban areas – could it be that the Govt. is not as popular as it believes?!!

22.4.73

Monday and Tuesday were devoted to legislation on N. Ireland sitting until 2am. Wednesday 1922 lunch at Savoy for PM. He made the most dreary speech – not a note, nothing prepared, no humour and no leadership – just the sort of speech for the Ramsgate Conservative women! He really does show a remarkable contempt for his Party – this is the one occasion of the year when he should really rise above the average – he failed and most people knew it. Trade figures show a deficit of almost £200m – if this goes on it will be serious. Later that day we debated the Report (Interim) of the Select Committee on EEC secondary legislation – I spoke and apart from some detailed comments I went for the secrecy of law making in the Community, i.e., the Council of Ministers is the law making body and it sits and promulgates the law in secret – this won't do! House adjourned for Easter on Thursday 19 April for one week.

On Friday 27[272] I had a meeting for my critics! Really pathetic criticism and they wanted a declaration of love and adulation of Ted!! However it served as a letting off of steam. Meanwhile in Brussels, Joe Godber fighting a battle against the stupidity of the CAP arrived at a compromise which he presented as a victory – but it really wasn't.

20.5.73

Busy week catching up. Tues. 1922 Exec. saw PM – he was very bullish about economy and seemed to have no reservations about success – I wish he had!

27.5.73

Monday lunched with CBI – general discussion on economy – several from Exec. of 1922 went – it was good for them to hear the backbench non-specialist view. They rather shared our doubts of the PM's bullishness – they too pointed out the dangers which loom on the end-year horizon. At the moment though everything in the immediate short term looks good. On Monday Tony Barber announced £600m in 'cuts' – a touch of the brake! – hailed by the press as brilliant timing – perhaps it was – time will tell. My fear is that the accelerated growth rate of 5-6% will lead to overheating of the economy, foster inflation and back to square one. Better to settle for 4% growth rate and keep it going.

Tuesday to Paris with Joan and Anthony for the Christening of Torolf's oil rig at le Havre. That evening the 'scandal' of Lord Lambton[273] and the call girls broke. He had been photographed in bed with 3 call girls and as Under Secretary RAF there was a security risk (*a la* Profumo) so he immediately resigned. Also police found some drugs in his home! He subsequently made a brilliant TV broadcast for 1 hour with Robin Day which seemed to put him in a better light with

---

[272] The anomaly here is that this is in the entry for 22 April.
[273] Anthony Lambton, Lord Lambton (1922-2006), Conservative MP for Berwick-upon-Tweed, 1951-73. The scandal involving prostitutes led to his resignation from parliament.

the public. Then Lord Jellicoe confessed to call girl trouble and he too resigned as leader in the House of Lords – a double blow for Ted. He made an excellent statement on it in House, showing his obvious distaste, fairly spitting out the word prostitute with contempt! And there are rumours of a Duke (guess who?!) and a third Minister involved. The 3rd Minister was subsequently challenged and denied it. Made quite a diversion for a week! But in total, Maudling and Poulson, Sandys and Lonrho[274], Lords L and J – the image gets quite a bit tainted. Bye elections on Thursday and Cons did not do well[275].

17.6.73

Reassembled 11 June – NHS Reorganisation Bill, N. Ireland Constitutional Bill, and Maplin Development Bill on which we had a sensible amendment on it and defeated the Govt! Like the Immigration Bill, they were insensitive to the impending defeat and should have given in. But they didn't with the inevitable result.

24.6.73

Friday AGM for the re-adoption. Friswell, Webb and others had obviously done their damnest to make it as awkward as possible for me and had virtually rigged things as far as they could – it was a very unpleasant feeling. I spoke - and answered my critics - I took a tough line throughout and really put the question to them "whether or not we were to fight the next election together" implying (but not saying so) that if I wasn't adopted I would stand nevertheless (harping on Dick Taverne at Lincoln). I emphasised that I stood by Burkean philosophy of MPs[276]. In the event I was adopted by 128-26! This has now virtually isolated the opposition, Friswell has retired and Len Edwards is Chairman. The F&GP now looks much more pro-me. I appealed for unity. There will now be a lot to do. I had a fairly relaxing weekend – it is nice to know that the anxiety is now over.

---

[274] Duncan Sandys was chairman of Lonrho, who were criticised for their mining activities in Africa. Ted Heath had called them the 'unacceptable' face of capitalism. In March 1973 the board sought to remove its chief executive Tiny Rowland, alleging financial mismanagement.

[275] These were the relatively safe Labour holds in Westhoughton and West Bromwich.

[276] MPs as representatives not delegates.

1.7.73

The local papers very complimentary about my re-adoption. The *Oxford Times* had an excellent leading article right on point of not being a yes-man! This should go to isolate the small-minded men. Many congratulations, too, in Parliament. On Monday we voted on having a new Parliamentary Building – I voted against, being quite happy with the present accommodation – seems an absolute waste of money. Tuesday was an excellent short debate on EEC regional policy – not so much on the policy itself, which was unknown, as the right of Parliament to debate and vote on it when it was known. The Govt. moved an amendment, irrelevant, and said parliament could debate it but not vote on it. As the regional policy is the work of the Commission and not the Council of Ministers this is rule by Brussels Civil Servants. I voted against the Govt. (as if to celebrate my readoption!). Wednesday went to Leeds at the invitation of Lord Boyle[277], Vice Chancellor, to speak to our report on higher education. A terrifying experience to speak in front of an ex-Minister of Ed. surrounded by his academics on a subject in which I am not an expert. However, it went well and agreeable and I stayed the night with Ed Boyle and we came down together on the train. He seems much more relaxed since he left Parliament. A Manchester seat bye-election on 27 June put us well to the bottom of the poll with only 600 votes! Lost deposit. Any significance?[278]

Fairly busy w/end – meeting with John Lee, new CPC man for constituency, to discuss political activity. What a pleasure it is not to have Friswell any more as Chairman – now we can get on with the constituency. I wonder how the new man Len Edwards will get on? It is essential that he sticks to organisation and leave the political. I hear he might be a Friswell man – I hope not.

---

[277] Edward Boyle, Lord Boyle of Handsworth (1923-81), Conservative MP for Birmingham Handsworth, 1950-70. Minister of Education, 1962-64. Vice Chancellor of Leeds University, 1970.

[278] They were not quite bottom. The Conservative candidate polled 683 votes, embarrassingly close to the Marxist-Leninist candidate who polled 109. A very low turnout of 18% for the Manchester Exchange by-election.

8.7.73

Monday were two half supply days of little interest. Dined at Dorchester with Cosgrave[279], PM of Eire, but had to leave before his speech to vote – quite reasonable about the North. Tuesday Dick Sharples memorial – he was assassinated as Governor of Bermuda. A really beautiful service in Westminster Abbey and full of friends – PM downwards! In the evening went to a party given by Maurice Edelman at Hughenden Manor, Disraeli's old house, where Maurice lives – he wrote an excellent book on him. Lovely evening. Friday Joan and I flew off to Rheims to play in the annual tennis match v. French – no longer at Deauville. Small plane from Biggin Hill. Team John Hannam[280], Tom King[281], John Osborn[282], Peter Rost[283], Maurice Edelman and self. It was champagne from the word go! We were entertained by the Tattinger family to dinner on Friday night, tennis Sat. and dined at Tattinger Chateau in the vineyards (where Joffre and Haig conducted 1st World War). We won the match 6-3 first time since war!

15.7.73

On arrival back from France, straight to a lunch by Lord Nugent on terrace of House of Lords – sunny and cool! In the evening I opened a debate on Higher Education as Chairman of the Select Committee on Expenditure on Education and Art. A short debate – the Minister didn't like our recommendations[284]!

Thursday a ½ supply on export of live animals for slaughter. Labour put down a motion in reasonable terms. The Govt. put a silly amendment and was, quite predictably, defeated by 21 votes. It gathered the anti-CM votes because under Art. 34 of Treaty of Rome

---

[279] Liam Cosgrave (1920-2017), Irish Taoiseach, 1973-77.
[280] Sir John Hannam (1929-), Conservative MP for Exeter, 1970-97. Knighted, 1992.
[281] Tom King, Baron King of Bridgwater (1933-), Conservative MP for Bridgwater, 1970-2001. Held various offices in the Thatcher and Major administrations: Secretary of State for Transport, 1983; Employment, 1983-85; Northern Ireland, 1985-89; Defence, 1989-92. Ennobled, 2001.
[282] Sir John Osborn (1922-2015), Conservative MP for Sheffield Hallam, 1959-87. Knighted, 1983.
[283] Peter Rost (1930-2022), Conservative MP for South East Derbyshire, 1970-83; Erewash, 1983-92.
[284] The Minister was Margaret Thatcher.

we cannot do this. So we have a sovereignty test, same as heavy lorries, where parliament has said what it wants regardless of CM!

22.7.73

A bad week at Parliament – nearing the end of the session, sultry weather and people getting bitchy! Tuesday a dreadful debate on the visit of the Portuguese PM[285] – a very dubious article appeared in '*The Times*' about a massacre by Portuguese in Mozambique – source was a Catholic priest. Wilson took this up and without any confirmation (indeed there was doubt as to whether the village concerned actually existed!) castigated the Govt. for entertaining the Portuguese PM! This was done to embarrass the Govt. It was really shameful. Next day (Wed.) a vote of no confidence in Govt. over inflation – it was a yak-yak debate, you did this, we did that! The Govt. rightly decided that the House should rise early next week!

An excellent party at Carlton Club on Wed. evening to celebrate the 50th anniversary of the 1922 Committee – all old members present and PM. PM to 1922 on Thursday evening - slightly better than usual but no great shakes! High Sheriff's party on Friday night. All my critics from the past, bankers, landowners etc., the "well-educated" who wanted me to default on my CM pledge to approve entry, were charming to the point of nausea, saying they supported me all along and how glad they were that I had been re-adopted etc. – such is life (and upbringing!)

29.7.73

The last week of this rather awful session. Lunched on Monday with Sir Cyril Kleinwort[286] who is Chairman of the Invisible Exports Committee to hear his views on the Government and the PM – not all together complimentary! After the 10 O'clock vote on Prices and Pay Board I had my motion on EEC proposals for driving licences. The Euro Commission have produced a draft directive about harmonising driving licences – quite the most dotty thing, harmonisation for the sake of harmonisation. They wanted to raise the age to 18 for cars amongst other things. I have for months been trying to get this

---

[285] Marcelo Caetano (1906-80), his government was overthrown in 1974 and Portugal transitioned to democracy.
[286] Sir Cyril Kleinwort (1905-80), banker.

debated so as to establish the principle that Parliament can express a view and establish an instruction for our Ministers to obey when they get to the Council of Ministers. The Govt. provided time and accepted my amendment! This, like heavy lorries, Parliament has said it is not going to have it. The interesting thing is what will happen if the Minister has to compromise and come back to Parl. having exceeded our wishes and instructions. Will he, I wonder, obey Parliament's instruction? Anyhow it was all generally regarded as a victory for the anti-CM lobby! Tuesday tennis v Livery Club followed by lunch at House of Lords. One hour with PM in the afternoon – again not very impressive – he seems to be over confident of success in Stage III[287] and places too much trust in Trades Unions. Wednesday saw the pound in trouble – Bank lending rate up to 11½% highest since 1914! Stock Exchange tumbles. Germany puts up overnight interest rates to effectively 30%! This drew money away from sterling – just what Germany should <u>not</u> do - no cooperation in CM!!

Parliament rose on Wednesday (25 July) earlier than expected – PQs in the morning were to the Foreign Office - plenty on the Common Market and the Govt. looked distinctly dodgy. Then John Davies came to the box to announce that the CM had demanded a further £33m for the common agricultural policy – all hell broke loose! Apparently the sum had been fixed only the day before. John Davies did badly and the House was generally furious with him and furious that this amount of money had to be spent to help the inefficient French farmers instead of our own needs. Thursday two bye-elections Ely and Ripon – both Tory seats and we lost both[288]. Ely was a Cons. majority of 9,600 and Ripon 12,064 – the Liberals won both – we did about twice as badly as Labour. A shock to the Govt. which it deserved. The Govt. has panicked over unemployment and got itself into an awful position over its Prices and Incomes policy. It is losing support everywhere. Talk of a major Liberal revival – thank goodness I have not been an obvious Heath-man. There could, in a great crisis, be an upsurge of a feeling that Enoch Powell is the only man who could save the Party!

Front-page article in *Sunday Times* saying that Civil Servants in Treasury and Brussels had made a report to Govt. that CM was a

---

[287] The third, and final, piece of the government's prices and incomes policy.
[288] The Ely by-election was caused by the death of Sir Harry Legge-Bourke. The Ripon by-election was caused by the death of Sir Malcolm Stoddart-Scott.

<u>disaster</u> for Britain! Excellent article – quite made my day! Date of article 29 July.

14.10.73

We did not go away, during the recess, for a holiday – on reflection I wish we had as we never get a real rest at home in the constituency – always work to be done and people ring up and mail pouring in! Then a trip to Canada and USA as Chairman of Expenditure Select Committee on Education, looking at how they did their post-graduate education. Went with Eric Deakins MP and clerk Frank Allen. Very interesting and altho' I originally had doubts about whether we should go I certainly found it to have been very worthwhile. Washington hot and sweaty, visited Watergate investigation, met Senators and Representatives, lunched with Lord Cromer[289], our Ambassador, who was very nice and hospitable. Americans mostly alarmed at Watergate revelations and even if Nixon[290] and Agnew[291] are guilty they would prefer to see them imprisoned and clean the place up.

Meantime, at home, the Liberal surge goes on. *The Times* poll by ORC showed Labour 34%, Libs 32% and Cons 31%!! A big shock for the Govt. The Lab. Party Conference was very leftish and they must have offended many who would vote Labour. Saw the PM at No. 10 on 2 Oct. to discuss Phase III with '22 Executive – he looked tired and so will Phase III, I suspect. CM becoming more and more unpopular every day – even Lord Stokes[292] is now attacking it! So far, no visible dividends coming through and just frustrations. Rather as we expected and, locally, people are recognising it – am <u>so</u> glad I did not yield to pressures to change my vote.

---

[289] Rowland Baring, 3rd Earl of Cromer (1918-1991), Governor of the Bank of England, 1961-66; British Ambassador to the United States of America, 1971-4.
[290] Richard Nixon (1913-1994), 37th President of the United States of America, 1968-74. Resigned office over the Watergate scandal where five operatives from Nixon's Committee for the Re-Election of the President were caught trying to break into the Democratic party offices in the Watergate building in 1972.
[291] Spiro Agnew (1918-1996), 39th Vice President of the United States of America. Resigned in 1973 when he was investigated in connection with extortion, bribery, and tax evasion.
[292] Donald Stokes, Baron Stokes (1914-2008), chief executive, British Leyland, 1968-75. Ennobled, 1969.

21.10.73

On Mon. 15th the F&GP was held. I was invited for only the second time in 14 years so suggested having it at Swalcliffe House. It went well – but amusingly the first item on the agenda was 'minutes of the last meeting', read out at great length by Harry Webb, the agent. V. embarrassing because they were apparently discussing <u>me</u>. But the interesting point was that the discussion centred on what canvassers should say between now and the election – they apparently didn't think there was yet much to say about Government achievements so they had decided to use me as the canvassing point and extol my virtues as a constituency MP etc. <u>and</u>, believe it or not, to extol the fact that I was not a rubber stamp and to highlight the fact that I had taken an independent line!! And that from an F&GP which only a few months before had been criticising my independence!! All of which goes to show that it is a good thing and that one has some friends on the F&GP for stormy weather. Drove up to London after the meeting was over.

The week was overshadowed by the Arab-Israeli war (round 3!). The Arabs (Egypt and Syria) attacked and one by one the other Arab countries joined in – not exactly whole-heartedly! The Israelis were caught on the hop as the attack took place on the 'day of atonement' when they were all praying[293]. However in the days that followed a lot of tough fighting took place, tank battles and air battles in the Golan Heights and Sinai. The Israelis seem to have been successful in the Golan Heights and we are now awaiting the major tank battle in the Sinai to start. In the meantime Britain stopped all arms deliveries to both sides; this aroused a lot of Jewish fury who said we should supply ammunition and spares to the Israelis as they had our tanks. However, if we had done that then we would have had to supply arms to the Arabs and we might well have had to supply anti-tank weapons to them which would have been counter-productive. Also we were holding ourselves in reserve to deal with the peace negotiations because this time it must be a <u>permanent</u> settlement not just a cease-fire. There was a good debate on Thursday (although the Jewish MPs 'wailed' too much) and the Govt. won by 70 odd votes – a lot of cross voting. The Labour Party forced a division and it is believed that they did it in order to get the 7,000 Jewish votes in the forthcoming Hove bye-election!!

---

[293] Hence it was known as the Yom Kippur War.

28.10.73

Mid East ceasefire due to Kissinger[294] (West) and Brezhnev[295] (USSR). – UK really did seem to play a minimal part in the whole affair – I believe it was because we were waiting on EEC who were so wet it wasted time. Our voice has now been effectively silenced by entry into CM – we were totally ineffective in protesting on behalf of Cwth. over French nuclear tests, our voice was gagged in the International Sugar Agreement talks which failed and now this. The point must surely be coming apparent to the public. Tuesday went to Chatham House to hear Commissioner Simonet[296] on harmonising banking in CM – the City doesn't like it one bit – altho' they supported entry. Lloyds Insurance also disapprove. And so do many other organisations. Printers and publishers angry about possible VAT on periodicals and papers if EEC harmonisation comes about. On Tuesday we had for example Tate and Lyle complaining (rightly) about EEC and sugar and they had supported entry! Opposition is very clearly mounting. Wednesday debate on sugar on Labour's motion reaffirming our undertaking on 1.4m tons of cane sugar from Cwth developing countries. Margin for refiners was a vital part in the argument – if these are cut cane refiners in UK could either go out of business so we could say we can no longer take the cane or they would have to merge with the beet refiners and so become dictated by them. The Govt. knew it was in a tight corner and so having had a 3-line whip they decided they could only accept the Labour motion and not have an amendment. A victory for the antis – the real crunch will come if they fail to get an agreement. Thursday a debate on Channel Tunnel – unfortunately the Government won!

4.11.73

Tuesday the State opening – a mild legislative programme was announced as a run up to the election although there are enough problems to cause the Party plenty of anguish in the meantime! The

---

[294] Henry Kissinger (1923-2023), diplomat and academic. US Secretary of State, 1973-77.
[295] Leonid Brezhnev (1906-1982), General Secretary of the Communist Party of the Soviet Union, 1964-82.
[296] Henri Simonet (1931-96), EEC Commissioner, 1973-77.

debate on the address was opened by Wilf Proudfoot[297] who was quite unbelievably dreadful and seconded by Gerry Vaughn[298] who was quite good – then the yak-yak of Harold Wilson and Ted Heath! Oh, how boring! In the evening we took our new Chairman Len Edwards and wife to the United and Cecil Club reception and introduced him to the PM, Chancellor and various Ministers – a successful operation, I hope!

11.11.73

Tuesday, a briefing at Shell on the M.E. oil situation – outlook depressing! Wednesday lunch with reps of newspapers anxious about EEC proposals for VAT! Thursday, Channel Tunnel (abstained) and Rhodesian Sanctions (abstained, because Govt. not being tough enough against CM partners who are sanctions busters). Re-elected to Executive 1922. General trend of elections to Party Committees was to right. Friday spoke for D. Walker-Smith at Bishops Stortford – awful drive.

Bye-elections on Thursday – we held Hove and Edinburgh – lost Berwick[299] - and did badly in Govan. Conclusion, Labour did really badly – Libs did well, Cons. held out. Looks as though if Lab. don't pull themselves together they will not win general election.

18.11.73

Air of self-satisfaction among Tories at Westminster on Monday and utter gloom in the Labour Party – many Lab. MPs felt they could not now win the General Election. But how true it is to say "a week is a long time in politics". Next day – crash! A balance of trade deficit of £300m for two months – miners' strike and a state of emergency declared!! Bank rate up to 13% - highest ever - and we all feel there is more to come.

---

[297] Wilfred Proudfoot (1921-2013), Conservative MP for Cleveland, 1959-64; Brighouse and Spenborough, 1970-74.

[298] Sir Gerard Vaughn (1923-2003), Conservative MP for Reading, 1970-74; Reading South, 1974-83; Reading East, 1983-97.

[299] The Berwick by-election was caused by Lord Lambton's resignation from parliament. The Hove by-election was caused by the death of sitting MP Martin Maddan. The Edinburgh North by-election was caused by the resignation of sitting MP John Scott, the Earl Dalkeith. Upon his father's death in 1973, Scott succeeded to the Dukedoms of Queensberry and Buccleuch.

Tony Barber (Chancellor) came to the 1922, spoke and answered 19 questions all critical – he did not seem to me to be very convincing. Enoch Powell just sat there – no need for him to ask any questions! Tony harped on a policy of steady expansion – growth was 5% and is now to be reduced to 3½% - clearly 5% had been too much and had overheated the economy. Massive special deposits called in and cuts planned in state spending over next years. Many speakers said we should not go ahead with Maplin and Channel Tunnel – others recommended import controls (!EEC?!). All in all a very shaky experience for PM who only a week before had spoken of an unprecedented boom and that these were merely the problems associated with success!! What success, might one ask?!

To my mind there is a distinct lack of candour in Govt. speeches and the public is seeing through it – at any rate they are completely confused. M.E. oil[300] may cause fuel rationing, miners' strike against Phase 3 will cause shortage of coal if not settled – the Govt. has promised not to give in! Balance of payments will obviously suffer yet more due to increase in oil prices – outlook thoroughly grim – Labour should have a hey-day – but one wonders if they are capable of it? Therein lies a quiet threat to Parliamentary democracy.

On Wednesday some enjoyable relief – Princess Anne married Mark Phillips – we watched from the pavement outside H. of C. – glorious sunny day and blue skies – all very moving and incredible loyalty to the Crown shown by the people – they got it just right between formality and informality.

25.11.73

Monday was a censure debate in the Govt. Stupid 'yak-yak'! Govt. won. Tuesday the Anglo-Norwegian group – gave a lunch to the Norwegian Ambassador – a friendly affair. Mass lobby by the anti-abortionists etc. although not much in the Parliamentary week. The miners' 'go-slow' goes ahead, the Arabs mostly still shout about keeping up the oil embargo; while King Faisal[301] makes the running the Shah of Iran[302] says they should lift the embargo while peace negotiations are on. If it goes on the West could be brought to its knees – but I doubt if we would allow that to happen.

---

[300] Embargo.
[301] King Faisal of Saudi Arabia (1906-75).
[302] Mohammad Reza Pahlavi (1919-80), Shah of Iran, 1941-79.

2.12.73

Tuesday a debate on EEC – rather a general one but the antis won hands down in the argument simply because there are no solid reasons for justifying our membership – John Davies was pathetic for the Govt. Dined at the Savoy Grill after the debate – with Smedvigs, Newman[303]. Thursday had Colin Cowdrey[304] to lunch to discuss the Sports Council – a <u>charming</u> person. Friday several constituency engagements ending up with the Caledonian Ball – during my speech a Scot. Nat.[305] walked out.

The issuing of petrol coupons has started altho' rationing has not yet started – driving is being reduced all round, particularly on Sundays. The Govt. came in for quite a lot of cynical mirth at the main 1922 meeting – largely for saying that it was impossible to give into the teachers over pensions and then finally doing so! No one seemed inclined to defend them – at the 1922 Executive it was even hotter for the Govt. Enoch Powell made a speech on Thursday saying he feared for the PM's mental health! That caused a turmoil! Cabinet changes in the offing.

9.12.73

Spoke on Wednesday a.m. at Wilton Park to a most prestigious audience on defence and CM – great sport. Elected to be Chairman of Commonwealth Industries – Lord knows why! Dined with National Union – v. dull. Thursday read the lesson at St. Margaret's Westminster at the memorial service for Gerald Nabarro[306] – sad that he's gone

Main problem of the week was still the fuel crisis – many people advocating rationing – Govt. says it is not necessary – but real crisis looms stock exchange really getting the jitters.

---

[303] Frederick Newman (1916-2012), Chairman, Davies and Newman Shipbrokers.
[304] Colin Cowdrey, Baron Cowdrey of Tonbridge (1932-2000), international cricketer. Ennobled, 1997.
[305] Scottish Nationalist.
[306] Sir Gerald Nabarro's health had not been good in 1973 and he had announced his intention to retire at the next election shortly before his death.

16.12.73

During this week the volume of criticism grew against the Prime Minister for not giving a lead to the nation over the fuel/economic crisis. He certainly waited a long time before doing or saying much. But on Thursday with really awful trade figures again, go slow by the miners really hitting the power stations and the Arabs still cutting back on oil, the PM came to the Commons and made an emergency statement. The major item was that due to the miners go slow and the running down of coal at the power stations, the country would go to a 3-day working week after 1st Jan. This will bring home to the working population that they are being made to suffer for the miners' pay claim. The Coal Board offer will give them 8 ½% above the average industrial wage – not bad in the circumstances but now that the Arabs have put up the price of oil some are suggesting that the price of coal could go up to accommodate the miners' pay claim. The miners' Executive is Communist dominated, and the question is whether they are trying to dominate Parliament in a confrontation or whether they are merely using the present situation to extract the maximum pay settlement and establish that the miners are a special case for high pay in view of their work. If they do not give in, in this Arab situation, there could well be unemployment of several millions by Feb. and then there <u>could</u> be an anarchical situation. This of course is exactly what the Communists would like to see. Should the Govt. yield? If they did it would be interpreted as rule by the Unions – but if they didn't yield (and the PM re-affirmed that he would <u>not</u> yield on Thursday) the consequences could be shattering. A dilemma!

23.12.73

Christmas on the way! Tuesday – 8.55am a car bomb exploded 400 yards away from our flat – quite a stir but the Services of ambulance, police, and fire brigade were very efficient and 2 helicopters in the air within minutes. 60 to hospital but more very seriously injured. Then next day an MP received a letter bomb so we were all warned against them – on return to the flat there was a small brown parcel addressed to Ian Gilmour who is now Minister for Defence and responsible for the Army in N. Ireland and also lived in the flat below some 2 years ago. Rang police and they came and sent for the bomb squad who eventually came at 2am and collected it – no news as to whether it <u>was</u> a bomb!

Wednesday meeting with PM for Exec. of 1922 – he was in good form and the conversation wandered agreeably and informally. Miners' ban on overtime continues to reduce coal supplies to power stations, railwaymen's go slow makes chaos of the railways and on Thursday evening I left House of Commons at 6.45 and got home at 12.45am! (by train!) – shades of wartime. So Christmas is well launched in an atmosphere of gathering economic gloom.

20.1.74

On return on Wednesday 16 Jan. all the talk was about a General Election – absolute fever and most MPs assumed it was on. I am against it as I fail to see what it would achieve. If we won what would be the difference – we would have to follow the same policies as we have now and would announce at the election – if neither side got an absolute majority the Liberals would hold the balance of power - and if we lost – well, HW back again! Our lead in the polls puts us 2-4% ahead of Labour with Liberals still 20% - not nearly enough to be certain of victory. Few of my grass roots want one and I believe Ted H. would be very suspect if he went – it would be divisive in the nation when we want a united nation – if it was a Union bashing election this would drive many Trades Unionists into Labour's arms. But we must wait on Ted. This topic dominates all. Enoch Powell came to see me when I got back and told me what he would do if an election came – surprising, so I will not record it here!![307]

27.1.74

Talk of an election faded! Ted said he would meet TUC again early in the week and have a final shot at a settlement. He did so, but it ended in no agreement. The TUC offer was that no other union would use the increased miners' settlement as a precedent when negotiating their claims – this the Govt. said was not good enough because they would use other reasons for being special cases so now the miners have agreed to hold a ballot over the strike – if they say yes we really will be in a difficult situation because the mood of the miners' leaders is very left wing and militant and if the railways come out too we will be heading for a General Strike – some say we should then have an

---

[307] See entry 10 February 1974.

election – it is hard to see how we could. TU solidarity will make a lot vote Labour. A great dilemma.[308]

3.2.74

Election talk subsides a bit but still bumbles on. Dull Parliamentary week except 10 min. rule Bill to televise Parliament on Wednesday. I took it upon myself to act as a Chief Whip for Conservative anti-TV MPs. I canvassed 89 MPs in 24 hours, got pledges from 87 to vote against and 79 did so. As Enoch Powell said, "And, Neil, you succeeded as Chief Whip without any patronage in your hand!!" We won again by about the same majority as last time.

Drinks with Victor Montague[309] in evening (Lord Hinchingbrooke Earl Sandwich) he told me an amusing story. He was dining at Pratts and Harold Macmillan was sitting at the head of the table. Suddenly HM said in a low voice "I made a mistake as PM" – everyone was agog – he continued "it was in choosing middle-class lieutenants" – Hinch said this was obviously one at Ted H.! I then went and dined at the Carlton with a gaggle of MPs – but did not repeat the story.

10.2.74

On Monday the Executive of the 1922 dined with Humphrey Atkins, the new Chief Whip – the discussion was mainly about a General Election or not. We all left with the <u>firm</u> impression that Ted would not want an election – Humphrey, too, seemed against it. The crisis deepens and the NUM will not give in nor will Ted – everyone is being v. obstinate but it is quite clear that many would favour a marginal settlement – the Party is divided on this and on the calling of an election. We booked the PM to come to the 1922 on Thursday and explain the position. Backbenches and 1922 Exec. completely in the dark about what is happening and about policy if there is an election. Major debate on Wednesday on Economic Affairs while the talk of election builds up.

On Thursday (7th) PM at midday announced an election. He came to 1922 and explained – basically we can no longer let militants

---

[308] On 24 January 81% of NUM members voted to strike.
[309] Victor Montagu (1906-1995) known as Lord Hinchingbrooke (1916-1962), Earl of Sandwich (1962-64), before disclaiming his peerages. Conservative MP for South Dorset, 1941-62.

run the country. But what he never said was how he would settle the strike! So we are "off". Enoch Powell announced he would not be standing – and now I can say he came to see me to tell me this in advance as he didn't want me to feel let down by him. His view is that he could not stand for Cons. Party led by Ted and when he believed the election was a sham. We shall watch with interest how he intervenes if he so does – I advised him to go to Andorra for the duration! I doubt he will! This could have an effect on the Cons. turnout. This will be a curious election – Feb., cold, wet, windy, power restrictions, issues confused. I do not look forward to it one bit. Supporters returning to the fold – but John Schuster and his gang still at me over voting. I will return to the election when it is over – at the start Cons. had about average 5% lead in 3 polls.

24.2.74

The end of the election is in sight – it has been intensely boring as a political exercise but it has been nice to be at home and to get around the constituency and meet people. Cons. started off with a bang on the "who governs" - Parliament or the militants – question – we had a good lead in the opinion polls – then, quite rightly, Labour diverted to food prices, N. Sea oil, and all the usual bits and bobs. At the end of the 2nd week (today) we still held the lead (generally) in the polls with the Liberals coming up fast and apparently taking from Labour – we shall see – but Jeremy T has made a good impression on TV altho' he might lose his seat!

The public have been soused in politics – far too much of it – great mistake – they hate "yah-boo – we did this you did that". Locally it is encouraging for me – lot of support for having stood firm on Common Market and taken an independent line on things. Betting at Ladbrokes is 10-1 on me, 7-1 against Liberal, 20-1 against Labour! Canvass returns show 50% or more for me – hard to be too accurate, with new part-constituency, in my traditional forecast this time. Ted will be in a very silly position personally if we don't increase our own overall majority – he will have been judged wrong to have an election. Meetings mostly better attended than 1970 – in spite of TV – 3 or 4 a night – weather not too bad – Sat. night Woodstock usual riot! Dined after with Duke of Marlboro[310].

---

[310] John Spencer-Churchill, 11th Duke of Marlborough (1926-2014).

3.3.74

It was difficult to keep myself from getting bored in the last 3 days. However, I changed the pattern and at all but the large meetings I merely had a question session – this was good as it gave more time for 'communication'. The Chipping Norton and Banbury Town Hall meetings were fairly mild and we completed over 50 meetings. Less strenuous than 1970 as fewer meetings and smaller constituency. Polling day revealed how the organisation had deteriorated due to the activities of Friswell, Schuster and Webb and in the new part it was virtually non-existent. Canvassing was poor and therefore the machine couldn't work. But, in the event, all my CM opponents returned to the fold and worked hard – a lesson for MPs who take a firm line. Snow came around 7pm but nothing serious. Len Edwards, Chairman, drove me around in his very fast car. And, after a good supper, we settled down to watch the first results come in. And there were Labour gains and soon the swingometer gave no overall majority and then a slight Labour majority. In the end it was Lab 301, Cons 296, Libs 14 (altho' Jeremy Thorpe had indicated he might have the biggest party – "I'm going for the jackpot" he said!), Ulster Loyalists 10, Scot Nat 7, and odds and bits.

The count was at Banbury Town Hall for the first time and went _very_ well. Labour Candidate (Booth) said I would win with a 2,000 majority. The Lib. cand. (Fisher) said I would win by 1,500 – in fact I won by 6,878! But Libs took a lot, 21.6% compared with 10%.

As I see it, Ted H has brought his Government down. He had 15 months to go, a working majority and should have soldiered on. Now he has landed his Party and his country in a fantastic mess - and the responsibility was _entirely_ his. He must go – I imagine he will - he has left the country in a _shocking_ mess. He is now approaching the Liberals but I doubt if they will play. He has not surfaced since defeat, keeping himself in Downing Street. He is constitutionally correct in trying to do a deal with the other parties – but I doubt if he will succeed. Then H. Wilson will try! Anyhow it looks that the Common Market has had it as there must now be a majority against it in Parliament!

Mon. 4th after clearing up at home I drove to London in the afternoon for a meeting of the 1922 Exec. (caretaker) at Ed. du Cann's home in Lord North Street, (being opposite the house of H Wilson!). There the Committee assembled and for 2 hours we discussed the situation and were joined by Chief Whip Humphrey Atkins. The news was that Ted H having failed to get agreement with the Liberals had gone to the Palace to hand in his resignation and that Wilson was at that moment going to the Palace. The Libs said they would cooperate on things in the National interest but would not join a coalition. It seems Jeremy Thorpe and Joe Grimond would have accepted Cabinet posts but the Lib MPs did not want any compact with the Tories. They stated they would have a 'Broad Alliance' whatever that is! The feeling in the Exec. was that we would not win the next election with Ted as leader but that silly 'loyalty' thing made them duck the issue. But it is bound to come out as next day, Tues., the 1922 meets at 11.30am to hear what Ted has to say.

Robin Maxwell-Hyslop was to raise it but he was obviously worked on to make a more modest contribution merely raising the question of how election to the leadership was to be meted in the future, i.e., was the leader to submit himself for re-election – it didn't cause much of a stir! Ted spoke for about 15 minutes – he looked tired and somewhat beaten but did not apologise in any way for having brought his Party and the country to this situation – instead he dwelt on the future, of playing fair with the Lab. Govt., supporting them unless they did anything stupid etc. He gave the impression that he intended to stay as leader. The contributions from the floor were 'rigged' – Derek Walker-Smith (too long and wordy), Nigel Fisher[311], Denis Walters[312], Angus Maude, David Renton, Hugh Fraser (not rigged!) – but the general sentiment was to keep the tempers cool as it was too early to do anything and to start the bitching process.

The trouble is that the alternatives are not up to it. Keith Joseph is my choice but people say he is indecisive – I am not so sure. Robert Carr is not strong and too 'lefty', Tony Barber is too 'light' – so who else? To remove Ted, who could lose us the next election, is not going to be easy. Willy Whitelaw hasn't got the brains – he is too emotional and liable to go off his rocker in a temper. So Ted got away with it! But for how long will this continue? H Wilson will probably settle with the miners, get everyone back to work, sterling will improve, and gloom will settle in the Tory Party by May – a hot summer, bitchiness and will there then be a move to get rid of him before the party conference? If he goes to the Conference and gets away with it, and then there is an election, we could lose again and

---

[311] Sir Nigel Fisher (1913-1996), Conservative MP for Hitchin, 1950-55; Surbiton, 1955-83. He was on the 1922 Executive with Marten.
[312] Sir Denis Walters (1928-2021), Conservative MP for Westbury, 1964-92.

then he will be in trouble – but Labour would be in for the N. Sea oil bonanza and would for a long time profit by it. So that is what is at stake.

Tuesday evening I went to see Enoch Powell at his home by his invitation. Pam obviously unhappy about his position outside Parliament – but he is determined to come back – how? – he doesn't know but events will provide the opportunity he believes. We talked for 2½ hours – relaxed, coherent, and a really enjoyable conversation exploring all the avenues open. Mostly about the Common Market and how Labour will move either to make the CM impossible to operate by blocking it or by renegotiation and a referendum – we kicked the ball around and around and in the end I said I thought it was a decaying tooth and he had better make a series of well planned speeches on real Tory policy outside the Market comparing it with what Labour would do outside the Market. Then the Cons. MPs would nod their approval. What a loss in the meantime to Parliament – we shall miss him.

Wednesday we elected the Speaker, Selwyn Lloyd, again. I find more and more people who feel Ted should go – quite a lot feel Keith Joseph should take over. Thursday sworn in.

17.3.74

Monday attended an excellent lecture at Chatham House by Prof Grosser[313] of the Science Politique in Paris on an interpretation of French Politics – he explained how Pompidou is strengthened by the Communists in their Parliament as people fear the Commys and will turn to Gaullists – also Franco-Russian friendship keeps the Commys deflated in Parlt.! French fear German-USA tie up so they counter with Franco-Russian tie up. On EEC the French regard it as something which benefits France and everything is to this end! Good! As to political union they see it rather like our relations with Cwth. and should be so treated!

Tuesday the Queen, brought home to deal with the election, opened Parliament without the usual State ceremony – a fairly modest (for Labour) Queen's speech but a firm determination to renegotiate the Treaty of Accession to CM – that is good if Lab. remains in power! The dispositions of Ministers by Labour looks good for this purpose: Peter Shore and Eric Deakins at Trade, Fred Peart at Agriculture,

---

[313] Professor Alfred Grosser (1925-2024), political scientist.

Callaghan at F.O. etc. But they will have to get on with it before they are thrown out or before the tentacles of the F.O. get at Callaghan and soften him.

What I would like to see is a quiet renegotiation which gets nowhere and then the lot put to a referendum – I feel sure it would be defeated. Wednesday and Thursday and Fri. the debate drifted on. The Shadow Cab. put down an amendment regretting that the compulsory incomes policy was being scrapped. A great division in the C. Party over the wisdom of this course – some thought the public would not like the Govt. being defeated so early without being given a trial, others thought now was the time to do it before Lab. got established, others wondered why we were doing it and what the long term objective was, others thought it should only be pressed home if it brought about a national coalition Govt. (which had the advantage of ditching Heath! But equally the disadvantage that the CM renegotiations would not take place) - and so it went on at the 1922 meeting – chaos and <u>complete</u> lack of consultation with the backbenchers. Now <u>at last</u> the backbenchers are waking up and can begin to exercise control over the leadership. Also, the Scots, Irish and Welsh Nationalists are unknown quantities in every vote so the whole system is a very precarious one for any whip and any party. In some ways this is no bad thing as it will make Governments much more careful and responsive to their parties and to the public but it is all very unstable for the country. Today it is cat and mouse politics and the country will get fed up with it. Yet HW could hang on for some months, have an early and long summer recess and then call an autumn election and get back with a firm majority and then get the N. Sea oil bonanza in 1978/80!

24.3.74

Monday received congratulations from Sir Arnold Weinstock on my TV programme – this is interesting because he is one of our biggest tycoons and said my case for a Free Trade Area was the only sensible one and the CM was no good! That's progress. I will follow up. The Cons. amendment to the Queen's Speech was withdrawn! About 40 Cons. said they would abstain and this would have made the Govt. look silly – so they withdrew it, pleading that Michael Foot[314] had promised to keep Phase III until something else was put in its place.

---

[314] The new Employment Secretary.

They really looked silly – there was chaos and they came in for a lot of criticism from backbenchers. Robert Carr opened for us and was awfully dull – Michael Foot opened for Labour and was superb – rated the best ministerial speech for a long time – no notes except when he had to read out a page of departmental stuff which he did in a broad monotone and with contempt! Willy Whitelaw was awful winding up and Ted Short couldn't be heard for the row – it seemed to me to be the 1970 vintage showing off to the 1974 vintage!

Tuesday did BBC 'world at one' broadcast on the leadership and got a large fan-mail. The groundswell of anti-Heath is growing and Keith Joseph's name is now the front runner – that's good.

Thursday went to USA on British-American Parliamentary Delegation with Lord Shepherd[315], Douglas Jay, Peter Thomas, John Langford-Holt[316], Winston Churchill[317], Roger Moate, Arthur Davidson[318], Jack Diamond[319]. Started by meeting Dr Kissinger at the State Dept. – an amusing man – I mentioned to him the need to have an Atlantic Free Trade Area and will be following this up. The Conference came at a time when Anglo-USA relations are at their lowest. I explained this was due to Britain being in CM and trying to speak with one voice which was always the lowest common denominator and this was the French who are anti-American. The CM I said would either break up or so change as to become a free trade area and therefore we should prepare the way by formulating plans with USA to prepare this – far better to have NATO, FTA, energy, finance etc. all in one strong grouping. USA having encouraged us to go into CM now regretted it.

31.3.74

Tuesday, Healey's first budget – he did well in 2¼ hour speech – although the Labour policy is full of subsidies on the one hand and increases in coal, electricity etc. on the other! No incentive for

---

[315] Malcolm Shepherd, 2nd Baron Shepherd (1918-2001), Labour peer. Leader of the House of Lords, 1974-76.
[316] Sir John Langford-Holt (1916-1993), Conservative MP for Shrewsbury, 1945-83.
[317] Winston Churchill (1940-2010), Conservative MP for Stretford, 1970-83; Davyhulme, 1983-97. Grandson of former Prime Minister Sir Winston Churchill.
[318] Arthur Davidson (1928-2018), Labour MP for Accrington, 1966-83. Made Queen's Counsel, 1978.
[319] John Diamond, Baron Diamond (1907-2004), Labour MP for Manchester Blackley, 1945-51; Gloucester, 1957-70. Ennobled, 1970. Joined the SDP in 1981.

investment and this is bad for cash flow – shares right down – little left! Rest of week on the budget. Anti-Heath movement simmers.

7.4.74

Monday the budget debate was concluded – Keith Joseph wound up for us putting forward the view that if you clobber the decision-makers in industry you clobber industry itself and growth etc. – a good speech and a Conservative one! Tuesday lunched with Arnold Weinstock who said it wouldn't matter if we were out of the Common Market – I asked him to say so in public – I don't think he will! Wednesday 1922 lunch at Savoy for Ted – only 170 out of 295 turned up! A dull speech by Ted – he simply <u>cannot</u> uplift people – he spoke fast as though he was nervous. Enoch Powell came to the flat in the evening for a gossip on the CM – he hopes to return to Parliament I am glad to say!

14.4.74

Monday R GP[320] and Enoch met in my flat to review CM – a useful meeting. Generally a rather morbid atmosphere in Parliament with few divisions and a lot of dissent.

28.4.74

Encountered one more example of the nucleus of the old constituency gang warfare! At the start of the Election in Feb., Len Edwards the Chairman mentioned that he still found people who would not help because of my votes. I replied that "I found it very odd because I had never voted against the Government on a vote of censure and had no intention of doing so, and a Govt. is only brought down on a vote of censure – it brings itself down if it loses a vote of confidence!" He replied, "well if only you would say that at your adoption meeting it would overcome their objections." So I did. But when, quite by chance, I saw the draft minutes of the meeting, it was written in that "I had pledged myself never to vote against the Government on a vote of confidence"!! So I took this up with Harry[321] who said he had destroyed his notes but he heard me say it! I produced my notes to

---

[320] Renegotiation/Referendum Group.
[321] Harry Webb, Marten's constituency agent, part of the anti-Marten cabal.

show that I used the other words about censure and not confidence. I spoke to Len and he said that Harry's words would be better!

I was furious at their attempted misinterpretation because it was <u>exactly</u> what I had always been fighting against pledging - and they knew it. It all stems from John Schuster's earlier attempts to pin me. It was a very dirty trick and this was emphasised by the fact that the draft was not shown to me – the idea was presumably that it should be read out at the AGM and I would therefore be committed. I said that if it was I would object to the Chairman signing the minutes as a correct record of the minutes and the row would be opened up again. After 1½ hours discussion Len admitted he has never heard me use the words vote of confidence nor had the Treasurer. At that point they agreed to my account of it and to insert the correct note in the minutes. I hope they have done so! It really does show that the vendetta is still on. Pathetic, with so much else to do.

The AGM was on 26 April. I spoke about why we lost the election based on letters I had received from branches in reply to my letter inviting their views. I then spoke of what I thought Cons. policy should be. Seemed to go down well.

Photographs supplied by Anthony Marten

Joan and Neil in uniform.

Neil and Joan with Nora and Torolf Smedvig. He was leader of the Norwegian Resistance in Stavanger with Neil during the war. Subsequently a leading shipowner and lifelong friend.

Off-duty weekend while serving in the Foreign Office in Turkey.

Devoted couple in the garden prior to opening a fête.

Election Day triumph at Banbury Town Hall.

With Indira Gandhi, Prime Minister of India, when visiting as Minister of Overseas Development.

Queen Elizabeth II is welcomed by Francis Pym, Foreign Secretary, Douglas Hurd, and Neil at the Ministry of Overseas Development.

Top row L-R Richard Luce, Peter Blaker, Douglas Hurd, Lord Trefgarne, Neil Marten, Nicholas Ridley
Bottom row L-R The Foreign Secretary Lord Carrington, Sir Ian Gilmour.

Just received his Knighthood. With Joan and children Anthony and Judith.

Inside No. 10 with PM Margaret Thatcher.

Joan and Anthony unveiling a plaque inside Banbury Church.

In action as a member of the Lords and Commons ski team at their annual race against the Swiss Parliamentarians in Davos.

Captain of the Parliamentary tennis team surveys a revealing poster!

Part Three:
The Rise of Thatcher

5.5.74

Cons. supporters are wondering what we are doing in Parliament. We seem to vote and not defeat the Govt.! They fail to realise that, ideally, before an election, we must re-organise our policy on which we were defeated in Feb. and we cannot do this overnight. So we don't want an election until we have done this. The entire Parliamentary tactics are now in a new dimension. A row brewed up during the week over Ted Short, leader of the House, having a year ago accepted £250 from Dan Smith recently gaoled with Cunningham for corruption[322]. A small matter, painfully indiscreet, but one which was blown up by the press. MPs are under great attack by the Press for their outside interests. It all looks very sordid but only a very small proportion of MPs are involved in abusing their positions.

12.5.74

Another nonsense over voting. We had a debate on Agriculture on Wednesday and were whipped on a 3-liner. At the previous Thursday 1922 the whip announcing the business said it was a serious 3-liner and "anyone not obeying it would get into serious trouble" (Walter Clegg[323]). The Liberals voted with us and so did Scot. Nats. – logically we should have won – but we failed by 11 votes much to the derision of the House. Fury abounded. A number of Conservatives didn't vote and rumour has it that the N. Irish were asked not to vote. This has all made a nonsense of 3-liners.

19.5.74

Monday was a debate on Defence – but, nowadays, it seems a dull subject and only the usual people take part – it revolves around how

---

[322] In 1974 T Dan Smith, the former leader of Newcastle City Council, pled guilty to charges of corruption and bribery in the Poulson affair. These included cash payments to Andy Cunningham, former chairman of Durham County Council, who was sentenced with Smith.

[323] Sir Walter Clegg (1920-1994), Conservative MP for North Fylde, 1966-83; Wyre, 1983-87. Knighted, 1980.

much defence is to be cut by! Took part in a discussion on the Common Market in the morning in the CPA – my view was something the Commonwealth delegates wanted to hear and they loved it, much to the irritation of Sir Bernard Brain [sic], the Chairman. In the evening, a nice party given by PM at No. 10 for the delegates – he was in great form and we chatted about the CM. Tuesday dined with Enoch and Pam Powell and Chapman Pincher[324] and wife – after the latter had left we stayed on and talked about Enoch and N. Ireland – it seems that the only way he can get back is via N. Ireland if someone (Willie Orr?[325]) gives up his seat at the next election – but someone must find a job for Willie Orr! Then if he leads the N. Irish he can rejoin them to the Conservative Party and himself too and then bid for leadership? A circuitous route! Meanwhile the bubbles against Ted continue and a few MPs are beginning to drop hints in speeches.

26.5.74

R Group met (with Enoch) to discuss the CM. At 9pm the 1922 met to discuss our attitude towards the registering of Members' interests – we mostly objected but when it came to the vote we were heavily defeated, many Cons. voting with Labour! Tuesday, first meeting of the European sub-committee of Foreign Affairs Committee under Tony Royle – it is obviously going to be rigged to get the answers the pro-CM want. Wed. we (1922 Exec.) met Ted Heath for an hour's discussion – it was inconclusive and Ted seemed, as someone said, like a wet pudding! He was off to China the next day. Then we dined with the Area Chairmen and had a good discussion – clearly they were not very happy. On Friday the House rose for 2 weeks Whit recess – meanwhile the Protestants are creating hell in N. Ireland against the Sunningdale Agreement and having a general strike, bringing the Province to a halt[326]. Friday visited a pig farmer and a beef farmer in

---

[324] Chapman Pincher (1914-2014), journalist known for exposing secrets in the intelligence services. Published *Their Trade is Treachery* in 1981 alleging that former MI5 director Roger Hollis had been a Soviet agent.

[325] Captain Laurence 'Willy' Orr (1918-1990), Ulster Unionist MP for South Down, 1950-October 1974. Marten was right. Orr stood down in October 1974 and Enoch Powell replaced him and re-entered parliament.

[326] Between 15 and 24 May the Ulster Workers Council called a strike in Northern Ireland to protest the Sunningdale Agreement signed in 1973. The agreement attempted to implement a power-sharing administration involving Unionist and Republican politicians. The strike forced the collapse of the power-sharing administration on 28 May.

the constituency, both feeling the pinch from higher prices. I am advocating a return to the old system of guaranteed support prices and getting away from the intervention system of the Common Market.

9.6.74

N. Ireland caved in and Parliament was recalled for a 2-day debate on Mon./Tues. 3/4 and direct rule was resumed. It only goes to show that it is fatal to "impose" a theoretical solution on a country unless it has the general support of the people. Looking back this is just what Ted Heath did over the Industrial Relations Act (without the cooperation of the TUC), the Common Market (without the cooperation of the people) and Sunningdale. These things cannot be done without feeling the heart of the people, something Ted (the ex-Chief Whip) has never really understood. Yet some of the responsibility must rest with the Conservative Party in the Cabinet and on the backbenches. The stranglehold of Heath on the Party is dangerous when combined with too many docile MPs.

16.6.74

We had 2 days on the Committee Stage of the Finance Bill on the floor of the House and the only other event was a debate on Tuesday on the details of the Government's renegotiation of the Common Market. Callaghan was under attack from his left wing for what they thought was going soft on the renegotiation. Callaghan was very clever in coping with them and said he had stuck precisely to the election manifesto – but his own party (anyhow the antis) are deeply suspicious of him. The Conservatives cooed at Callaghan and supported his line. This is convenient for Cons-antis! And I sensed that the Party might (wisely) be taking a softer line on a referendum. The negotiations will certainly have to be watched <u>very</u> carefully.

23.6.74

Monday started off with a bang – got to the House at 10.15 to find Westminster Hall on fire after a bomb had been placed in the canteen leading off the Hall and the bomb – an IRA 20lb one – had fractured the gas main and set the place on fire. It was blazing quite hard and destroyed part of the Grand Committee Room, MPs desk room and secretary's room. The latter two blazed furiously and the floor collapsed – an awful sight – but the Hall itself was not badly damaged – no one killed thank goodness.

Wednesday we defeated the Government on their proposal to repay the TUC £10m! First defeat. In the afternoon we set up a Committee to study the effects of leaving the CM – a private enterprise effort by Cwth. Industries employing experts to do it – should be useful. Thursday defeated the Government again by 21 with Libs. and Nats. over Wedgewood-Benn's proposals for nationalisation. Then later we were going to do it again over increased tariff rates for all night storage heaters but thanks to a revolt by Lab. backbenchers the Govt. gave in. On Friday the Govt. was defeated again on a Private Member's Bill over lotteries – can they go on like this? Will we have an election before the summer? An interesting position. In the meantime David James has circulated a letter to MPs asking if they want Heath to go now or later or not all! This has stirred things up a bit.

30.6.74

But after the weekend he [David James] seemed to give in on the grounds that Willy Whitelaw had been appointed Party Chairman and that Willy had the common touch which Ted hadn't got!! He told me that the replies he had received showed 40% wanted a change at once, 30% wanted a change but not now and 30% wanted no change. I imagine he gave in to his constituency and the Whips. So now Ted must stay until at least after the election.

On Tuesday spoke in the City on the CM with Enoch Powell. Government defeated again over Rates on Tuesday! And they "gave in" on Wednesday over agriculture and gave the farmers a better deal over beef rather than face another defeat. I must say that minority government has its points in the way it can be controlled by Parliament – one good thing, at least, is that it has shown the government can be defeated and not resign – this is something I have always advocated.

7.7.74

On Wednesday we had our first reference to the House by the Scrutiny Committee on EEC legislation – it was to take note of a 'decision' of the proposal to agree to economic guidelines – in many ways this was not a satisfactory way to deal with it altho' we voted on it 107-70 against – not bad in the circumstances.

14.7.74

Dull week for me – had to go into hospital to have a hernia sewn up for 3rd time! Went in Monday, operation Mon. evening, out Thursday lunchtime! Record turnaround, so they said. One good thing, after all the pre-op tests of blood etc. the surgeon said he had never operated on someone of my age so fit – does that mean I drop dead tomorrow?! Some exciting votes in my absence – 2 ties on Trade Union Bill – Lab. refused to pair me, the rotters! Commodity prices falling fast so I wonder if PM will delay election to cash in the steadying effect this should have on prices – he might be wise to do so.

21.7.74

Well, Harold Lever was not on the premises when he was nodded through – he was dining at the Savoy! So he should not have been counted![327] On Tuesday he made a statement to the House and after a lot of argument the vote was amended, we won our amendment to the TU Bill – the Bill was actually being debated that day in the Lords and it was called back and amended formally!

A bomb exploded in the Tower of London killing one and injuring many children – IRA again. On Tuesday and Wed. we had the report stage on the Finance Bill and defeated the Government on 4 occasions. Got my amendment accepted for disabled passengers. Cyprus taken over by Greek Army officers[328]. Makarios[329] escaped to UK. Subsequently (and rightly) Turkey invades Cyprus! Could be serious.

On Wednesday launched my pamphlet "No middle way"[330] and it got a good lot of press though not enough. Thursday stitches out, lectured at Civil Service. French MPs over for tennis but couldn't

---

[327] On 12 July two divisions on the Trade Union and Labour Relations Bill were tied, giving the Speaker the casting vote. If Lever had not been counted the Government would have lost.

[328] A coup took place on 15 July.

[329] Mikhail Khristodolou Mouskos, Archbishop Makarios III (1913-1977), President of Cyprus, 1960-74 and December 1974-1977.

[330] With reference to the Common Market, not the earlier work by Harold Macmillan.

play – we dined at Lancaster House, match at Wimbledon, dinner at Hughenden Manor Disraeli's old house where Maurice Edelman lives – sat next to Lady Pamela Berry[331] who was insufferably rude because I didn't agree with her over the CM.

28.7.74

Completion of the Finance Bill on Monday and Healey announced his mini-budget which totally failed to deal with the situation and was a political cosmetic. At least he gave some money for interim rate relief. Tuesday/Wednesday an economic debate on which the Conservatives put down a critical motion. Labour amended it in such a way that it was difficult for us to vote against it – some did vote against it as a protest – Ted under criticism for a bad speech and failing to vote – shambles! Everyone ready for the House to rise.

Enoch P and Pam came to lunch at the flat on Thursday – it is impossible to find out what his intentions are about standing again for Parliament – but it was good to see him again – so sad he is not in Parliament.

Cyprus looked dangerous mid week after Clerides[332] (ex RAF pilot) had been made President, the Greek Colonels[333] had given over to Karamanlis[334] (v. good) and then the Turks started putting more troops into Cyprus and this upset the Greeks and Geneva Conference[335] looked like breaking down. Common Market selling part of the beef mountain to Russia! Peter Shore accused Rippon of being mis-led by the assurance of 1.4m tons of sugar from developing Commonwealth – this <u>could</u> be a major factor. Labour Party are showing signs of splitting into right and left – we'll see!

4.8.74

Tuesday was the Lords amendments to the Trades Union Bill and the Govt. was defeated five times on fairly major issues – a healthy

---

[331] Pamela Berry, Baroness Hartwell (1914-1982), daughter of F. E. Smith, Lord Birkenhead.
[332] Glafcos Clerides (1919-2013), President of Cyprus, 23 July-7 December 1974 (interim), 1993-2003.
[333] The military junta that had led Greece since 1967.
[334] Konstantinos Karamanlis (1907-1998), Prime Minister of Greece, 1974. He was called back to Greece from exile to head a unity government.
[335] To discuss the situation in Cyprus.

situation. Wednesday, we adjourned: many felt too easily although Parliament was as usual getting tetchy and boring. Had a meeting in the afternoon with Lord Campbell about sugar which is in shortage in this country – he said the Cwth. could well supply 1.7m tons.

And so ends our first experience of minority Government – it has its advantages! Election expected 3 or 10 Oct. – oh, what a bore for everyone.

22.9.74

Oct. 10th it is. Wilson, at 12.45 on Wed. 18th announced it. No real surprise! All of August I have been preparing it and, for once, am therefore reasonably ready. As of now it is anyone's guess as to the winner – my bet is on a small Lab. majority and still a minority Government.

20.10.74

Wrong – Lab got an overall majority of 3!! I believe we could have won had we had a different leader than Heath – far too many Conservatives said they would not vote as long as Ted was leader, particularly the younger ones and older ones. It was not so much his policies but his personality which repels.

Had 48 meetings and carried the same theme all the time, i.e., that the crisis facing the country was the worst since 1931 and the only way to overcome it was by a national Govt. and the only Party offering to form one was the Cons. Party[336] – I said the Social Contract (TUC and Lab.) was a mere charade. It was odd in many ways because I did not really mind if Lab. was a minority Govt. as we would then get the chance of a referendum on the Common Market - and it now looks as though we will. However, after a somewhat unexciting campaign I was returned with a slightly lower majority but an increase of 2% in my vote on a lower turnout. Weather was dreary and mostly damp – enthusiasm was ok on the day. Liberals suffered a lot, 5.2% - I feel they have been rumbled and so had Thorpe. Polls showed Labour well ahead all the time – sometimes 14%!

The 1922 Executive met on Monday after the election in Edward du Cann's home in Lord North Street – we entered to a battery

---

[336] This is interesting given Marten's concerns in late 1973 that the policies of the Labour and Conservative parties were becoming indistinguishable.

of press photographers – so much for security! The meeting had been arranged before the election to discuss the date on which to call the main Committee but inevitably the press assumed we were meeting to discuss the leadership. This we had to do because it affected the date of the meeting. The press blew the whole thing up as 'King makers' etc. – v. funny. The Exec. was <u>unanimous</u> that Ted should go altho Ed du C thought it should be at once – everyone else thought as soon as decently possible. This was communicated to Ted who was very off hand. We met the next day in E du C's office in the City (in Milk St.) – press called it the Milk St. Mafia! It was there decided to summon the full 1922 for Oct. 31. I personally felt we should have met on Wed. 23rd (the day of swearing in) but it was decided to give more time and meet on the normal day – this will give plenty of time for the Central Office/Whips machine to go into action – but we shall see.

Between meetings No. 1 and 2 I saw Keith Joseph and discussed the future – he is my choice and he is the one not too associated with Ted. We made plans which will evolve interestingly! (around 30 Oct.). Ted has written to E du C says he will meet the 1922 Committee when the new officers have been elected! A direct challenge to get a 1922 which is <u>pro</u>-Ted – if we are re-elected this will be a slap in the eye for him – if we are not, well! The Central Office machine has ill-advised him – but it may be to our advantage. Ted is making an ass of himself in his bid to hang on to power – the Party will never unite behind him.

27.10.74

On Tuesday we re-elected Selwyn Lloyd as Speaker – after the usual speeches which were good Jeremy Thorpe dropped a brick by making a rather silly speech on proportional representation and came in for criticism.

On Wednesday after lunch I swore in then had a meeting with Keith Joseph and David Mitchell[337] (his PPS) about Keith and the leadership. We got a skeleton organisation set up to canvass for him should there be an election for the leadership. He regretted having included in his speech (which was an excellent one on re-moralising Britain) a piece about birth control – this hit the headlines for about 3 days! – he said he was unwise to have included it in <u>that</u> speech – if

---

[337] Sir David Mitchell (1928-2014), Conservative MP for Basingstoke, 1964-83; North West Hampshire, 1983-97. Knighted, 1988.

only, he said, he had shown it to his wife first she would have struck it out! Anyhow, every leftie commentator and politician jumped down his throat! But he will ride it. Then had a meeting of 1922 Exec. – still fury over Ted's behaviour, he published a reply to E du Cann in the press, when Ed had marked his private. The Exec. still wants him to go. The whole question is rather nasty - one can see the hand of Central Office and Ted's supporters taking the line that we should leave it for the moment – obviously because they want to give him time to re-establish himself. This, for us, is a great danger – then it will be said it is too late to change.

3.11.74

The Queen opened Parliament on Tuesday – nothing very startling in the speech – most of it had been foreshadowed in the Election. The first day's debate was pretty bad. Ted Heath got little support from his backbenches and made a bad speech. Wilson was not much better.

Most of the week was devoted to discussing the leadership, in the corridors and over the tea table. The great moment arrived when the 1922 Committee met on Thursday. Ed du Cann explained the activities of the Executive and in the event there was little or no criticism of us. About 20 people spoke, 12 said Ted should go, 3 stay and the rest talked about new rules for the election of leader. The mood was clearly to get rid of Ted. The radio reported him as saying afterwards that he would stay on! What a man. He has no feeling and is absolutely clinging on to power. If this goes on the Party will have to remove him.

10.11.74

Thursday the great day of the elections to the 1922 Committee. Every strategy seemed to be used to get us off by the Heathmen. I was given two lists of people they wanted on which were being circulated – they were unsigned and created a very bad impression. In the event E du Cann was re-elected as Chairman and received the longest applause I have ever heard – it was really most heartening as it was saying that the Party disapproved of all the things the Heathmen had been trying to do to smear us and probably an indication that a change of leadership was wanted. The vice-chairmen were both opposed by Heathmen yet won handsomely, so was the Treasurer and he too won. Then all the retiring members of the Executive were re-elected with, I am told, massive majorities. Only two new ones join us – Paul Bryan and Mark Carlisle[338] to take the place of Tom Boardman (defeated)[339] and Marcus Worsley[340] (retired).

And yet, after that slap in the face, Ted made a speech the next evening saying virtually that he would stay on! He comes to the 1922 next week! To Paris for the week-end to attend a dinner to celebrate the 30th anniversary of the landings in Algiers – dear old General Maste[341] was the host – all very elderly and nice!!

17.11.74

Monday voted against the reintroduction of the Channel Tunnel Bill, partly because I dislike it but also because it sets a precedent for Bills which have not had Royal Assent continuing from one Parliament to another – a very risky thing to start. However, it got through. Then later in the evening we debated the Common Market orders to do with sugar. I spoke. It was all about the 'bankable assurance' from the CM to import 1.4m tons from the developing Commonwealth. The CM produced a cocked up scheme for 200,000 tons to be imported into the CM and to be subsidised – it was just a wangle to stop us acting unilaterally and buying Australian sugar. The whole thing illustrates the practical way in which we have lost the independence, power and sovereignty to buy and import sugar ourselves. At the end of the day, if the CM does not agree the price and duration for the importation of Cwth. sugar, we shall be short of sugar and we can all fairly blame this direct on the CM as it would never have happened if we had not joined. To boot, we see the pressure of the French beet lobby to make us use beet sugar, put our cane refineries out of work and then we will rely on beet only. Nigel Spearing[342] had an amendment and we the

---

[338] Mark Carlisle, Baron Carlisle of Bucklow (1929-2005), Conservative MP for Runcorn, 1964-83; Warrington South, 1983-87. Secretary of State for Education and Science, 1979-81. Ennobled, 1987.

[339] Tom Boardman, Baron Boardman (1919-2003), Conservative MP for Leicester South West, 1967-February 1974; Leicester South, February 1974-October 1974. Chief Secretary to the Treasury, 1974. Boardman did not stand in the 1922 Executive election as he had lost his seat at the October 1974 election.

[340] Sir Marcus Worsley (1925-2012), Conservative MP for Keighley, 1959-1964; Chelsea, 1966-October 1974.

[341] Gen. Charles Mast (1889-1977), chief of staff of the French Nineteenth Corps, 1942.

[342] Nigel Spearing (1930-2017), Labour MP for Acton, 1970-74; Newham South, 1974-1997.

all-party antis agreed to vote against it[343] – so the Government gave in and accepted it!

Tuesday we had an anti-CM meeting and supper at the *Spectator* to try and form a national organisation for the referendum to join all anti organisations together. It will be difficult – there are so many prima-donnas like Dick Body and Christopher Frere-Smith. But we must keep trying. Tuesday was also budget day, the third this year! Not too bad a budget in some ways but the left wing was furious.

Thursday was the long awaited meeting of the 1922 Committee with Ted Heath. He got a cool reception – it was difficult for him. He spoke of new procedures for electing the leader and said he would set up a committee consisting of the Chairman of the Party, the Chairman of 1922, of National Union and Leader in House of Lords. He did not give the impression of speedy action. Later that evening the 1922 Exec. met and were not satisfied with what he said. The Exec. wanted the sovereignty of any decision to rest with the 1922 and wanted a quick election based on the Electoral College of the MPs alone. We decided to go inform Ted and would await the meeting of the full 1922 next Thursday to see how they felt.

And so off to the West Indies for 2 weeks.

8.12.74

In my absence bombs went off killing 17 in Birmingham so at last the Govt. has proscribed the IRA and we are to debate the death penalty! Returned to a massive pile of work hence the brief description of my trip.

15.12.74

Wednesday debate on Capital Punishment – voted to bring in death penalty – but we lost! Spent Monday interviewing candidates at Central Office. Economic crisis goes from bad to worse – terrible trade figures, pound sags again and shares down.

22.12.74

On Monday the PM made his delayed statement on the Summit Meeting of EEC – he was very long winded! He said there was "still a

---

[343] The government motion, Spearing was an anti-marketeer.

long way to go before terms could be satisfactorily agreed". Jim Callaghan told me later in the week that "while he was edging towards staying in the CM the PM was still far from convinced and had by no means made up his mind" – whether this was merely to soothe me or not I cannot say. But it begins to look as though they will recommend the terms to the nation.

Tuesday a Government lunch to the Grenada High Commissioner and then a session of the EEC Scrutiny Committee at which Fred Peart (Ag) and Roy Hattersley (FO) gave evidence. After that a meeting of the various anti-CM organisations to discuss the formation of a coordinating Committee for the referendum campaign – I was elected Chairman! It's going to be a big job – but it cannot last too long. Thursday a debate on the EEC six monthly report – it went on until midnight – quite good but not entirely satisfactory. I spoke for 5 mins at the end pleading that, before the referendum is held, we should be told precisely what is meant by 'political union' – but it fell on deaf ears as usual, everyone ducking it. Friday, with some relief, the House rose for the Christmas recess until 13 Jan. The country is in poor shape, the Conservative Party is drifting and demoralised, the Labour party is on the brink (as usual) of internal splits.

12.1.75

The New Year was heralded by strikes in the motor industry, the collapse of Aston Martin, and Burmah Oil!! However, Harold Wilson did at last speak up and said to the Brit. Leyland workers on strike that if they did not behave themselves they could not expect to be nationalised! But they still went on strike!

On Tuesday we announced the formation of the National Referendum Campaign at a press conference in the morning. I thought about 10 would come – in the event about 42 came! Great success although the news was somewhat blanketed by a hijacked aircraft at Heathrow! Anyhow, it was generally welcomed – good reactions. TV and radio galore for me that day.

19.1.75

Reassemble Mon. 13 Jan. I found on the order paper a motion to pay salaries to political parties – I raised this on grounds that it needs more thought and many of us objected and it was not right to do it on first day after recess etc. – eventually the Leader of the House conceded the point and was withdrawn for another day – minor (and popular) victory but disapproval by the establishment at my views expressed on BBC as Tory Party is broke and needs money! Tues. and Wed. mainly meetings on Common Market, interviewing journalists and cranks! Thursday more interviews and then 1922 discussed the new rules for the leadership elections – most agreed to get on with it and get it over in spite of deficiencies of the new rules! Attempt by Heathmen to alter them (and delay) or to have a vote of confidence in the 1922 on Ted. – some obviously tying to delay and get Soames[344]! (some hope). Should all be over in Feb. – the first ballot will obviously be treated as a vote of confidence in Ted. Went hare-coursing to see how it was conducted – it seemed fair to me.

26.1.75

The party leadership continues. The election (1st round) is to be on Feb. 4. Margaret Thatcher is standing against Ted Heath, and Hugh Fraser is standing to get the votes of the anti-Heath folk who won't vote for a woman. Margaret's bandwagon is rolling well with Keith Joseph supporting her. Ted probably getting worried as M has done exceptionally well on the floor of the House on the Finance Bill (as did Ted in 1965!). But if there is no final decision on the first round anything could happen on the second – rumours have it that Willie Whitelaw, Jim Prior[345], du Cann, Joseph, Amery[346] could stand against Ted. But I don't expect they will! The other play is that du Cann might stand, ask the Ulstermen to take the Whip and then, in next autumn, stand down and let Enoch in. This really seems to be the best answer because none of the others come anywhere near him.

Meeting of National Referendum Campaign on Tuesday and it went well: gradually smoothing things out. Wed. interviewed candidates at Central Office, lunched with Sir Michael Wright, Sir

---

[344] Christopher Soames, Baron Soames (1920-87), Conservative MP for Bedford, 1950-66. UK Ambassador to France, 1968-72. Vice President, European Commission, 1973-77. Governor of Rhodesia, 1979-80. Married Mary Churchill, daughter of Sir Winston Churchill, 1947.

[345] James Prior, Baron Prior (1927-2016), Conservative MP for Lowestoft, 1959-83; Waveney, 1983-87. Held office in Heath and Thatcher administrations: Leader of the House of Commons, 1972-74; Secretary of State for Employment, 1979-81; Northern Ireland, 1981-84. Ennobled, 1987.

[346] Julian Amery, Baron Amery of Lustleigh (1919-1996), Conservative MP for Preston North, 1950-66; Brighton Pavillion, 1969-92. Son-in-Law of Harold Macmillan, he married Catherine Macmillan in 1950.

George Bolton and Peter Jay[347] at Norwegian Club to discuss the CM – then in the afternoon a series of visits from people interested in the CM.

On Thursday the PM made his statement on the Referendum – much anger from the pro-CM Tories! I went on ITV and BBC to speak about it. It all seems quite sensible but a bit of a joke about the Cabinet being divided and free to speak!

2.2.75

Monday was on Panorama. The subject, with an invited audience, was the question of sovereignty and the CM. Peter Kirk[348] and David Marquand[349] opposed me and George Wigg[350] supported me. I did a 5 minute introductory piece and so did Peter and then it was a general discussion, ending up in a fair shambles of the invited audience. Maybe it was good entertainment but it was not good discussion – most people agreed – convinced we won the argument!

Still having trouble with 'Get Britain Out' (GBO)[351] over cooperating in National Referendum Campaign – they are being very tiresome. Tuesday lunched with Fred Corfield who told me how he was sacked by Ted from being Minister for Aviation. He was first starting a tour of French aviation industries and was in South of France and got a message to return at once – he went straight to No. 10 – he asked if he had done anything wrong or failed and was told no but he was being dropped – in fact he was a good aviation minister. Very odd behaviour by Ted. Tuesday the House debated the Stonehouse affair[352] and rightly set up a Select Committee to report on it all – some Tories opposed this! Wed. lunched with Air-Marshall Don

---

[347] Peter Jay (1937-2024), economist, journalist and diplomat. UK Ambassador to the United States of America, 1977-79. Son-in-law of James Callaghan, he married Margaret Callaghan in 1961 and they divorced in 1986.
[348] Sir Peter Kirk (1928-1977), Conservative MP for Gravesend, 1955-64; Saffron Walden, 1965-77. British Member of the European Assembly, 1973-77.
[349] David Marquand (1934-2024), Labour MP for Ashfield, 1966-77. Principal of Mansfield College, Oxford, 1996-2002.
[350] George Wigg, Baron Wigg (1900-1983), Labour MP for Dudley, 1945-67. Paymaster General, 1964-67. Ennobled, 1967.
[351] Headed by Christopher Frere-Smith.
[352] The Labour MP had faked his own death in 1974. It was also alleged he had been a Czech spy.

Bennett[353] as NRC wanted me to assess if he was connected with National Front – he assured me he wasn't and never had been altho' people tried to establish it.

Wednesday the Govt. was defeated on the earnings rule for pensioners when 9 Lab. members voted with us – 280-265 – the limit which an OAP can earn before they start forfeiting their pensions is now £13 a week – it will be raised to £20 in 75/76, £35 76/77 and £50 in 77/8.

Had a long talk with Margaret Thatcher in the evening – the leadership elections are next week – she is impressive but I do wonder if she can really lead the Party. We are in need of a man – we don't really want Ted any longer, he cannot lead a united Party. Had a meeting with Enoch Powell on Thursday: he cannot and will not predict his future – he cannot rejoin the Conservative Party until the CM is out of the way and until N. Ireland has settled down in 1½ years' time. From his point of view he would probably like Ted to remain until then.

One interesting conversation with a Central Office person (nameless) who was furious at the 'dirty tricks dept' of CCO. The 'Milk Street Mafia' story – (see 20.10.74) – apparently Charlie Morrison[354], vice-Chairman of 1922 Committee, quite naturally told his wife[355] of the feeling in the 1922 Committee after the Election. She was furious and rang Ted and told him about the meeting the next day (she is female Vice-Chairman of the Party) – Maurice Trowbridge (of CO) apparently told the Press to photograph the 'Milk Street Mafia'! It was the same person (and David Knox[356]) who planted stories about Margaret Thatcher and the food stores[357] and Keith Joseph and the nervous breakdown and the latest one is that they have supplied the

---

[353] Air Vice Marshall Donald Bennett (1910-1986). One of the shortest-serving members of parliament. Elected unopposed as Liberal MP for Middlesbrough West 14 May 1945 and lost at the general election on 5 July. In February 1974 Bennett stood against Edward Heath in Sidcup on an anti-EEC platform.
[354] Sir Charles Morrison (1932-2005), Conservative MP for Devizes, 1964-92.
[355] Antoinette Sara Frances Sibell Long (1934-), wife of Sir Charles Morrison, divorced 1984. A vice-Chairman of the Conservative party, 1971-5.
[356] Sir David Knox (1933-), Conservative MP for Leek, 1970-83; Staffordshire Moorlands, 1983-97. Firmly on the 'wet' wing of the Conservative party.
[357] Anti-Thatcher stories suggesting that Mrs Thatcher was hoarding food and goods purchased at a lower price to hedge against future inflation.

YCs[358] with T-shirts saying "we want the Grocer[359] – not the Grocer's daughter" – unbelievable behaviour.

Friday spoke Nottingham University on CM and they said afterward that they had never heard the other side of the argument and it had done them good!

9.2.75

Monday, the day before the first ballot on the leadership, the 1922 Exec. met in accordance with the new rules to hear the views of the Lords, the National Union and the Scots and, unofficially, the Ulster Unionists about the leadership. They all reported a substantial vote for Ted Heath in the region of 75% except the Scottish Students who were pro-Thatcher. But as we questioned them it became apparent that the consultations were a bit dubious to say the least! It certainly struck me as being rather cooked up. Peter Rost, a Derbyshire MP, blew the gaff in public when he said that his agent had been invited to "bend it" in favour of Ted by Central Office. The agent, a 27 year old girl, said she was not going to do this and then Central Office said she must make a statement contradicting her member. She said she wouldn't. So Central Office reminded her that she was centrally employed and paid by Central Office. Then the Chairman of the Party rang her and told her a statement was being prepared for her to sign. She caved in. But what a way to behave by Central Office. The Agents are all furious with Peter Rost because he gave the impression that all agents were bending the results!

Then Tuesday, the vote and at 4pm the result was Margaret Thatcher 130, Ted Heath 119 and Hugh Fraser 16. At about 5pm Ted decided to resign. A cloud thus lifted off the Party. I have rarely felt such general relief in the Commons. V. sad for Ted – a bad twelve months for him – 2 elections lost, 1 boat sunk with loss of godson[360], house bombed[361] and now turned out of office! But he has himself to blame – he failed to listen to advice, was contemptuous of colleagues,

---

[358] Young Conservatives.

[359] The media nickname given to Ted Heath. Thatcher's nickname 'the Grocer's daughter' had nothing to do with being Heath's successor, rather that she was the daughter of a grocer in Grantham.

[360] On 2 September 1974, Heath's yacht Morning Cloud sank and his godson Christopher Chadd drowned.

[361] 22 December 1974, Heath's house in Wilton Street was bombed by the IRA. Heath was on his way to Kent at the time.

surrounded himself with virtual yes-men, fixed the Party machine for himself, and in the end, in his fight to retain the leadership, he (or at least his surrogates in Central Office) played it dirty. The press, with exception of the *Mail*, were odiously for Heath. His obstinacy, his near-arrogance, his near-conceit, lost him the support of his colleagues. His manner was off-hand. If he had been able to tolerate criticism from colleagues and had had a family around him he might not have developed this way. Yet, to be fair, he was very competent, technically, devoted to his causes, tough and single minded. But it takes more than that to hold the leadership. The leader must carry the Parliamentary Party with him, his supporters in the country and the majority of voters. He only carried one group – his supporters in the country and I am not certain if this was very healthy being based on the doctrine of loyalty to the leader rather than loyalty to Party and Country.

By Thursday Willie Whitelaw, Jim Prior, John Peyton, Geoffrey Howe had joined Margaret for Round Two. Maurice Macmillan and Julian Amery did not run and made fantastically pompous statements! My bet is that Margaret will get it but some will desert her and it may go to Round Three – I hope not. Anyhow it has all been conducted in a good humoured way.

16.2.75

Monday lunch at Lloyds Bank and afterwards 1922 Exec. met to hear from the Peers and the National Union about the candidates for leadership. The Peers were largely (no figures) for Willy Whitelaw – predictably, because he is from the landed gentry class! The constituencies were 2-1 in favour of Margaret Thatcher (my constituency was marginally for Willy) and the Scots evenly divided. The next day we voted and the result was 146 for Margaret, 79 for Willy, 19 for Prior, 19 for Howe, and 11 for Peyton – only two spoilt papers! A super outcome. And once again the Press and the bookies were for Willy! It was humiliating for Willy and the others but no doubt very good for them. The Party was delighted – except for the Heath/Whitelaw boys whose patron has been removed. She came to the 1922 Committee on Thursday for a brief appearance and was superb – immediately established a rapport and in good humour. She warned of Front Bench changes saying that people could take a sabbatical year or so as [a] backbencher!

She said away with labels of left, right and centre in the Party, stressed the need for policies based on a return to Tory principles, distinctive not blurred, which the people want – the people must get a clear message that the Tories stood for home ownership, education (choice), reduction of taxation, personal responsibility – she also said she did not want to be isolated! In fact she said everything that Ted would not have said - that is what the Party wanted to hear. What a change!

On Wednesday evening, the day after the election she took her seat on the Front Bench and acquitted herself well. In the evening I had ½ an hour with her alone in the Shadow Cabinet room when I put to her my views on the Common Market. I asked her not to be absorbed with it as Ted Heath – she agreed. I then went on and explained my fear of federalism and she seemed to wake up to the danger. She said that these matters had been largely kept from Cabinet by Ted! I gave her a copy of my pamphlet[362] and an article I had written on the subject and she promised to read it. What a change – she listened and it went in – so unlike Ted. I felt relieved that I had got my point over so early (within 24 hours!) of her leadership – we shall see what happens!

Spent a busy week on Common Marketing. Saw the Lord President of the Council (Ted Short) to give him our views on how the referendum should be conducted – he was receptive and will publish a White Paper in 2 weeks. Wednesday met the Chairman of the BBC for an hour – Sir Michael Swann[363] and discussed how the BBC should handle TV and on Thursday met Lord Aylestone[364] Chairman of IBA for similar discussions. There are difficult problems to overcome but we hope the media will be even-handed.

Had supper in the canteen with Jim Callaghan, Foreign Sec., on Wednesday. He is veering towards staying in the CM. He modestly boasted of his good relations with Kissinger saying that K was the only Foreign Sec. in the world who looked at things on a world basis. But K was not a politician and Jim said the mix between himself the politician and K the academic was very fruitful!

Lunched on Wednesday with the Australian High Commissioner, drinks with Norwegian Ambassador in the evening to

---

[362] *No Middle Way.*
[363] Sir Michael Swann (1920-1990), molecular biologist. Chairman, BBC, 1973-80.
[364] Herbert Bowden, Lord Aylestone (1905-1994), Labour MP for Leicester South, 1945-50; Leicester South West, 1950-67. Ennobled, 1967. Chairman, Independent Broadcasting Authority, 1967-75.

say one of many farewells to him and on Thursday lunched with Tony Kershaw[365] and Enoch Powell at Whites – first person I met there was the Duke of Marlborough who had recently written a lovely letter to me about the CM – anyhow he was as friendly as ever. We discussed Enoch's return to the fold but obviously not yet.

23.2.75

On Thursday Margaret Thatcher was 'crowned' Leader of the Party and made a short speech.

2.3.75

On Monday Parliament debated television and radio of the House. An experimental radio trial was agreed but TV was rejected by 12 votes, thank God. Tuesday I did the 'It's your line' programme on BBC with John Mackintosh and Robin Day in the chair on the question of sovereignty – answering telephone calls for listeners – quite fun. Wednesday we debated the grant to the Queen and 90 voted against it – I didn't think by any means they were all republicans – they really wanted her to be taxed – but as she is above the law it doesn't make sense. The White Paper on the referendum came out on Wednesday – much press conferencing and comments required for all and sundry! It showed considerable bias towards staying in by a variety of ways, the question is slanted, the setting up of information centres is a great mistake etc. – if it is to be successful it must be seen to be as fair as possible.

During the week, on Wed., John Schuster (President) and Jack Whiteley (treasurer) of my Association came to House of Commons and said that they could not recommend the proposed new agent Tim Statham who has been a trainee with us and had done very well. They had built up a most curious case against him in my view just a heap of straw – it didn't stand up to examination for a moment. It seems obvious that they want Harry Webb to stay on and they recognise that Tim is 'on my side'. I am not going to have his career wrecked like this so we agreed to postpone this interviewing of agents for the moment – during that time I will examine their evidence and if it proves to be false I really am going to create a row.

---

[365] Sir Anthony Kershaw (1915-2008), Conservative MP for Stroud, 1955-87.

9.3.75

All the evidence shows that it was a 'heap of straw', and I am astounded at their absurd behaviour. There has obviously been a lot of dirty work behind the scenes – this constituency association is really getting a bad name and much of it can be traced back to Harry Webb and John Schuster.

It was a week of rows in the Commons. The Govt. timetabled the Finance Bill which means that much of the complicated legislation about Capital Transfer Tax[366] etc. has had to go through poorly debated. I have rarely heard such a noise in the Chamber when it was introduced! At least it meant that we ended the Finance Bill by midnight and avoided all night sittings – which is probably part of the reason for introducing it as the Lab. Party is not very good at stay[ing] too late and they might have been defeated! There was also the timing element to get it into law on time. And there is now the prospect of another budget next month – we are permanently in a state of budget!

16.3.75

A bad week in Parliament – a strike for more wages by ancillary workers so little heating, no hot meals, and no tea! Pickets outside and rubbish inside! Disgrace. No parliamentary papers "allowed in" by the pickets. On Monday evening I had a long talk with Reggie Maudling about the Common Market – he has just taken over as Shadow Foreign Secy. I outlined my objections to the Market and he said it was an interesting point of view which has not occurred to him before! He said he was not an enthusiast about CM but, on balance, he thought we ought to stay in! So it looks as though the Cons. are going to be less obsessed over the whole thing – I hope so!

Tuesday I lectured at Wilton Park on the CM and as most of the students were European I succeeded in shocking them somewhat. Back in the House after lunch I got a note to say that the tea party arranged for Trudeau[367] (Canadian Prime Minister) was cancelled because due to the strike, they could not boil the tea!! But as I was anyhow in the debate on the referendum I wouldn't have gone. The debate was on the White Paper about the referendum proposals but

---

[366] A tax levied on capital transfers, gifts or inheritances. It applied to transfers upon death in 1975.
[367] Pierre Trudeau (1919-2000), Prime Minister of Canada, 1968-79 and 1980-84.

much of it was on the principle of referenda as such and not the details of the machinery. I spoke and got a nice compliment on my speech from the Minister winding up for the Government (Jerry Fowler – my opponent in 1964 election!) Plenty of broadcasting about it. Meanwhile, Wilson and Callaghan were over in Dublin at the Summit Conference finalising the renegotiation of the CM. Next day Wed., PM announced the results of the renegotiations in Parliament but did not say what he thought of them because the Cabinet had not discussed them! When they do there will, of course, be a furore and a split – should make interesting politics. In the evening, supper with CPA delegates and then theatre to see "The Dame of Sark' about German occupation of the island – excellent - and then to No. 10 for PM's reception for Trudeau – he was very chatty and the PM pulled my leg about the way my constituency had treated me over the CM and related it all to Trudeau who seemed appropriately shocked. During question time that day I had pulled PM's leg and referred to the "Wilson fan Club" in the Tory Party and then asked him to compare his election pledges with the results – this got the headlines in the press!

23.3.75

Monday Press Conference for Douglas Jay's new pamphlet on alternatives[368] – went well – good press. In the evening a meeting of National Referendum Campaign – long meeting but it went well – Frere-Smith rude as usual. Tuesday lunch with Lord Kings-Norton[369], an anti-CM peer. PM then announced the terms of the re-negotiation – it was dull and he was obviously shifty as he knew he hadn't met the election pledges. Went on TV and said so. Thursday evening Christopher Soames came to the 1922 – he was hopeless and bumbled – the worst attendance ever of 1922!

    Friday NRC Conference all day going over organisation and tactics – I hope it helped – we got some clearer definition of GBO's position. Back to Banbury and straight out to a drinks party at Len Edwards dressed as 'Caribbeans'. Sat Surgery. And, in afternoon, a most tedious Executive dealing in part with the Agent question and then the attitude which the Association was to take over the Common

---

[368] To Common Market membership.
[369] Roxbee Cox, Baron Kings Norton (1902-97), aeronautical engineer. Chief Scientist, Ministry of Fuel and Power, 1948-54. Ennobled, 1965.

Market – the latter was a ludicrous shambles. Prime Minister is in a real mess over the CM!!

30.3.75

Short week with the House rising for Easter on the Friday. Mostly spent getting the National Referendum Campaign group – Frere-Smith still being very awkward and disruptive. Did French TV on Wednesday. Govt. White Paper on renegotiations out on Thursday and very much on the same lines as the 1971 White Paper!

13.4.75

Really wretched Easter recess of 1 week when it snowed and froze most of the time – it was no rest for me with the CM coming up! First week back was really terrible – 3 day debate on the CM. I spoke on the 2nd day and had to attend the Chamber when I could. But I also was responsible for drafting the 2000 words for the anti-case – this took up <u>all</u> my time during the week – we had 7 drafts and it was a terrible job getting in everyone's wishes!! <u>Never</u> again. Everyone will complain when it comes out! Saturday spoke at a meeting at Conway Hall, Red Lion Square – the National Front came and broke it up fighting and throwing chairs about in front of TV. Hopefully we turned it to good advantage as what they were complaining about was that NRC would not affiliate them! So in fact they helped us! Once it settled down it went well. I spoke first, then Sir John Winnifrith and then Peter Shore. A lot of press the next day! Sunday the constituency Executive met to choose a new agent – awful rows and they rejected the lot including our trainee agent Tim Statham – the constituency Mafia war again! How very depressing.

20.4.75

Budget on Tuesday – a nasty one with taxes up all round designed to take back the tax of those who have broken the Social Contract[370] – but, of course, at the same time it hits those in the same income group who have had no pay rises at all. Budget all the week and Common Market all the week for me! Spent Thursday morning with Lord Snowdon over the disabled. To Devon on Friday a.m. – spoke at Taunton to a

---

[370] The trade unionists who achieved higher pay settlements.

good meeting on CM – stayed night at Edward du Cann's glorious Manor 'Cothay'.

27.4.75

Final day of Budget debate. National Referendum Campaign Committee meeting on Monday evening attended by the dissenting Cabinet Ministers for the first time. Tuesday a meeting at No. 12 to finalise the programme for TV and broadcasting and the draw for the last TV broadcast which we won. Lunch time spoke at Chatham House on sovereignty although I don't think the academics really liked my views.

Tuesday, Wed., and Thursday the House went through all stages of the Referendum Bill and changed the count from national to county basis – this was good. The whole week seemed to be CM all the time ending with the Labour Party Conference which voted 2-1 against the Market! Friday lunch at General Foods, then spoke at Banbury Tech against Uwe Kitzinger, Christopher Soames No. 2 from Brussels – 300 there - and a good meeting.

4.5.75

Busy day Monday, NRC meetings all day. The campaign gears up but due to obstruction mainly from Frere-Smith and GBO we have not got off the mat quickly enough. But now we have the £125,000 available from the Govt. we can get moving with advertising, leaflets, etc. Spoke at Tottenham Chamber of Commerce on Wednesday – good meeting – James Hill[371] put the case for pros – very badly. Wed. evening news that the 2,000 words had leaked so it had to be published. Quick decision needed! I am suspicious that it was done by the Government. However, we had a press conference 10.30 the next day (Thurs.) and BBC TV and news carried my views, so we did well. But it has not helped our cause to have it deployed too early altho' everyone agrees that our 2,000 words is better than the Pro's – although the pro-market Press will of course pick it to pieces!

---

[371] Sir James Hill (1926-1999), Conservative MP for Southampton Test, 1970-October 1974 and 1979-1997.

18.5.75

Tuesday the 1922 Exec. went to see Margaret Thatcher for the first time since her election – what a change! She listened and took in – so unlike Ted. She is keeping a very low profile at the moment which is probably right as we are in an awful muddle over policy. The Party is in an awful mess, little money to get good research going - and the City is being advised to withhold financial support unless we agree to proportional representation – apparently Jeremy Thorpe is canvassing this idea.

25.5.75

A very busy week on CM. We had the last meeting of NRC Committee on Monday – we had our battle orders and decided to get on with it. Frere-Smith of GBO seems to have baled out and gone his own way – he _is_ a curious character! Monday CPA dinner and theatre. Tuesday a.m. O Group, then Thames TV meeting about TV programmes and spoke in evening at Lewisham with Ian Mikardo[372], John Mackintosh, Kenneth Clarke[373] – 500 there.

    The CM referendum debate is going full blast – we seem to be winning all the arguments but not the votes according to the opinion polls. However things can swing in the last days.

1.6.75

The latest private poll shows a significant drop in the Yes vote, mostly going to the don't knows and slightly to us. This is at least a move and we still have time to go and on TV we can make an impact. Tony Benn, the 'ogre' to the pros, has made a big impact on unemployment and we have done well on food – the pros continue their scares and fear tactics – all very negative. Press Conference at the Waldorf very well attended, meetings everywhere and all the bally hoo of a General Election. Fascinating and am learning a lot. Aunt Ada (90) died in the

---

[372] Ian Mikardo (1908-93), Labour MP for Reading 1945-50; Reading South 1950-55; Reading, 1955-59; Poplar, 1964-74; Bethnal Green and Bow; 1974-83; Bow and Poplar, 1983-87.

[373] Kenneth Clarke, Lord Clarke (1940-), Conservative MP for Rushcliffe, 1970-2019. Held office in the Thatcher, Major and Cameron administrations: Secretary of State for Health, 1988-90; Education and Science, 1990-92; Home Secretary, 1992-93; Chancellor of the Exchequer, 1993-7; Lord Chancellor, 2010-12.

middle of the week and had to organise the funeral which I attended on Friday at Worthing. Meeting in Banbury Friday night – with Ernest Wistrich[374] we discussed integration vs cooperation theme – excellent debate. Joan went to Brussels with Barbara Castle on a shopping spree to show that prices of the food basket was 60% higher in CM – then a good press conf. at which Joan was v. good. Altogether a more encouraging week.

8.6.75

Monday started early – 8.15 at Royal Commonwealth Society to do a Granada TV 'State of the Nation' programme for 2 hours. It was in the form of a debate as standing committee which they 'mocked up' v. well. Taking part for the pro-marketeers were Ted Heath, Reggie Maudling, John Davies, Roy Jenkins, Roy Hattersley and David Steel[375] – for the antis, Enoch Powell, Peter Shore, Judith Hart, Douglas Jay, Douglas Henderson[376] (SNP) and self. We debated 3 motions on the Common Market in fine parliamentary style with Betty Harvey [sic] Anderson as Chairman. General impression seems to be that the antis won the argument – it was well received by the public. Then a long session agreeing the script for the next anti TV broadcast which went v. well – well produced by Ken Little[377] and George Gale[378] with Patrick Cosgrave[379] and Paul Johnson[380]. BBC TV at 6.15 to the 'Nationwide' programme. This I enjoyed – a relaxed 20 mins. chat with the interviewer – I got a lot of praise for this one – it must have come over well because it was not hurried. Tuesday a.m. TV again in the morning, Davies and Newman AGM at midday! (re-elected a director) and then 'O' Group meeting in the afternoon. Wednesday final press conference at the Waldorf, self in the chair, and guests were Norwegian anti-CM leader, Peter Shore, Barbara Castle, Enoch Powell,

---

[374] Ernest Wistrich (1923-2015), Director of the European Movement.
[375] David Steel, Baron Steel of Aikwood (1938-), Liberal MP for Roxburgh, Selkirk and Peebles, 1965-83; Tweeddale, Ettrick, and Lauderdale, 1983-97. Member of the Scottish Parliament for Lothians, 1999-2003. Leader of the Liberal party, 1976-88. Ennobled, 1997.
[376] Douglas Henderson (1935-2006), Scottish National Party MP for East Aberdeenshire, February 1974-1979.
[377] Ken Little (1945-2015), BBC TV Producer.
[378] George Gale (1927-90), journalist. Editor of the *Spectator*, 1970-73.
[379] Patrick Cosgrave (1941-2001), journalist and author.
[380] Paul Johnson (1928-2023), journalist. Editor of the *New Statesman*, 1965-70.

Jack Jones[381], D. Jay, R. Moate, R. Bell, Michael Foot – quite a bag – it went well and the press enjoyed it. And that was the end of the campaign.

Polling Day, Thursday 6 June. All opinion polls show 2-1 for Yes and staying in. As it happened the turnout was 64.5% (about what we expected). ITV did a survey of 10,000 voters after they left the polling stations and got it almost exactly right. The count, by counties, was on Friday and the first results coming in showed the polls to be only too right. I was at Earls Court with Sir Philip Allen[382] the national counting officer in case of a recount. TV and Radio all day – about 5 TV appearances and 6 radio commentaries. By 4 in the afternoon I conceded defeat but took the view that because of the large margin it was no use calling 'foul' – although there were plenty of them! The result was Yes 17,378,581 (67.2%) No 8,470,073 (32.8%) majority 8,908,508, out of an electorate of 40,086,677. Yes votes 43.4% of total electorate, No votes 21.1%. – 'full-hearted consent'. So that was that – I gave a party that evening in the House of Commons for about 80 workers - and we all went home. Enoch said nice things about me. Mary Louise[383], who had done magnificent work for NRC throughout, was highly praised by all – I felt very proud of her – she went on TV that night with David Dimbleby[384] and was excellent. Then home to Banbury with Joan and Maggie and a simply <u>glorious</u> week-end of hot sun – rest, relax, tennis. Unwound.

It has been a long fight and we have lost for the moment. We lost because we had all 3 political parties against us, the press, TV, City, CBI etc. etc. We had only the £125,000 given to each side plus a little extra and they must have spent several millions. An example, their 4 TV broadcasts cost about £135,000 – ours £2,300! But ours were better I think. They played it dirty, too, with the Press. The Press and the pros centred on Tony Benn as an ogre, said that if the verdict was No we would be taken over by the Communists etc. This affected most of the Tory voters – they were simply scared to vote No. Tony Benn intervened over unemployment and gave 500,000 unemployed because of the CM. The pros, whose case was weak, used every ploy to keep the debate off the CM. They never said what was their

---

[381] Jack Jones (1913-2009), General Secretary of the Transport and General Workers' Union, 1969-78.

[382] Sir Philip Allen, Baron Allen of Abbeydale (1912-2007), civil servant. Permanent Under-Secretary, Home Office, 1966-72. Ennobled, 1976.

[383] Neil's daughter had been employed by the No campaign.

[384] David Dimbleby (1938-), TV presenter and journalist.

meaning of political union, they never said what their views were about federalism – the vital question. We could not get our case out in the popular press. But we all tried hard and I believe we won the argument but the Press won the vote.

So now we, the people, have had our chance to get out. And we have lost. So Phase II begins, to stop any move towards federalism – this should widen the opposition in the Tory Party. The options are: The CM will throw us out for blocking federalism, the CM will break up and we will come out because we don't like it. I cannot in the long run see us remaining in. Possibly the Germans, French, and the low countries will go ahead with a closer cooperation on economic and monetary union and step by step to federalism leaving us, Italy, Denmark and Ireland in the outer second division joined possibly by Norway and Sweden. This could be one answer. But now we are in a different ball-game. It will be interesting to see who was right.

On return to Parliament on Monday 9 June everyone was very nice to me on all sides, Labour, Conservatives, Liberal, Nationalists, whether pro or anti – shouldn't say it but, for the record (!), I got lots of letters from all over the country, with thanks and congratulations etc. Even the Prime Minister, when making his statement on the referendum in the House said:

"I am sure that I am expressing the view of the whole House when I say that the Hon. Member for Banbury, although he expressed views different from those that I was expressing, conducted his campaign with great dignity during the referendum".

Part Four:
The Hung Parliament

22.6.75

Anti CM 'unusual channels' met to discuss the future and decided to maintain the group to deal with on-going legislation and resist moves to a federal situation. Tuesday tennis a.m. and lunch with Peter Hardiman-Scott[385] of BBC to discuss referendum. In evening David Butler led a 'seminar' on the referendum under the 'Media Society' and I let go at the Press! They didn't like it at all and all gave wet defences for their attitudes – on the other hand I gave credit to TV and broadcasting. We shall see what comes out in David Butler's book! Wed. meeting of NRC bods to go through finances – it looks as though our books will balance, thank God. Lunch at Lancaster House with Jim Callaghan and Norwegian Foreign Minister who spoke well. CPA Executive at which I was appointed to CPA General Council for two years – this is excellent and just up my street. Conference in India in Oct/Nov.

29.6.75

Monday the Association Chairman came to see me at House of Commons to discuss the AGM on Friday! He has <u>at last</u> seen through Harry Webb and all his machinations and is furious with him – I believe he now sees how Harry has been working with John Schuster against me and if only he will come off the fence we can get cracking with the Association. John Schuster and his hunting/country friends, who pack meetings of the Executive, are still after my blood to make me their puppet – this I will resist not only for myself but for the sake of Parliament. They have decided to hold a meeting of the Executive to discuss me 2nd week in July! Then they might want to see me – this should be interesting.

Tuesday Bob Harrison[386] (TGWU) came to the flat to see me armed with presents from TGWU! We had a most interesting discussion on the views of the Unions and I hope we can keep up the dialogue for the benefit of all sides as, one day, we shall be in office

---

[385] Peter Hardiman Scott (1920-1999), journalist. BBC political editor, 1970-75.
[386] Research Officer for the Trade and General Workers' Union seconded to the National Referendum Campaign.

and together we must work! Lunch with regional CBI and discussion – 5 MPs (Tory) most of whom disagreed about everything! It was a fascinating view of our Party today, with the Heath-men wanting a return to statutory prices and incomes policy and the Thatcher men wanting a non-statutory system. Ted has been making speeches (really anti-Margaret) in various countries and seems to me aiming at a Coalition with the Labour right wing and Libs in which he will lead (?). This has caused great offence to the Cons. MPs and Ted and his friends like Peter Walker are unpopular. This was raised in 1922 by Peter Rawlinson[387] on Thursday – the Press has got the message and the *Daily Mail* has told him to stop it!

Friday was my AGM and I expected a lot of trouble over the CM – so I designed my speech to pre-empt all outcomes. I said that everyone, pro – anti – in Cons. Party had been v. nice to me (as Cons. always are!), PM and EEC had congratulated me on CM campaign, that Margaret wanted no backbiting, leave that to Labour! This stemmed any really bad criticism and John Schuster looked <u>furious</u>. Then the Exec. agreed to hold a meeting to discuss me in July!! I am not interested! 'They' are still trying to pin me down to be their servant – I refuse.

6.7.75

Monday was such a lovely day I decided to go up to London late – but in the event I got a message to go and see the Belgian Prime Minister[388] at the Belgian Embassy after lunch to give him my views on the future of 'political union' in Europe! This I did in no uncertain fashion, making it clear that the result of the referendum was achieved on the basis of no federalism and any move toward it would be heavily resisted by MPs and people. Several others did the same yet at his press conference at the end he gave the impression that the British were all for it! Later that day I held the final meeting of the National Referendum Campaign, an argument with Frere-Smith over his deficit! An agreement to set up a successor organisation with Hugh Simmonds[389] in charge to do research and to publish a quarterly paper

---

[387] Peter Rawlinson, Lord Rawlinson of Ewell (1919-2006), Conservative MP for Epsom, 1955-74; Epsom and Ewell, 1975-78. Ennobled, 1978.
[388] Leo Tinedmans (1922-2014), Prime Minister of Belgium, 1974-78.
[389] Conservative activist. He was an ally of Ronald Bell in Beaconsfield and worked on his successful re-adoption campaign in 1972. He committed suicide in 1988.

- and so ended, except for the accounts, the umbrella organisation of the National Referendum Campaign.

13.7.75

On Tuesday the constituency Executive met to discuss me! It was arranged without me being consulted. Apparently John Schuster went into a diatribe against me and read out pages of stuff! At the end Jack Friswell and Tom Roach attacked John Schuster and sent him packing! It seems quite clear that John Schuster and Jack Witley and Harry Webb have been plotting this exercise for some time with a few of their cronies like Terry Molloy and Judy Hutchison. As a result they agreed "not to seek an alternative candidate at this juncture"! Just as well for them! Len Edwards, the Chairman, still seems to sit on the fence but I understand he has at last hoisted in the Schuster plot. We shall see how it develops.

27.7.75

All the week on inflation and prices and incomes. Govt. bringing in Tory type legislation again – it seems it will fail – Michael Foot very unhappy and will resign if they have to bring in compulsory powers. Thursday Committee Stage of Prices and Incomes Bill (called something else[390]) and all night sitting until Friday 4pm! Michael Foot still v. unhappy but attended all the debate.

3.8.75

Petroleum nationalisation Bill on Monday – drinks with Margaret Thatcher at St. Stephen's Club – she was v. charming but Ted H, who came was, we thought, positively rude to her. Tuesday back to Prices and Incomes – it was incredibly hot and stuffy in London and much liquid refreshment was consumed on the Terrace in the long hours of the night!
    Wednesday Employment Protection Bill – again very, very hot 86 degrees in London and relief on Thursday with slightly cooler weather and the un-whipped Consolidated Fund. Margaret T came to the 1922 and was excellent – she really <u>can</u> communicate and she got

---

[390] The Remuneration, Charges and Grants Bill.

a great reception. John Schuster is still getting at me and Crossbencher[391] carried the story naming him.

10.8.75

On Monday, in the report stage of the Housing Finance Bill, the Govt. was defeated on a Lords amendment dealing with the Clay Cross councillors[392]. This was an amendment to disqualify councillors who broke the law, i.e., it was a vote to maintain the rule of law. This was a good example of parliament defeating the Government of the day in spite of 3-line whips – George Strauss[393] and Crawshaw[394], 3 Lab., voted against the Govt. and several abstained = very encouraging. Wednesday was the debate on Court Line[395] - I advised Willy Whitelaw to play it in a low key – but Heseltine, opening, didn't and got fairly chewed up by Tony Benn[396]! After that I went home and started the recess – Parliament rose the next day 7 Aug. – the weather has been <u>unbearably</u> hot up to 90 degrees in London and we all felt whacked.

26.8.75

On 18th meeting with F&GP (my 3rd in 16 years) to hear the result of the Executive meeting about me! 6 weeks ago! We went over the usual ground – all very puerile but agreed, in the end, to issue a cooling statement at next Executive. My 'crime' is that I am too independent! John Schuster gave me a copy of his speech at that famous executive –

---

[391] Marten knew Robin Oakley who wrote the Crossbencher column, see entry 25.7.71.
[392] In 1972 Councillors in Clay Cross refused to pass on rent increases mandated in the 1972 Housing Finance Act.
[393] George Strauss, Baron Strauss (1901-93), Labour MP for Lambeth North, 1929-31 and 1934-50; Vauxhall, 1950-79. Ennobled, 1979.
[394] Richard Crawshaw, Baron Crawshaw (1917-86), Labour MP for Liverpool Toxteth, 1964-81; SDP MP for Liverpool Toxteth, 1981-83. Created Baron Crawshaw of Aintree, 1985.
[395] Court Line was Britain's largest air travel operator and collapsed on 15 August 1974.
[396] Anthony Wedgwood Benn (1925-2014), Labour MP for Bristol South East, 1950-60 and 1963-83; Chesterfield, 1984-2001. Held various ministerial posts in the Wilson and Callaghan administrations: Secretary of State for Industry, 1974-75; Energy, 1975-79. Contested Labour deputy leadership, 1981, and leadership in 1988.

it was odious, libellous and offensive. I will have to deal with it at next Executive as I cannot allow him to get away with it.

12.10.75

The last 2 weeks have been the weeks of the conferences at Blackpool. Labour's was dreadful with a lot of in-fighting with the very left-wing and gave a very nasty image of envy politics. By contrast the Conservative Conference was sensible if slightly boring and a general low-key demand to move back on track to being a proper Conservative party again. Margaret Thatcher wound up the conference in a really splendid speech – no statistics just good common sense straight from the heart and restating Conservative values. She got a terrific reception – the Party honours, broadly, the philosophy we have. Ted Heath bogged it and apparently, at a private party, called Margaret and Keith Joseph traitors! This leaked and he had to issue a denial! "It is said" he was tight[397] and was put to bed and then got up to join the party again!! How true it is I don't know – probably only gossip.

The referendum accounts were published showing the pros spent 10 times as much as the antis – they were amazing accounts. I did TV and radio broadcasts on them. I think the public was somehow surprised. The *'Economist'* tipped me as one who might succeed Ed. du Cann as Chairman of the 1922 Committee! V. unlikely.

19.10.75

Parliament reassembled on Mon. 13 Oct. and straight away we had 3-line whip on the Community Land Bill and Trades Union Bill. On Friday we debated the EEC document on agriculture and I spoke on the theme that the CM was trying to clobber the UK dairy industry and fill the vacuum with EEC surpluses – I am deeply suspicious.

16.11.75

The following days spent in a general rush! Joan and I preparing to go to the Commonwealth Parliamentary Conference in India, Judith and Peter John preparing for their departure to Malawi for 2 years, Anthony and Maggie involved in negotiating loans for their house and

---

[397] Drunk.

Mary Louise causing us anxiety in the West Indies over her job with a curious outfit! However we got off to India having said our goodbyes flying out by Air India 747 – packed plane – with Lord and Lady Shepherd, leader of our delegation and a few delegates. A long flight but excellent service. On arrival at Delhi we were met with garlands and much ceremony by the Speaker of the Indian Parliament Dr. D[h]illon[398], a really super chap. We were accommodated in the Ashoke [sic] Hotel in New Delhi, a really magnificent place with excellent service – recuperated by the swimming pool fairly rapidly. The Conference was held in the new parliamentary annexe, a splendid building. I have never come across such efficiency in the way the conference was run. We had about 10 days of conference debating a wide range of subjects. What was so outstanding was the quality of the speeches from the delegates, no matter where they came from and the togetherness of the Commonwealth, although we didn't always agree on everything! But it certainly led to a far better understanding between us all and we met and became friends with many colleagues.

Mrs Gandhi[399] opened the conference in great style – very impressive. The President arrived in carriage with Household Cavalry and trumpets and all! Very vice regal! Mrs G. was in an emergency situation as her parliamentary democracy was under threat from extra-parliamentary forces and she had locked up the baddies and 'stretched' the constitution to the maximum[400]. But I had the impression that, in the circumstances, she had done the right thing altho' the British Press and Radio were very anti-her. The Indians, for internal political purposes, still seem to blame us for their troubles but in their hearts they know this not to be true. Here follow merely aide-memoires – it would take a book to write it all up.

Reception like Buckingham Palace Garden Party by President of India[401] in ex-Vice Regal Palace – nothing changes! All splendour. Tennis with Jerry Regan[402], Premier of Nova Scotia, at Canadian High Commission and again at British High Commission with ex-champion of India! Dinner at ex-Nizam of Hyderabad house in Delhi – 500

---

[398] Dr. Gurdal Singh Dhillon (1915-1992), Speaker of the Lok Sabha, the Indian lower House.
[399] Indira Gandhi (1917-1984), Prime minister of India from 1966-77 and 1980-84. She was assassinated by two of her bodyguards.
[400] On 25 June Gandhi's administration announced a state of emergency that lasted until March 1977.
[401] Dr. Fakhruddin Ali Ahmed (1905-1977), President of India, 1974-77.
[402] Gerald Regan (1928-2019), Premier of Nova Scotia, 1970-78.

present and scrumptious fare – Nizam had 47 wives living there (once!). Display of dancing – quite excellent. Joan got tummy troubles and was out of action for 2 days. Reception at Red Fort, Delhi – Gurkha pipe band – *Son et Lumiere* in the fort with anti-British ending! Vast dinner after given by Lt. Governor and again pipe band and dancing girls. Visit to Agra to see Taj Mahal and Fort. It really is a wonder of the world – our plane flew round it at 1000ft! Superb lunch etc. Fort was fascinating – the occupant used to have 300 concubines! Lunch with 'opposition' – rather weak. Dinner with Mrs Gandhi and farewell speeches. Then on tour. First to Kashmir – lunch with Sheikh Abdulla[403], the rebel leader, stayed on house-boats on lake, went up to Gurung 9000ft in Himalayas from Srinagar (5000ft) where we were staying. Autumn visits and shows snow. We want to go back for a trekking holiday. Our host on the house boat said Mrs Gandhi was irrelevant to Kashmir as long as we have Sheikh Abdulla! On to Chandigarh in the Punjab – a town laid out in 1950s by French Architects – wonderfully done broad streets. Visited hospital and university and then dancing display and dined in fabulous gardens of ex-Maharaja of Patiala. Art galleries, machine tool factory, lunch in Guest House and departure for Jaipur – getting absolutely whacked! But reception in Jaipur was really fantastic on arrival – I collected 20 garlands of French marigolds! Dancing girls again and dinner at ex-Maharaja of Jaipur's palace – we had to pinch ourselves to believe we were not dreaming. Toured the palaces next day, rode on elephants, saw observatory, lunch with the Governor, elegance again! Then reception and final speeches in Jaipur Parliament. Showered with gifts all the time – such generosity I have never experienced – but behind it all the poverty of the public. Home again by Air India and back to the all night sitting in Parliament. Cold and frosty weather. All a super experience!

23.11.75

Visited the local Association office for the first time since Feb. Have boycotted it until Mon. since last Feb. when I was disgusted by their behaviour over the selection of an agent. Now we have a new agent Ken Axford – excellent, it seems - and it is really great to have someone who is not working behind your back. Len Edwards, the Association

---

[403] Sheikh Mohammad Abdullah (1905-82), leader of Kashmiri independence movement.

Chairman has at <u>last</u> realised the trickery which has been going on between Agent Webb, Schuster and Treasurer Whitley. I now look forward to some peace!

Wed. the Queen opened Parliament, the speech from the Throne was <u>dreadful</u> (not the Queen herself!) but the content. The speeches which followed in Parliament were abusive and totally lacking in statesmanship. Francis Pym has decided not to stand against Edward du Cann for 1922 Chairman – some opposition to E du C about his Common Market speech during the Referendum[404] and his connection with Keyser Ullman. Hope it will all die as he is an excellent Chairman. CPC on Sunday afternoon; debate on whether the Cons. Party was moving to the right or not. I said it was and David Knox said it wasn't – I won 35-16! Actually in the mood of the Party it was a foregone conclusion.

30.11.75

Departed at 6am on Monday to London Airport to get plane to Copenhagen. The Select Committee on European Legislation, of which I am a member, went on a round tour of Denmark, Germany and Brussels to study the question of scrutiny of EEC legislation. Arrived Copenhagen in bitterly cold weather – straight to lunch with a foreign office Minister in the Folketing. The Danes take a cautious view of the EEC saying that before any changes are made there must be progress on a number of fronts – v. sensible! They have a healthy group of anti-marketeers and, being a coalition government, they must proceed with caution. They exercise more control over their Ministers going to EEC than we do – if Ministers want to exceed their mandate they must consult the scrutiny Committee again.

Tuesday p.m. flew to Bonn and in the evening dined with our Ambassador Sir Oliver Wright[405] – large dinner party and the antis in the Committee pulled the German legs quite a lot. Briefing by Ambassador in the morning during which he said that "the Germans want a federal state (on the lines of Germany itself) – unless we allow them their aims their energies will go down a more dangerous direction i.e. E. Germany". It seemed clear to me that they wanted a federal Europe of which <u>they</u> will be the bosses! We met their

---

[404] Du Cann declared in the final week of campaigning that he was voting against EEC membership in the 1975 referendum.
[405] Sir Oliver Wright (1922-2009), Ambassador to West Germany, 1975-81; United States of America, 1982-86.

Committee who seemed weak in that they did not want to offend EEC or their Ministers by blocking any EEC proposals! They want to hand over all EEC legislation to the European Parliament – naturally, as it is the first step to a federal state. Early departure next day for Brussels by train. Lunch at Commission HQ and then a meeting with Christopher Soames, chef de Cabinet David Hannay[406], a supreme example of a Eurocrat with his feet totally off the ground! In the course of conversation he confirmed that the Commission really wanted to become the Govt. of the CM! This shook the pros in the delegation as it was precisely what the antis had always said and they denied it.

The trip confirmed my worst fears, namely, that CM is not working well, it is dreadfully bureaucratic and out of touch and that its real aim is federalism – the direct elections to the EuroParl are the first step – achtung.

7.12.75

Tuesday a Bill to nationalise the aircraft and shipbuilding industries – Labour majority of 5! Thursday PM reported on the Rome European Council and we roasted him. Having let Callaghan stand out for months for a single seat at the Energy Conference[407] in a very Gaullist way the PM capitulated totally – altho' of course he presented it as a success! I called it appeasement and suggested that the next Council Meeting should be held at Munich! He didn't like that! Also attacked the Govt. policy over N. Ireland at question time – the Govt. is letting out all detainees. Fury.

14.12.75

Thursday we voted again on the death penalty and lost – for the death penalty 232 (217) against 361 (369) – 1974 figures in brackets – a 94% turnout on a free vote! After which I dined with the Speaker at a dinner for the Prince of Wales. He was very charming and intelligent and keen and made an excellent off the cuff speech having torn up his prepared one. After dinner had a long talk with the Prime Minister

---

[406] Sir David Hannay, Lord Hannay of Chiswick (1935-), diplomat. Permanent Representative to the European Community, 1985-90. Ambassador and Permanent Representative to the United Nations 1990-95. Created Lord Hannay, 2001.

[407] Wilson had agreed to a single EEC seat at a world energy conference to be held on 16 December.

and Lord Chancellor[408] – PM was endeavouring to tell me that the Cabinet was united! Rumours have it that if the Govt. bales out 'Chryslers' Varley[409] S/S Industry will resign – if it doesn't Willie Ross[410] S/S Scotland will resign! – Bill Rodgers will resign if there are defence cuts and Fred Peart if the Common Market doesn't let him continue with his beef premium scheme! And the PM went to great lengths to tell me that every dept. had been cut except for overseas aid! Discussed Australian elections with Lord Chancellor (Elwyn Jones) and he said he was very worried at the effect of the result on the constitutional position of the Monarchy in Australia. This brought the PM in to say that he had 46 relations living in Darwin! Prince Charles said, when we met, he knew all about me – Common Market! Three times last week unknown people stopped me in the street (recognising me from TV) to express hatred of the CM!

21.12.75

The political week was taken up with the affair of Chrysler motors. They have been doing very badly in UK and were going to close down their factories here introducing massive unemployment amounting to 25,000 people. The Govt. had recently announced a new approach to industrial strategy (!) which was not to support lame ducks etc. Chrysler offered its factories to the UK Govt. plus £35m – in the event the Govt. did a deal with Chrysler for propping up the lame duck at a cost to the Govt. and taxpayers around £200m. Most extraordinary! They couldn't face the unemployment involved. But Chryslers are not selling well and they will obviously come back for more money in due course. British Leyland are in a mess and have stopped investment in the company until productivity improves – Chrysler will now flood the market with more cars in competition with BL! Why should 25,000 jobs be saved for £200m when 1.3 million people are out of work –

---

[408] Elwyn Jones, Baron Elwyn-Jones (1909-89), Labour MP for Plaistow, 1945-50; West Ham South, 1950-74; Newham South, February 1974-March 1974. Created Baron Elwyn-Jones, March 1974. Lord Chancellor, 1974-79. Elwyn Jones was a British prosecutor at the Nuremberg trials after the Second World War.

[409] Eric Varley, Baron Varley (1932-2008), Labour MP for Chesterfield, 1964-84. Secretary of State for Energy, 1974-75; Industry, 1975-79. Created Baron Varley of Chesterfield, 1990.

[410] William Ross, Baron Ross of Marnock (1911-1988), Labour MP for Kilmarnock, 1946-79. Secretary of State for Scotland, 1964-70 and 1974-76. Created Baron Marnock, 1979.

preferred workers? Yes, because quite a lot are in Scotland and the SNP are making headway there against Labour! The Cabinet was very split over it all and this was done to patch it up – a costly Cabinet. When we debated the money resolution it was clear that the Govt. hadn't got its sums right, it hadn't thought it through and it hadn't allowed for inflation – an <u>extraordinary</u> performance. And so we rose for Christmas recess, the country in a spirit of gloom - and the Govt. up against the ropes. Xmas a relief for them!

11.1.76

N. Ireland erupted again after the new year with an awful series of murders – it had an instant effect of getting the parties together – but it didn't last long! The cod war with Iceland flared up nastily, the steel men went on strike and gales swept the country although the weather was warm.

18.1.76

N. Ireland debate on Monday about the Convention report which the Govt. couldn't accept. The idea was to achieve power-sharing and the elections to the Convention gave a majority against the sort of power-sharing the Govt. wanted – the Unionists were not prepared, if elected, to have members of other parties in their 'Cabinet' – don't blame them really – would a UK Govt. do the same? Anyhow the report has been put back to the Convention to have another go at it.

Then on Tuesday we started the debate on Devolution running for the whole week – 4 days of it! Both main parties are divided on the issue – a lot of Labour hate the idea. The Conservatives are in a mixed up situation – some say we are committed to it because it was in our Manifesto at the '74 elections, some say we will lose all Scottish seats if we don't devolve, some want to devolve legislative functions to a directly elected assembly. Margaret T., unfortunately, in opening the debate, implied that we would devolve legislative power to an Assembly. At the Committee on Wed. evening there was considerable confusion, the Scot devolvers wanting one thing, the anti-devolvers another and in the end the general mood was to urge great caution on any amendment and I urged that no mention should be made of direct elections and legislative powers. In the end a v. modest amendment was put down merely mentioning an Assembly without mentioning elections and legislative powers. Even then at the 1922 Committee it was raised again and many objected to even a mention of an Assembly in the amendment. Willy Whitelaw who is to wind up promised Betty Harvie-Anderson that we would not mention devolving legislative powers or direct elections: if he does (and he may well have to under pressure) then some will abstain on our amendment. We really have got ourselves in a mess due in large part to a failure of the leadership to consult the Party – the matter should have been brought to the main 1922 before a line was agreed in the Shadow Cabinet.

25.1.76

The devolution debate ended on Monday – the Govt. won the vote but there was substantial unhappiness all round! I voted for our amendment which called for an Assembly only and I got the Chief Whip's confirmation before voting that I was *not* voting for a directly elected Assembly with legislative powers. I wrote him a note 10 minutes before the vote and he wrote back and said that was so! I have kept that note in case of future trouble! After that experience we must be sure that the same does not happen over directly elected European Parliament. Thursday did a broadcast on BBC on direct election. Margaret T made a good speech on defence and irritated the Russians[411] – she obviously hit the nail on the head!

1.2.76

Margaret's defence speech has hotted things up – the Russians continue to attack her as the 'iron amazon'! Roy Mason[412], Def. Minister, made an absurd attack on her (which he will regret), Party partially supported her, Russians also attacked Callaghan and Chinese support Margaret (naturally!), so it was all a thoroughly good exercise which I hope has woken up the people to the dangers.

Thursday big debate on unemployment. Govt. put down a cunning motion against which we could not vote but we voted for our amendment. When it came to the main vote 52 Lab. lefties abstained! But as we didn't vote they had a huge majority. All rather frustrating

---

[411] This was Mrs Thatcher's 'Britain Awake' speech at Kensington Town Hall on 19 January 1976. The Russians used the 'Iron Lady' moniker on 24 January. The speech focussed on Russian military power and the threat to the West.

[412] Roy Mason, Lord Mason of Barnsley (1924-2015), Labour MP for Barnsley 1953-83; Barnsley Central, 1983-87. Secretary of State for Trade, 1964-67; Defence, 1974-76; Northern Ireland, 1976-79. Made Lord Mason of Barnsley, 1987.

for us. Apart from that no excitements this week except perhaps the report on Jeremy Thorpe's company collapse[413] which he was made to look irresponsible and a witness in a case said he had had homosexual relations with Jeremy! Not good for his image.

8.2.76

The Jeremy Thorpe thing grows in intensity – all sorts of allegations started flying about and Cyril Smith[414], that clumsy Lib. Chief Whip, seemed to be emerging as playing rather a nasty game and is after Jeremy's job – but Pardoe is keeping a low profile. There is more to come yet and it seems like a re-run of the Profumo affair[415]. He may have to give up the leadership of the Lib. Party?

Excellent debate on Procedure on Monday – the interesting thing was that the pros[416], who are constantly criticising us, were conspicuous by their total absence! Tuesday Selwyn Lloyd retired as Speaker and we had many glowing tributes to him – he <u>had</u>, on the whole, been a good Speaker. We then elected George Thomas[417] – I wonder how long he will be regarded as a good choice? Not married, non-drinker – non-smoker – Methodist lay preacher – but, anti-CM!! We shall see – some say he will not be a good Speaker – but at least he has a good sense of humour.

Dined with Margaret T but she was worrying about the speech she was about to make and didn't get very far! However, on Thursday I got a chance to speak with her and she seemed to be worried about direct elections to the Euro parliament and said we must think deeply about it – which I think is helpful. I am preaching that we should not rush into it and should first know the powers of the Parliament before we agree to it – that is what the pros do not want discussed!

---

[413] Thorpe was a non-executive director of London and County Securities that collapsed in 1973.

[414] Sir Cyril Smith (1928-2010), the disgraced Liberal MP for Rochdale, 1972-92. Smith was accused of paedophilia after his death.

[415] The scandal involving Minister for War John Profumo (1915-2006) and his affair with Christine Keeler (1942-2016) who had links to Soviet spies.

[416] Pro-Europeans.

[417] George Thomas, Viscount Tonypandy (1909-1997), Labour MP for Cardiff Central, 1945-50; Cardiff West, 1950-83. Speaker of the House of Commons, 1976-83. Created Viscount Tonypandy, 1983.

15.2.76

Tuesday 2nd Reading of Docks Bill – press said Govt. might have been defeated but it wasn't - by 8 votes! Odious bill to extend Dock Labour system[418] 5 miles inland – very dangerous. Govt. defeated on motor industry debate by counting the first vote inaccurately, so another vote was called and a lot had already left! Quite a joke! Then we seriously defeated the West Midland Council Bill, (opposed Private business) another odious piece of legislation to have state trading and all sorts of interference[419]. Thursday spoke in EEC Agricultural Price Review debate and heavily criticised the CAP – Fred Peart is going to get into trouble on this one – but will the Conservatives really hammer him and, by implication, the Common Market? Friday spoke at Oxford Union on Tindemans report[420], Sat. surgery and dance plus two interviews with farmers complaining about EEC! The chickens are certainly coming home to roost!

22.2.76

Healey cuts announced on Thursday – will cause trouble with left wing.

29.2.76

Another quietish week with the Coventry by-election coming up. The left keep up their shots at Healey about his proposed 'cuts' which are not really cuts – merely a reduction in the planned increase of spending! But they are paper tigers once again.
    Tuesday I took a delegation to see Margaret Thatcher about direct election to the Euro parliament. Peter Tapsell[421], Ken Lewis[422],

---

[418] A scheme introduced in 1947 to end casual labour in the docks. It gave dockers a legal right to minimum levels of work, holidays, sick pay, and pensions. It was abolished in 1989.

[419] Legislation designed to have the state set up its own businesses, such as caterers and butchers.

[420] A report by the Belgian Prime Minister into further European integration.

[421] Sir Peter Tapsell (1930-2018), Conservative MP for Nottingham West, 1959-64; Horncastle, 1966-83; East Lindsey, 1983-97; Louth and Horncastle, 1997-2015. Knighted, 1985. Father of the House, 2010-15.

[422] Sir Kenneth Lewis (1916-97), Conservative MP for Rutland and Stamford, 1959-83; Stamford and Spalding, 1983-87. Knighted, 1983.

Nic Budgen[423], Ronnie Bell and John Stokes[424] came. She listened well and took our points. It was clear that she wanted the Party to have more discussion about it and she herself is a *Europe des Patries*[425] and not a federalist. I have a feeling that she hasn't really thought much about it. Anyhow we left her in no uncertain state about our views.

7.3.76

Writing a week later we are back to sub-zero weather with freezing East winds and flurries of snow. Free vote on Monday on the use of seat belts which we lost – I am against making it compulsory. Tuesday discussed with John Boyd-Carpenter about the Civil Aviation Authority and their request to see the forward estimates of airlines accounts! Wednesday we defeated a GLC Bill again odious piece of local authority Labour legislation. Thursday went to Coventry by-election where Jonathan Guinness was fighting a 7,500 Labour majority on the death of Maurice Edelman. There was a fantastic turnout of only 2% below the general election and although we lost there was a 5% swing to us – this was good[426]. The Lab. man Geoffrey Robinson[427] was ex-managing director of Jaguar and was very popular with the workers who turned out well to support him. He will be a useful asset to Labour thinking.

14.3.76

Well, that was a week that was! The main item for debate on 10 March was the Government White Paper on Expenditure. Briefly, the Govt. under pressure of inflation, declining sterling, unemployment etc. etc. had to do something. It should have made massive cuts right now. Instead the White Paper set forth no actual cuts, merely a reduction in planned expenditure and even then only starting the reduction in 1977. This was absurd and sterling reacted by going below $2 to the £.

---

[423] Nicholas Budgen (1937-98), Conservative MP for Wolverhampton South West, 1974-97. Lost the whip in 1994 by voting against the EEC Finance Bill.
[424] Sir John Stokes (1917-2003), Conservative MP for Oldbury and Halesowen, 1970-74; Halesowen and Stourbridge, February 1974-92.
[425] Europe of Nations.
[426] Coventry North West by-election, 4th March 1976 result: Labour 17,118, Conservative 13,424, Liberal 1,062.
[427] Geoffrey Robinson (1938-), Labour MP for Coventry North West, 1976-2019. Paymaster General, 1997-98.

The Conservative Party obviously opposed this policy and voted on an amendment which was defeated. Then on the main motion the Tribune Group[428] 37 of them abstained because they wanted no cuts at all! And so the Govt. was defeated on its main economic strategy. The PM, altho' he voted, disappeared because it was his birthday (60)!! The inevitable row calling for the Govt. to resign took place and as a result the remaining business (CM skimmed milk) was adjourned – pity! – but the House was not in the mood to go on.

So next day, Thursday 11th the Govt. put down a motion of confidence in its economic policy and predictably the Tribune Group supported its Government! So it remained in power. But the legacy of bitterness with the left wing will remain very deep – the PM called them Marxists and Healey blackmailers, surrender and betray. During most of the debate the PM was absent again! So, what happens now? Either the Govt., having bashed the left, tries to make it up with them and gives in and reduces even the planned 'reductions' or it decides to ditch the left and increase the cuts with Conservative support or the Labour right wing rebels or the Government gives in to the left wing. Anyhow the Govt's. life is now terminal and although I don't expect an election until Oct '77, it could happen at any time. We did very well in two by-elections on Thursday Wirral and Carshalton with swings of 13% and 8% respectively with Liberals losing deposit at Wirral[429]. Libs. in an awful mess over Jeremy Thorpe's two scandals as director of a property company and allegations of homosexual relations with a Mr Scott! They are tearing themselves to bits.

21.3.76

During a board meeting on Tuesday my secretary telephones at 11.45 to say rumours were about that the PM had resigned. It was announced on the 12 o'c news. A <u>real</u> surprise to everyone including the Cabinet. He has just had his 60th birthday, he has broken many records as PM and I think, with his Party in disarray over last week's events, he is right to retire before he is thrown out. A good example to other PMs! And so the election process goes on for a new Labour

---

[428] Left wing group of Labour MPs.
[429] The Wirral by-election was caused by the resignation of Selwyn Lloyd and was won by David Hunt, a majority over Labour of 24,412. The Carshalton by-election was caused by the resignation of Robert Carr and won by the Conservative candidate Nigel Forman with a majority of 9,732. Both Lloyd and Carr took seats in the House of Lords.

leader. First choice on the announcement of PM's retirement is Jim Callaghan with Michael Foot second, Jenkins, Healey and Crosland third and Tony Benn fourth. So now we Conservatives can watch from the sidelines!

Common Market is looking sillier every day with so many things going wrong. The snake in the tunnel has broken up again, dried milk mountain is causing despair as is the regulation for eviscerated food, balance of trade is looking awful £3,368m deficit in 1975, and so on. When, oh when, will the penny begin to drop in the Conservative hierarchy.

28.3.76

On Monday Christopher Soames came to our Euro policy Committee. I have rarely heard such bumble from anyone. He has caught the disease of 'Euro-gook'. He said clearly that proposed Europarlt. would not have any additional powers (to soothe us) – I then asked him why he, as a Commissioner, had put his name to a report of the Commission, which advocated not only a legislative Europarliament but also a Euro-Government. That boiled him! He said he was looking far into the future! But he never mentioned it when he was speaking to us. Yet another example of the blatantly misleading tactics of the pro-marketeers.

The Govt. had proposed to debate 2nd reading of Metrication Bill on Thursday but had to withdraw it because of continued opposition of Cons. Party and some Labour MPs – Cons. saying it would be inflationary and needed more publicity before being brought forward – embarrassing for them as it stems from the Common Market! However, Parliament dominated the Government – that's the stuff.

Thursday evening ballot for Labour leadership announced at 6pm was Foot 90, Callaghan 84, Jenkins 56, Benn 37, Healey 30, Crosland 17. Crosland dropped out and Jenkins and Benn withdrew leaving 3 candidates. Anyhow given his support it will be Jim C – Michael F would be far more entertaining and an easier target for us to attack!

4.4.76

Monday and Tuesday we debated the question of direct elections to the European Parliament. A very interesting debate. I spoke and suggested that we should pause and think before we went ahead as it seemed, from remarks from Commissioner Lardinois[430] that the CM was in danger of disintegrating. I listed the failures (with great pleasure) and then questioned the failure of this Govt. and opposition to state anything about the powers in future of the EuroParl. whereas all the eminents had said that it really must become federal if it was to succeed. My speech was listened to but the Press didn't awfully like it! But I was well satisfied on this occasion. Anyhow we had been, via the 'usual channels', calling for a Select Committee to go into it all – I had seen Margaret Thatcher seeking her agreement. And when Jim Callaghan opened he accepted and agreed to a Select Committee! Triumph – the idea being to delay the whole project and to show up the many fallacies. In my speech I offered to be on the select committee. But the Chief Whip[431] told me quite firmly afterwards that he wouldn't put me on because I was against direct elections! Odd! And I must make him change his mind!

On Tuesday the PM (Wilson) came to answer PQs for the last time (he would be at the EEC Summit on Thursday) and I managed to ask him the last question! The Speaker told me after that as I had been the MP to ask him most questions it was appropriate that I should ask the last. I congratulated him on the dexterity with which he had answered questions and he said I had always been most courteous! Curtains!

After that we (1922 Exec.) went to see Margaret for 1½ hours – she was excellent the way she listened and dealt with us – she gives me confidence – I only hope she can stand the strain.

Meantime the EEC Summit meeting was a complete flop and they agreed to nothing! As regard direct elections, on which they were to agree to set things going, the French proposed no increase in the size of the Parliament from the existing 198 – this would mean constituencies of about 1½mn! Democracy?!! Callaghan is reported to have said that it was pointless to have direct election on this basis – well – well! This will cause gloom in the pro-camp. What now? Obviously Giscard D'Estaing[432] was under pressure from the Gaullists.

---

[430] Pierre Lardinois (1924-87), Dutch politician and EEC Commissioner for Agriculture, 1973-77.
[431] Humphrey Atkins.
[432] Valery Giscard d'Estaing (1926-2020), President of France, 1974-81.

11.4.76

On Monday, instead of a Ministerial Statement on the Summit meeting, a statement was made in answer to a written PQ. I created a row and the Speaker said he would look into it. That evening the result of the Labour election for leader was announced and as expected Jim Callaghan was elected over Michael Foot by 176-137 votes. So he became PM. Next day he answered questions quite well and at the end I raised the question of the statement and he said that it would not happen again! First victory! He did not get a tumultuous welcome when he came in from the left wing.

Budget on Tues. 6 April 2 hours 15 min speech from Healey. Not a good budget – he failed to get to the root of the problem of Govt. expenditure and he proposed a series of tax cuts on condition that the TUC agreed to 3% wage increase limit – an odd way to go about it and it caused considerable offence to those who were not Trades Unionists. We shall see how it works out – had he got the Unions prior agreement, I wonder?

Then on Thursday he announced his first lot of Cabinet changes. To my great joy Roy Jenkins did <u>not</u> go back to the F.O. – it would have been awful CM wise – instead it went to Tony Crosland who is agnostic about CM! So with Tony, Jim and Margaret things look better just at a time when the whole thing is looking more jaundiced than ever. Michael Foot became leader of the House, <u>excellent</u> and Peter Shore to Environment (pity). My feeling about Jim as PM is that he may lack decisiveness and will not be so clever with his left wing as Harold Wilson – he may lose the overall majority in the House for Labour[433] and this could make life difficult for Labour and what with the economic crisis which is far from over he may have to have an election before he wants.

18.4.76

Budget final day's debate opened by Michael Foot who, in his speech, said we must retrieve our lost sovereignty from the CM – a very encouraging start! Then after 10pm we had a debate on EEC regulations to do with skimmed milk mountains, disposal of. The Govt. accepted the Cons. amendment disapproving of the EEC regulation which had in fact become law already! So we are now in a

---

[433] Marten was right in these assessments.

fix - and we see the conflict of law. Michael Foot was really enjoying the occasion and next day he promised a further debate on it all. We shall see what happens!

2.5.76

A quiet week for me with dull business in the House. Thursday the new US Ambassador came to tea in the House - and was great – went down really well – Mrs Armstrong[434]. Meanwhile Healey talks to TUC over pay deal for next stage of prices and incomes policy – high drama and sterling goes down to nearly $1.80!

9.5.76

Healey announced his deal with the TUC – more than he said was the maximum[435]! But the press and commentators seem pleased and everyone made the right noises to strengthen sterling! But I cannot believe it will hold. However we must try. Local elections on Thursday and we did very well gaining some 1,900 seats. In Banbury we gained 3 from Labour and nearly 3 others. Great boost for Margaret T.

16.5.76

Monday had a meeting with EEC Commissioner Cheysson[436] about aid – he was smooth – but I went for him over all his fine flowing intentions, which were destroyed when it came to supporting our old Commonwealth sugar friends. The EEC is really doing them down, something we would never have done.

Big row in 1922 over devolution to Scotland. Margaret T had to make a speech at the Scottish Cons. Conf. on the weekend. Prior to this, for several months, Willy Whitelaw had undertaken a study in our Constitutional Committee and it was clear that the majority of MPs (Cons.) were against devolution. However, when he announced his prepared conclusions which were to be the basis of his speech the next day at the Scottish Conf. (prior to Margaret's) at the 4.30pm meeting of the Constitutional Committee, apparently nearly everyone was

---

[434] Anne Armstrong (1927-2008), US Ambassador to the United Kingdom, 1976-77.
[435] Healey said the maximum was 3%, the TUC got a 4½% pay ceiling.
[436] Claude Cheysson (1920-2012), French politician and EEC Commissioner, 1973-77.

against it! When the full 1922 Committee met at 6pm Julian Amery raised it and a fairly lengthy debate took place with about 11-3 against Willy's ideas. This was v. awkward! Anyhow Willy made his speech, somewhat softened, I imagine, and there was apparently a blistering row because no vote was allowed! Typically Tory rigging of the Conference, Teddy Taylor and Ian [sic] Sproat[437] led the anti-devolutionists. The whole thing hangs on whether a Scottish Assembly should be directly elected with legislative power. Not much harm in a non-elected Assembly which is a talking shop as some compromise on those lines. I believe we have once again fluffed it – it would have been better to have come out straight against any devolution. We shall have to see how it develops – anyhow, Margaret promised we would oppose Labour's devolution plans when legislation came before the House.

Friday was the constituency AGM and a big row was expected. Nominations are due in by end of Feb. for office. The sitting President, John Schuster, Treasurer Jack Whitley and v-Chairman Martin Wilkinson, all the old 'anti-Marten' group, forgot to get their nominations in whereas others Irene Johnson, President, Richard Ratcliffe and Heather de Freitas vice Chairman did and were accordingly due for automatic election. About a week later, when they had woken up to it, they sent in their nominations which were, of course, invalid. They then claimed that the rules were vague and that their nominations were in order! So I referred it to Central Office and Shadow Attorney General[438] for interpretation and both agreed that they were invalid. Their next move was to write to every member of the Executive and say they were <u>withdrawing</u> their nominations (which were invalid!) because they found it increasingly difficult to work with the Chairman, Len Edwards!! Very misleading. They sent their letters three weeks before local elections and of course it got into the local papers as Tory split – that was a cardinal sin. All a very unhappy incident. Anyhow along came the AGM and the elections went through and Jack Friswell raised the question of timing of nominations etc. but nothing more. Len Edwards, Chairman, went into hospital with something else and Martin Wilkinson was abroad. I made my speech which went well and we then heard eulogies about John Schuster from the 'hunting set'. The net result of all this is that

---

[437] Iain Sproat (1938-2011), Conservative MP for Aberdeen South, 1970-83; Harwich, 1992-97.
[438] Michael Havers, Baron Havers (1923-92), Conservative MP for Wimbledon, 1970-87. Attorney General, 1979-87. Created Baron Havers, 1987.

the 'hunting set' who were the group which tried to get rid of me in 1972 are now effectively out and it remains to consolidate the position and see that there is no return. They are a bit upset but I hope it will blow over. Quite a week that was!

23.5.76

Monday Finance Bill followed by EEC debate on New Zealand butter. This was a frightful mess. We were wanting to see that NZ got a fair deal on her quotas for butter and the debate was on a document which left the actual quotas blank! The next day the Ag. minister was in Brussels and might have agreed to a deal without the consent of Parliament. This was really the issue. Michael Foot, Leader of the House, was all on the anti-EEC side really wanting the House of Commons to control ministers – the pros didn't! I spoke at 1.45am. We will debate it all again. I spoke again at 2.30 on the appointments to the Select Committee on Direct Elections but we did not press it to an issue.

30.5.76

It was a dramatic week! The Bill to nationalise the Aircraft and Shipbuilding Industry had gone through its Committee stage with a record number of sittings. It was due for the report stage on Thursday when Robin Maxwell-Hyslop, MP for Tiverton, raised a point of order. Briefly it was that the bill was a hybrid bill, i.e., it treated different firms differently. That being so it should have followed a certain and different procedure, i.e., before going to Committee it should have gone to the Examiners of Public Bills and then the 'left out' firms could have petitioned – a right to protect private industries/firms. In this case the Bill excluded Marathon yards because apparently when the USA firm purchased it they were given an understanding that they would not be subject to nationalisation. The argument turned on whether this firm was building ships or oil rigs - and it was discovered that the rig was a ship! – or something like that! Anyhow the Speaker ruled that it was prima facie a hybrid bill - and this of course upset the active programme for the Bill and would have meant its delay, something the Govt. could not tolerate. So next day they moved a motion saying while accepting the Speaker's ruling (!!) they would suspend the rules relating to the hybrid bill, i.e., negativing the effect of the ruling and bending the rules to meet their ends. This was bad enough and with a strong 3-line whip and all the minority parties supporting us, the voting was 303-303 and the Speaker according to custom cast the deciding vote on the opposition amendment with the Government. The next vote was on the proposal to suspend the rules of procedure and the Speaker had to vote for the status quo i.e. against the Govt. Had it been 303-303 again the Govt. would have lost and the Bill would have been delayed. So the Govt. Chief Whip instructed one of his Whips who was paired with a Conservative overseas to break that pair without telling the Conservatives and they won 304-303. Not only did they go against the "referee's decisions" but they cheated.

There was uproar - fists flew in the shape of Denis Canavan[439], a left wing Scot, attacked SNP members, Conservatives intervened to stop it, the Tribune Group began to sing the Red Flag and Michael Heseltine who wound up for us seized the Mace and said to the Red Choir that "they might as well have the mace as well" – i.e., they had defeated parliamentary democracy. Jim Prior restrained him, putting the Mace back (the wrong way) and there was general uproar and the Speaker suspended the sitting. Humphrey Atkins announced that there would be no more pairing and that the usual channels would cease. Stern stuff! Next day Heseltine apologised to the House and Margaret T went to see PM but he refused to re-vote or withdraw the Bill. So warfare continues. The whole [thing] is a disgrace on the Govt. and will do them no good. Meantime sterling continues downwards - and there are rumours of impending cuts and a further loan from the IMF and a rise on the left wing. One scenario for an impending General Election?

13.6.76

On Monday (7) the Exec. of 1922 went to see Margaret T to discuss the future tactics. Some of our colleagues, Nigel Fisher, Charlie Morrison, Mark Carlisle were advocating caution! Nigel had even written a letter to *The Times* advocating a coalition because the £ had fallen to $1.70 – I think they are still really Heathmen! However, Margaret was tough and was determined to have a censure motion because, as she said, in spite of Healey arranging a £5 billion standby credit and the £ recovering there was in fact a continuing slide about everything, not only the £, and we needed to put down a firm marker of censure. I am

---

[439] Dennis Canavan (1942-), Labour MP for West Stirlingshire, October 1974-83; Falkirk West, 1983-2000. Independent MSP for Falkirk West, 1999-2007.

sure she was right and I fully supported her. Also she was determined to make no accommodation with the Labour party over pairing until, as she said, they had disregarded their ill-gotten gains, i.e., the Aircraft and Shipbuilding Nationalisation Bill. Good on her – I like her real toughness. But she was looking tired. So no pairing. And on Mon. the House sat until 4am and Tuesday we had every intention of going on all night on the Education Bill but Labour drew stumps at 2am – i.e., they couldn't take it. On Wednesday we had the censure debate which we lost by 19 votes – every Cons. voted. But the Liberals and UUU's[440] abstained. I understand on Tues. eve. the UUU were going to vote with us but decided on Wed. a.m. to abstain (Enoch Powell again) and Jo Grimond said he wanted his Party to vote with us but his 'lefties' didn't want to – so both decisions were fairly marginal and if they had decided otherwise the Govt. would have been defeated and we would have had an election. I am sure it was all worth it – but the Press did its best to criticise us. A few Labour MPs are very worried about their party having cheated over the vote and keep making comments indicating their guilt. I am sure that if we keep it up we can certainly damage the Govt. – already they have lost a lot of business and they may even have to dish the Aircraft and Shipbuilding Nationalisation Bill.

20.6.76

The 'usual channels' continued to be inoperative all this week. Margret T is quite adamant that they will not function until the Govt. has made amends; and there is accordingly no pairing. My pair said that Labour backbenchers were deeply suspicious of what had been done in their name and 'fury was brewing up' – I hope we will keep it up. Christopher Soames came to an EEC meeting and was all huff and puff again!

27.6.76

An olive branch from PM about the cheat in the vote. He admitted that there had been a misunderstanding and altho' not seemingly apologising he said we could have a re-run next week – but of course

---

[440] The United Ulster Unionists were a coalition opposed to the power-sharing Sunningdale agreement, bringing into it most of the Unionist parties in Northern Ireland including Ian Paisley's DUP, anti-Sunningdale UUP, and the Vanguard Unionists.

it won't be the same as they have since won a bye-election at Rotherham (with a much reduced majority and a 13% swing to the Cons!) and the motion in event of a tie will be so worded that the Speaker will vote with the Govt. Anyhow we'll see! But we are still not pairing and, altho' personal relationships are still good, the usual channels are still blocked. We didn't mind but Labour is getting very fed up with it and their programme is in an absolute mess! I must admit (a) Margaret T is being very tough (b) it is very worthwhile even if (c) it is unpleasant with temperatures at 85-90 degrees! On Wed. the French President came to Parliament and addressed both Houses – very well, too. Afterwards the Speaker gave a drinks party and I was talking to Alec D-H about the Test Match and the Speaker said to the President "I didn't think you have met Neil Marten" and the President replied, "No, but I know all about him!" Fame!! Interestingly he spoke about European unity and not Union – good for him.

4.7.76

Monday we debated Cabinet leaks – a Cabinet document had come into the hands of a paper called *New Society* and they had printed it to reveal the Child Benefit Scheme. Then we debated the scheme itself which was to transfer the child allowance given to the taxpayer to the wife – but TUC objected as it would mean less take home pay for the man as he had to pay more tax: so the Govt., having said they would do it, have now postponed it at the dictate of TUC. In the vote, when the Govt. would have been defeated by its own rebels and the opposition, the Govt. Party refused to vote to avoid revealing its split! Tuesday we returned to the re-run of the famous Aircraft and Shipbuilding Bill – but the Scot and Welsh Nats. abstained so we lost – the Govt. gave some assurances to the Nats. that they would have some identifiable Scot or Welsh set up for nationalising the shipbuilders and aviation firms – but in my view it was meaningless and they may well vote against 3rd reading. Then on Wednesday went back to the Education Bill to enforce 'comprehensivisation' of schools but not much progress was made because after midnight Labour MPs drifted away, fed up with the heat and the long hours and we only lost a division by 6 – had they gone on they would have lost subsequent clauses – so they drew stumps! Same again on Thursday night! Anyhow, normal relations will be restored on Mon 5 July and pairing starts but essentially on MP to MP basis and not block pairing by Whips office. We really have had a wonderful run of delaying Govt.

business by about 5 weeks – they have got their programme into an awful jumble!

11.7.76

On Tuesday my Select Committee on Euro Regulation went to Brussels and Luxembourg. In Brussels we had an Embassy briefing on Belgian attitudes and then went to lunch with the Speaker of the Belgian Parliament – an excellent and enjoyable meal. After that we went to see their Chamber in operation and had a meeting with MPs to discuss how they scrutinised Common Market legislation. It seemed as though they did very little about it! The Belgians are not too keen on being one country and would rather be part of a Federal State: then the Walloons and the Flemish would have to be separate provinces in the Eurostate – I see their points – the same as the Germans. Left Brussels in the evening by train for Luxembourg – it was a v. hot day but going through the Ardennes Forest just after a thunder storm and rain it was deliciously cool. <u>What</u> a forest.
    Next day (Wed.) went to the Euro-Parliament to hear question time. Oh, how dreadful it was too – it really was worse than I expected. The Minister answering from the Council of Ministers couldn't answer anything because there is no collective responsibility – it all seemed pointless. The new Dutch President in office, in his opening statement (he took the Chair on 1st July) used words like stagnation, decline, escapism, moving backwards, sterile, ineffective, signs of disintegration, advanced stage of erosion, political anaemia – I agree!! There was an atmosphere of depression – but the place was stuffed with elitists and busy-bodys and vastly over-staffed. The great racket of expenses per day means that they make a lot of money out of it and this seems to be the driving force of some of them. Had meetings with various Committees, lunch with the Secretary General, dinner with the MPs – it is obvious that no expenses were spared! All very stomach turning. Of course having virtually no power they are ineffective. It will never work until the whole structure is changed. Lunched with Luxembourg MPs – <u>very</u> provincial chaps but charming; and then went to their Parliament which was small (50 MPs) and <u>very</u> rowdy – reminded me of an Australian State legislature! After cocktails with our Ambassador[441] caught the plane home so as to

---

[441] Sir Anthony Acland (1930-2021), British Ambassador to Luxembourg, 1975-77; Spain, 1977-80; United States of America, 1986-91.

attend the debate in the House on Friday on the Select Committee's report on the numbers to be elected to EuroParlt. But on Thursday a debate had started on the Race Relations Bill and led by Enoch Powell and Ronnie Bell they kept it going on report stage all night and until after 11am on Friday so that no debate could take place on the EuroParlt. This is amusing because the Council of Ministers (Prime Ministers) is meeting on Monday and Tuesday (12/13 July) to settle (they hope) the numbers for the Europarlt. But UK cannot agree until Parliament has approved – so Enoch (perhaps with the connivance of the Michael Foot, Leader of the House?) has done us a great service! We shall see how it all ends.

18.7.76

Callaghan reported to the House on Wednesday on the EEC Summit meeting that agreement had been reached on the number of Euro-MPs – 410 instead of 198 – I expect a lot of trouble before it gets through!

25.7.76

Monday 3rd Reading of Finance Bill and then debate on EEC Budget in which I spoke in my usual castigating fashion saying we should vote against the CAP section of the budget when it is finalised. Tuesday a major show of disapproval when we voted against the guillotine – the Govt. had lumped together 5 Bills for guillotining into 3 debates each of 3 hours – most of these debates were spurious anyhow! Bed at 3am. Exec. of 1922 met Margaret and had a good session with her – she seemed right on top of the ball.

1.8.76

Much of the week was spent on the remaining stages of the Aircraft and Shipbuilding Nationalisation Bill – on the 3rd Reading vote on Thursday it got through by 3 votes – very sad but there are further possibilities when it gets to the Lords! As it was entirely a guillotined week, we were not too late to bed which was a relief. Played 9am tennis on Tues. and Thursday. The Labour National Exec. voted 16-2 against direct election to the EuroParlt which is <u>excellent</u> news – this could have some effect.

7.8.76

Had a private meeting with Margaret Thatcher at her request. She had seen my critical letter to *Daily Telegraph* about Common Market and asked me to discuss it with her. She has some sympathy for my views as she is a patriot/nationalist, altho' she is boxed in by Shadow Cabinet people who are committed Euro-jobs! We discussed direct elections and she doesn't want any directly elected Parlt. to have increased powers. I enlightened her on what is going on in the Scrutiny Committee front and agreed that I would keep her posted on events as they developed. This is good as I fear she might not get to hear the details. Later had a meeting with Nigel Fisher who is writing a book about politics and he wanted to get my views on the change of leadership (Alec for Ted). I took along my diary of that period and he was delighted that I was recording things and said I <u>must</u> write a book – so <u>he</u> thinks this diary is worthwhile!! And so it ended. The cheating vote, no pairs, the terrific heat and awful nationalisation Bills continued to make it a bad session – but the bad Bills still have to go to the Lords so will return at the fag end with presumably some major amendments. Stonehouse got 7 years in gaol!

25.8.76

It is remarkable what a short break does. Sleep, and generally feeling less tired, earlier bed, afternoon nap, exercise, fresh air and a most relaxing atmosphere. One's brain clears and work becomes more interesting, quicker and satisfying. Everywhere is scorched and brown and the water shortage is getting v. serious. No rain for 39 days! S. Wales only has water for 7 hours a day, everywhere in conservation of water, baths, loos, garden and so on – a crisis feeling. Forest fires all over the country – Govt. has been dilatory over doing anything about it – too late!

3.10.76

Conservative Party Conf. at Brighton – I did not go – too much work had accumulated in my absence and with Parlt. reassembling on 11 Oct. it was best to get things straight first – but I watched it on TV as much as possible. Ted Heath made a good speech – but it was just the same old character. He gave a lukewarm reception to the new document 'The Right Approach' and in my view, while he said he had confidence in Margaret, he was really saying he had been right all along and, by giving an accolade to the TUC, he was staking a claim for a Coalition Govt. Michael Heseltine made a rip-roaring speech and got a standing ovation demanding the Govts. resignation and Margaret wound up the Conf. with a <u>superb</u> speech – "she is right on the crest of the wave" said Bob Mellish – I agree!

17.10.76

Back on Monday 11 Oct. (too early?) to complete the fag end of the session – this used to be 3 days or so – this time it looks more like 6 weeks or even more. Many Bills, important to the Socialist Govt. such as Docks Bill, Aircraft and Shipbuilding Nationalisation, still await completion in the Lords. Their amendments will come back to the Commons etc. so with a bit of luck we may delay the opening of Parlt. for quite some time. One point of importance is that we (Commons) are trying to get the Lords opposition to move that the Shipbuilding Bill, which they now have in Committee, is hybrid and for it to be referred to the examiners. This time, with a Cons. majority, it could be so referred and it would probably be declared hybrid – then it could take say 40 days hearing petitions – the Govt. is so keen not to lose it by prorogation, they would delay opening of Parlt. Our objective must be to delay until mid-Dec. By then the £2.9bn loan from IMF would be coming through complete, we hope with strong strings attached. The 'Left' won't support this and the PM will turn to us for support to get it through Parlt. But we will say "yes you can have our support if you drop your Socialist measures which have not had the Royal Assent!" Fine in theory – will it happen in <u>practice</u>!

Great debate on Monday on Economic situation – Healey v. bad and obviously in a corner. Margaret T gave the best speech of her life winding up – really on <u>top</u> form and held the House, entranced by her non-stop flow of economic expertise. But we lost by 13 votes – Liberals and Nats. absent. Tues. and Wed. dull on Health Services Bill. Big discussions on Rhodesian conference with the right wing being very pro-Smith – this needs watching.

24.10.76

The only major debate this week was on Rhodesia based technically on the order to renew sanctions. It was a curtain raiser to the negotiations in Geneva to give majority rule in Rhodesia (Zimbabwe) based on the Kissinger proposals. The Right in our Party, led by Julian Amery, carried out a campaign supporting Smith trying to establish that the Kissinger proposals were a package which was unalterable so that if the blacks deviated on one item then they could be blamed for the breakdown after which they would then ask for sanctions to be removed. I argued that the negotiations were negotiations and that we had to take a fairly flexible approach to the package and get a settlement on the basis that black majority rule was inevitable in the end and that we as a Party had better be seen to be reasonable and not dogmatic as, if we are to be the Government, we will have to deal with the black leaders. I urged that sanctions should be continued and not lifted now (or necessarily if negotiations broke down). The debate itself was represented on our side largely by the right-wing altho' Reggie Maudling was quite reasonable from the Front Bench. When it came to the voting I was walking to vote for sanctions – the Whips tried to persuade me not to in order to avoid a 3-way Party split as the Party itself was abstaining. Twenty-two voted against sanctions and while I was engaged in argument with the Whips, the doors closed and I couldn't vote! So in effect I abstained. My fault! But it was an example of the stupidity of the desire of the Whips to regiment the party. What about trying secret voting in Parliament for a change?!

Another interesting 'side light' – in the Finance Committee on Tues. evening the question of VAT proposals by the EEC was raised and discussed. For the first time, the pro-marketeers are waking up to the reality of the amount of control which will be exercised by the EEC. I made the point that, due do the lack of interest of the Conservative Party, much of the EEC proposals was leading to Socialism, officialdom, bureaucracy etc. After the meeting several MPs came to me and expressed their doubts about the EEC! We might have opened up something here! Opinion polls going our way – the last 3 have given (with a week between them) 11%, 14% and 19% lead to Cons. - and 3 bye-elections coming up!

31.10.76

An interesting incident on Thursday – Mr Ponomarev[442], the Russian "Himmler", visited Parliament and we spent all the 15 mins of PM's question time saying what a shocking thing it was of the Labour Party

---

[442] Boris Ponomarev (1905-1995), Soviet politician and member of the Secretariat of the USSR.

to have invited him over etc; he was sitting in the gallery all the time! Eventually, Nic Ridley[443] "spied strangers" and there was a vote. By when Mr P had left. He certainly must have gained an odd impression of Parlt.!

During the week sterling fell to $1.57 to £ - and the depression deepens.

7.11.76

A dullish week in Parliament – the quiet before the storm! Started off with Joan and me going to do some canvassing for the bye-election in Walsall N – vacated by Stonehouse going to prison – long dreary roads of poor housing, raining and many out – some Lab. going to vote Conservative, many Lab. to abstain (see later!). But it was worthwhile, show the flag, give a lead, etc., and always interesting. Tuesday we at last debated the CM eviscerated chicken and lost by 7 votes – a pity as it would have faced the Govt. with a conflict between our Parlt. and the EEC – failure of promised votes to turn up at 11.30. Thursday was the bye-elections – we turned out Labour in Walsall N from a majority of 15,885 to a Cons majority of 4,379 – a swing of 22.5%!! And at Workington (ex-Fred Peart) from a majority of 9,551 to a Cons. majority of 1,065 with a swing of 13.1%. In both cases Cons. vote was well up – Walsall by 4,000 and Workington by 6,000 and Libs down from 6,000 to 1,000 in Walsall and 4,700 to 2,400 in Workington. A great credit to Margaret and "boo" to her critics! This gives Lab. a possible overall majority of 1 and a majority of 34 over Conservatives.

14.11.76

We started the week with guillotine motions on six Bills each motion being debatable for 2 hours. The usual rumpus! The guillotine was being used to guillotine the Lords amendments to the Education Bill to make comprehensivisation compulsory, the Docks Bill to extend dock labour to 5 miles from ports and rivers and warehouses etc., the Aircraft and Shipbuilding Nationalisation Bill, Rent Agriculture to

---

[443] Nicholas Ridley, Baron Ridley of Liddesdale (1929-93), Conservative MP for Cirencester and Tewkesbury, 1959-92. Financial Secretary to the Treasury, 1981-3. Secretary of State for Transport, 1983-86; Environment, 1986-89; Trade, 1989-90. Created Baron Ridley of Liddesdale, 1992.

abolish tied cottages[444] and the Health Bill to abolish pay-beds. A good measure of Socialism! The Lords, to their credit, had taken out the Socialist nonsense from the Bills but after a lot of exciting votes (several ties with the Speaker giving his casting vote) we only killed the Docks Bill by eliminating the essential clauses to do with the 5 mile limit. However the Lords can re-institute their amendments and we can try again. The Lords amendment to keep ship repairing out of nationalisation was defeated by 1 vote! Two Labour, Walden[445] and Mackintosh abstained on the Docks Bill which caused us to win. But many of the votes were won by 1 and this was the Irish Republican (ex-internee)[446] who never or hardly ever came to the House - and he was virtually dragged over and kept under surveillance by the Whips and fitted with drink! And presumably he extracted the price out of the Govt. and got some detainees either released or better conditions.

The PM's questions are getting stupid – the Speaker let No. 1 run for 21 minutes and no one else got in their question – I was No. 3 – this on Thursday. I raised this as a point of order and he gave some lame excuse. I just wonder if he is protecting the PM from subsequent questions? The PM asked me, coincidentally, the evening before why I was no longer questioning him – I replied it was the Speaker's fault! How true.

Jeremy Thorpe approached me and said he was trying to get the Liberal Party to vote against direct election to the Europarliament because they did not cater for Proportional Representation. Good if he does! Contact has been established with Michel Debre[447], ex PM of France who is also opposing direct elections.

The Govt. is looking very tattered – economic policy in ruins.

21.11.76

Monday lunched in House of Commons with Miss Worlds – v. agreeable! An intelligent lot, by and large. At F.O. questions Tony

---

[444] A dwelling owned by an employer and rented to an employee, hence it 'tied' the employee to the employer.
[445] Brian Walden (1932-2019), Labour MP for Birmingham All Saints, 1964-74; Birmingham Ladywood, October 1974-77. After leaving the Commons, Walden became a prolific TV presenter and political interviewer.
[446] Frank Maguire (1929-81), Unity/Republican MP for Fermanagh and South Tyrone, October 1974-81. In the confidence vote of March 1979, Maguire abstained in person, and thus brought about the fall of the Callaghan government.
[447] Michel Debre (1912-96), Prime Minister of France, 1959-62.

Crosland, S/S Foreign Affairs, said that both he and I were old fashioned patriots because we didn't like the EEC passports! I am very worried by this – it is being done by use of the Royal Prerogatives and not via Parliament – a typical FO way of handling it. Thursday we had the Aircraft and Shipbuilding Nationalisation Bill Lords Amendments for the second time and were defeated. I hope the Lords will return their objections to shipbuilding being included – if so this means that the Bill will not get through this session – one wonders how it will all end. On Friday the House, very unusually, sat until 5pm to debate Lords amendments to the pay-beds Bill and we were defeated. During the morning Margaret T announced her front bench changes – the major one was the dropping of Reggie Maudling as shadow F.S.[448] and replacing him with John Davies – Reggie really has been too lazy and I am delighted that we are not sending John Davies to Brussels as he wanted. He is a person of vast knowledge of business and financial matters. Apparently Roy Jenkins the new President of the Commission wouldn't have him! Many suggestions why but I believe it was because John knew so much more about it than Roy that he would have put Roy to shame and dominated him. So he chose Christopher Tugendhat[449] the MP for Westminster a relatively minor character - @ £47,000 a year! Dropped were Tim Raison[450], Cranley Onslow[451] and Tom King came in to the Shadow Cabinet – an excellent and sensible choice – so did Teddy Taylor – so we now have 2 anti-CM in Shadow Cabinet. Peter Tapsell went as No. 2 to John Davies – he is anti-direct elections. Margaret told me how sad she felt when Reggie walked out of the room – having been dropped – end of his political career? His business career is over too after Poulson. If only he had tried harder and supported his supporters it might have been different.

---

[448] Foreign Secretary.
[449] Christopher Tugendhat, Baron Tugendhat (1937-), Conservative MP for Cities of London and Westminster, 1970-February 1974; City of London and Westminster South, February 1974-77. European Commissioner, 1977-85. Vice President of the European Commission, 1981-85.
[450] Sir Timothy Raison (1929-2011), Conservative MP for Aylesbury, 1970-92. Succeeded Marten as Minister for Overseas Development, 1983-86.
[451] Cranley Onslow, Lord Onslow of Woking (1926-2001), Conservative MP for Woking, 1964-97. Chairman, 1992 Committee, 1984-92. Created Lord Onslow of Woking, 1997.

28.11.76

Back in Parliament the final stages of the Shipbuilding and Aircraft Nationalisation Bill when we rejected by 6 votes the Lords amendments; and so it went back to Lords again who insisted and it was dropped and Parliament prorogued in the late afternoon. The Bill will be reintroduced again next week the day before the result of the Cambridge bye-election where David Lane[452] has retired to do Race Relations and Robert James[453] (ex-Clerk) is coming in – so we shall be one down – they don't miss any tricks! Tuesday a non-day and I was in the flat all day started work at 9am and finished at 11.30pm – non-stop but I really got on top of all outstanding letters – relief! Wednesday (24th) state opening – usual stuff in the speech – devolution and direct elections will take up a lot of time. Thursday debate on address then Francis Pym to 1922 Exec. to discuss devolution – he was given pretty firm advice that the Party was far from united.

5.12.76

Monday evening there was an EEC debate after 10pm on VAT harmonisation. We made circles round the Minister (Bob Sheldon[454]) and showed up the process of debating legislation before it was firm. The pattern is developing that we get an out-of-date legislative proposal which has been verbally altered and we do not see the precise amendments. We are therefore debating vague proposals and the Minister goes off the Bench and agrees it and it becomes law without any precise debate on the definitive legislation. It should be agreement subject to the approval of the House of Commons i.e. ad[455] referendum. Tuesday, broadcast on rising food prices to show that CM is causing the major part of the rises – the penny is certainly beginning to drop.

---

[452] Sir David Lane (1922-98), Conservative MP for Cambridge, 1967-76. Chairman, Commission for Racial Equality, 1977-82. Knighted, 1983.
[453] Sir Robert Rhodes James (1933-1999), academic, historian, and Conservative MP for Cambridge, 1976-92. Knighted, 1991.
[454] Robert Sheldon, Lord Sheldon (1923-2020), Labour MP for Ashton-under-Lyne, 1964-2001. Financial Secretary to the Treasury, 1975-79.
[455] Advisory.

In the evening Garfield Todd[456], ex PM Rhodesia, came over from the Geneva Conference[457] to talk to us. He was splendid and very anti-Smith! He had been detained for years by Smith. He continued that the Kissinger proposals were only a "basis for negotiation". He made the point that Rhodesia had little time to organise political parties because Smith had prohibited them. He favours a Brit. Governor and Brit. Chief of Staff until majority rule. Wednesday we went back to the resurrected Aircraft and Shipbuilding Bill where the Govt. is once again changing the rules to get the Bill through. Devolution Bill now comes to the fore and after a lot of prevarication the Cons. Party had decided to vote against on a 3-line whip. This has caused umbrage to the pro-devolutionists (and Ted Heath!) (cf Common Market!!) who yelp that they cannot defy a 3-liner. In the 1922, I indicated that they should do so if they felt deeply and were committed – I quoted myself and the CM in 1972 - and a number of MPs said they advised my doing so – v. embarrassing! We shall see how it turns out – this will show the stuffing people are made of. The decision to vote against will be very helpful in the debate on direct elections! The French are going well on direct elections demanding a firm statement that if there are direct elections there must be a firm understanding that the powers of the Assembly are not extended – if they get this then why have direct elections? An interesting discussion in the 1922 executive with Lord Carrington[458] on the reform of the House of Lords and of Parliament generally. Politics is becoming interesting again!

12.12.76

The big discussion of the week has been the so-called division in the Cons. Party over devolution. Ted Heath has said he will not support Cons. Party in voting against the Bill and some 20-30 will follow him. This is a clear one-in-the-eye for Margaret. We, in turn, are in a mess

---

[456] Sir Garfield Todd (1908-2002), Prime Minister of Rhodesia, 1953-58. A relatively liberal, reforming Prime Minister, he was put under house arrest by Ian Smith in 1965.
[457] A conference on the future of Rhodesia.
[458] Peter Carrington, 6th Baron Carrington (1919-2018). Held several posts in government and opposition from the Churchill administration to serving as Mrs Thatcher's Foreign Secretary from 1979-82. During the Conservative opposition years between 1974 and 1979, Carrington was Shadow Leader of the House of Lords.

over devolution because most Cons. want nothing to do with it and Willie Whitelaw and Margaret said in Scotland in May that we were committed to a directly elected assembly. Anyhow, Alec Buchanan-Smith[459], who <u>was</u> shadow Sec. of State, duly resigned from the Shadow Cab. when, after <u>much</u> discussion, Margaret put on a 3-line whip as he was committed to devolution – 3 others with him[460] – very right and proper to resign. She appointed Teddy Taylor, a strongly anti devolutionist, to take his place – (another anti-marketeer in Shadow Cab!) and John Nott[461] (nearly an anti-marketeer) to take Teddy's place in Trade – so we are progressing – that is 3. Anyhow, the devolution row will potter on – but we are in <u>opposition</u>! The press, of course, are enjoying it all and exaggerating it all.

19.12.76

This was the week of the second reading of the Devolution Bill – Scotland and Wales Bill and it got a majority of 45 after certain cross voting on a 3-line whip and about 30 Cons. abstentions including Ted Heath! That puts me in the clear with my constituency Heath-men who criticised me for not obeying the CM 3-liner!

Tuesday, M. Bortreand came over from Paris as the emissary of M. Debre, to tell us about the Debre group's opposition to direct elections – v. interesting and very similar to our situation – we will both be trying to delay things and they are doing so by trying to get the matter regarded as a change in the constitution requiring a referendum – that will cause a lot of inter-party disputes in France!

Wed. the Chancellor Denis Healey made his expected statement on the cuts resulting from negotiations for IMF loan of 3.9bn dollars. He didn't do very well and I doubt if he has done enough. We will be debating it next week.

26.12.76

---

[459] Alick Buchanan-Smith (1932-1991), Conservative and Unionist MP for North Angus and Mearns, 1964-83; Kincardine and Deeside, 1983-91.
[460] Malcolm Rifkind was the only other junior member to resign from the shadow cabinet.
[461] Sir John Nott (1932-2024), National Liberal and, from 1970, Conservative MP for St Ives, 1966-83. Secretary of State for Trade, 1979-81; Defence, 1981-83. Knighted, 1983.

Reg Prentice, Min. of Overseas Development, resigned from the Cabinet on Tuesday – he made a very splendid speech which was greeted with opposition cheers. Cause of the resignation was Healey's cut in overseas aid and a lot of other matters with which he disagreed.

16.1.77

Started the week with a letter in the *Daily Telegraph* on the Common Market, a speech in the House on the CM and a broadcast after the 10 O'clock BBC news on the debate with Michael Stewart. Well satisfied with that day! Wednesday a debate on defence where 77 Lab. voted against their own Govt. – but, as we didn't vote on the lefties' amendment, the Govt. was secure. We met to discuss the Devolution Bill – that is, the anti and not devolution group called the 'Union Jack Group' run by Betty-Harvie Anderson and George Gardiner[462]. While I share their views and will support them, I am watching them keenly to see the analogy with direct election to the European Parliament if and when that comes up – I feel sure that what the pro-Market anti-devolutionists say about devolution will (or should!) equally apply to direct elections to the Euro-Parlt! We had the first day of the Committee stage of the D. Bill on Thursday and as with the European Communities Bill it started with hours of points of order! I am being consulted by the Union Jack Group about how to organise the opposition based on my CM experience.

23.1.77

During the week Sam Silkin[463] the Attorney General was in the Court of Appeal defending his decision over the proposed strike by Post Office Workers Union intention to interrupt mail to S. Africa as protest against apartheid. A very interesting case, as in Dec. I had asked him to prosecute P.O. workers for intercepting mail to Grunwick Co. where P.O. wanted to influence the firm to give a better deal to the workers

---

[462] Sir George Gardiner (1935-2002), Conservative MP for Reigate, February 1974-97. Joined the Referendum party briefly before the 1997 general election after being deselected by his constituency association. Knighted, 1990.
[463] Samuel Silkin, Baron Silkin of Dulwich (1918-88), Labour MP for Dulwich, 1964-83. Attorney General, 1974-79. Created Lord Silkin, 1985. His brother was Labour MP John Silkin.

in that factory[464]. He had refused. He seems to use his A-G hat for political convenience and not in the public interest as he should. The judges in the case have turned it into a major political/constitutional affair between the Bench and Parliament and who should have the right to decide these matters.

6.2.77

On Wed. 26 I went to Washington with Charles Morris[465], Minister of Civil Service – we are joint Treasurers of the Brit-American Parliamentary Group and we went to contact the new Congressmen on Capitol Hill and to arrange the conference in Bermuda and UK. We had some interesting talks with the Chairman of Senate and House Committees. On the whole I was not too impressed with them because the Chairmen seem to go mostly by seniority rather than ability. Washington was in a freeze and lack of gas was enforcing the closure of factories and snow was piling up in some cities like Buffalo and Pres. Carter[466] was meeting his first problem. Some reserve was expressed over Carter and his policies, at that stage, were not clear. Charles (anti-CM) and I were able to fly the anti-CM flag successfully and had many arguments with our Embassy officials!

Devolution Bill is going very slowly and the Cons. seem to think the Govt. is in a mess with the Bill and will soon have to introduce the guillotine and there is some doubt if they will get it. All of this made the House of Commons very tired and bored and tetchy.

13.2.77

Monday debate on Direct Elections to Euro-Parlt. on private motion – put in to speak but didn't get called. Inconclusive but Govt. showed itself to be in no hurry to introduce a Bill – good news. The Tories are furious! The irony is that the Tories will oppose the guillotine on the Devolution Bill and hope to keep it running all the session and kill it – but in so doing they will keep out the direct elections Bill for which

---

[464] A long-running dispute at the Grunwick photo processing factory in North London. An industrial dispute over the right to recognise a trade union turned into a symbolic campaign by the trade union movement which led to clashes between sympathetic protestors and police.
[465] Charles Morris (1926-2012), Labour MP for Manchester Openshaw, 1963-83. Father of future Cabinet minister Estelle Morris.
[466] Jimmy Carter (1924-2024), 39th President of the USA, 1977-81.

they are screaming! Hoisted by their own petard! The Devolution Bill is moving very slowly and suddenly the Govt. introduced the referendum into the Bill as a sop to get more support for the guillotine. More and more people are beginning to see the measures involved in the Bill and the PM may have to make the question of the guillotine a question of confidence (as did Heath over the CM Bill!).

20.2.77

Devolution again on Tuesday and Wednesday although not much voting. The two days were spent on debating the Referendum – it is not without interest to me that the Conservatives are seeking precisely the type of referendum which I had advocated in my amendment to the European Communities Bill in 1972, i.e., a consultative referendum and not a binding one which would have taken away the sovereignty of Parliament! How well I remember all the speeches against me and the criticism I received from my Association when I proposed it in 1972 (and earlier in 1969 in letter to *Times*). Ah, well, I always was an advanced type!!

Thursday I went to see Margaret T to give her the latest NOP on the Common Market which I had commissioned, i.e., is CM a good thing, bad thing and neither – 35% good, 41% bad, 24% neither. If it was scrapped tomorrow would you be pleased, sorry or not care – 40% pleased, 31% sorry, not care 21%. Food prices up because of CM – great deal 41%, fair amount 29%, little 16%. She was seriously impressed and I advised her to show not too much enthusiasm and not get too involved and we discussed it generally and I felt she had a lot of sympathy with my views but, of course, she is surrounded by pros and this makes it difficult. Fri. Bicester AGM and Banbury dance. Bicester AGM was well attended and I enjoyed the speaking and questions. After questions I left and they got on with electing the officers. Dear Irene Johnson, elderly school mistress, who had been chairman for years and done so much work and is President of the Association, was defeated – apparently a group of people moved in and packed the meeting and voted her out. We shall have to watch the implications!

The previous week was overcast by the news that Tony Crosland, our Foreign Secretary, had had a bad stroke. It soon became clear from reports from the Radcliffe that he would not live and indeed on Saturday he died. Really a great loss to all of us – a fine politician, a v. good Foreign Secretary and a nice chap. Joan did what she could for the family but there was little to do. The Labour Party have had a great loss, in a matter of months Harold Wilson resigned, Roy Jenkins in EEC and now Tony C. David Owen[467] aged 38 was made Foreign Secretary – a remarkably bold choice – regrettably very pro-CM[468]!

27.2.77

The week started going to Paris with my Select Committee on European Legislation. All very French! Started with an 8 course lunch with M. Poher President of the Senate – magnificent. Then vague talks with Senators and cocktails with our Ambassador followed by a dinner party. Next day talks with the National Assembly for which we concluded that the French leave it very much to the Government and the Civil Service to look after EEC legislation. After lunch we all trooped back to Westminster to vote on the guillotine which the Govt. had proposed for the Devolution Bill. The Govt. was defeated by 29 votes – they had expected to win by 3. Super, not only because the guillotine was defeated but because Parliament had exerted its will over the Executive. Gradually we are winning this battle. It is essential for the image of the party.

Next morning on to Rome for similar discussion with the Italian Parliament. They seem to take a somewhat more detailed interest in it all but nothing nearly as concrete as ours. I think that all the characters we met were members of the Euro Assembly and Eurofanatics except at lunch in the French National Assembly when Couve de Murville said that the more the EEC is expanded the more it will be divided!

6.3.77

A very easy week. The Govt. is in such a mess that it is not putting forward controversial Bills at the moment. The Aircraft and Shipping Bill <u>was</u> declared hybrid and the shipping part of it was dropped!! Triumph for Robin Maxwell-Hyslop and the House of Lords. Foreign Affairs debate on Tuesday and David Owen made his debut as new Foreign Sec. – not very inspiring. Direct Elections to Europarliament

---

[467] David Owen, Lord Owen (1938-), Labour MP for Plymouth Sutton, 1966-February 1974; Plymouth Devonport, February 1974-83. Co-Founded SDP, 1981. Re-elected as MP for Plymouth Devonport, 1983-92. Foreign Secretary, 1977-79.
[468] In 2016 Lord Owen campaigned for Britain to leave the European Union. One wonders what Marten would have thought of that.

looks even further away – Govt. proposes a White Paper with Green after and they say it will cover every possible snag!

13.3.77

We are still in calm non-controversial waters – no votes this week at all! Monday Tony Crosland's memorial service in Westminster Abbey – very impressive – masses of people there and it was quite socialist with a reading from Tony's book on Socialism – but all in good part.

20.3.77

On Tuesday the Aircraft and Shipbuilding Bill went through on Lords Amendments without the ship repairing part – victory for the ship repairers. We then squashed the proposal to have a new size Hansard and then had an EEC document on safety signs at work. Wednesday was a debate on the EEC Price Review proposals – it was a good debate in which the EEC got a good roasting for the CAP. At last the consumers have revolted about the cost of food and they have kicked in the EEC. Silkin was v. good and we got him to accept our (anti-EEC) amendment calling for easier access into the UK for efficiently produced food stuffs from outside the EEC – the Cons. were in a spot and had to agree with it! But Thursday was the great day. The debate was on the Govt's. White Paper on Public Expenditure. Naturally the motion is to approve it but they dared not put this one down because their left wing would not have voted for it: so they had the debate on the adjournment so that we could not amend it. In the event when it came to the vote they did not put in tellers so the SNP did and then the Labour Party did not vote. This was an outrage – where Margaret T next day called for a vote of censure and we are to debate it on Wednesday – it will be a cliff hanger for the Govt. and forecasts are that they might loose [sic] – if so an election – target date 28 April – ooh!

27.3.77

The week was dominated by the censure motion – rumours and counter rumours. It centres round the Irish and the Liberals. The SNP and the Welsh were voting against the Govt. and had clearly said so.

I concentrated on the Irish working to Airey Neave[469]. The majority [of Unionists] wanted to vote with us and Callaghan saw them and offered more seats in N Ireland for the UK Parliament and some vague promises about regional administrative devolution. Margaret T didn't want to deal with anyone (rightly) – in the event, 7 out of the 10 voted with us and 3 abstained (inc. Enoch Powell, who I feared might persuade them all to vote with the Govt. because of his curious dislike of Margaret because she was in Ted Heath's Cabinet!). Enoch was under pressure from his Irish constituency and the UUU party generally. So it all hung on the Liberals. On Monday evening they had voted 11-2 to vote against the Government but then David Steel started talks with the PM and in the event they voted with the Govt. It was sickening to see the PM at the box "giving in" to the Liberals but when one analyses what he had "given" it really isn't much at all. There is now an 'alliance' between Libs and Lab. to last for the rest of this session – I think they will find it increasingly difficult and they will be dragged down the Socialist road until the "break", when we shall be able to say 'we told you so' and they will look v. silly. They have only done it so to save an election at which they would have been trounced. 'A vote for the Libs is a vote for Labour' will now stick – it can never again be denied. The other theory is that it is the beginning of the centre Social Democrat alliance – but I doubt this.

On Monday Joan and I canvassed in Stechford bye-election[470] – had a smell of victory but, since when, the Lib/Lab pact has taken place and we shall have to see the effect of it.

3.4.77

The smell of victory was correct – we won it[471]. A remarkable victory converting a Labour majority of 11,935 into a Cons. majority of 1,949! The Lib/Lab pact obviously failed in spite of their having claimed beforehand that they had one of the best organisations and would win (!) and David Steel having spent three days there since the Lib-Lab pact explaining it, they lost their deposit and halved their vote from 5,860 to 2,901! The Cons. vote increased by 4,500. Taking all the other recent

---

[469] Lt. Col. Airey Neave (1916-79), Conservative MP for Abingdon, 1953-79. Escaped Colditz concentration camp. Masterminded Mrs Thatcher's leadership election victory in 1975. Murdered by Irish Republican terrorists, 1979.
[470] Vacated by Roy Jenkins to become President of the European Commission.
[471] The Stechford by-election was won by Andrew Mackay for the Conservatives.

bye-elections together this does show a consistent massive swing to Cons. continuing. Good for Margaret.

Budget day on Tuesday. A fairly modest affair but he put tax on petrol and cigarettes[472] and the Libs have said they would vote against the petrol tax - and that they might not – a big muddle which typifies the muddle they will get into.

10.4.77

Monday budget wind up – the Liberals abstained on petrol tax so it went through! Otherwise it wouldn't have, i.e., before the Stechford bye-election they said they would block the tax, once the bye-election is over they reverse their decision.

Interesting meeting on PR for direct elections to Europarlt. on Mon. evening – the well-attended meeting spoke 2-1 against PR. We also ran an early day motion on it and got 21 signatures against PR in the afternoon – this was to put down a marker before Shadow Cab. met the next day – result, a free vote! Tuesday Michael Foot before the Scrutiny Committee when he agreed with me that we needed a Select Committee to investigate the CM

Wed. Bishop Muzorewa[473] came to speak to us on Rhodesia, the main point was he wanted a referendum of all races in Rhodesia to elect a leader to do the transfer to majority rule – Smith would have one to elect a black leader who would then negotiate with him – but Bishop M believes that this would only lead to Smith not agreeing to anything and as a result war. He's probably right.

1.5.77

The week starting 18 April was much taken up with preparations for the CPA Exec. meeting to be held in Sierra Leone which I was to attend as Hon. Treasurer. Meanwhile the Commons had debated direct elections and no decision was taken on the system of elections. So now we await the Bill and presumably the Govt. will include PR in it to satisfy the Liberals. The House of Commons will throw that out and we will revert to first-past-the-post and this will take such a long time that first the Bill won't get through in time and second, the Boundary

---

[472] Petrol up 5½p, cigarettes up by 4p.
[473] Abel Muzorewa (1925-2010), bishop and the first black Prime Minister of Rhodesia-Zimbabwe, 1979-80.

Commission won't have time to get its work done, together with appeals, for the elections to take place in time for May/June '78.

On Thursday 28th there were 2 bye-elections. Grimsby (ex-Crosland) where Cons. only required a 7% swing to win it, was held by Labour largely because the Lab candidate was anti-CM and the Cons. pro, a lesson I hope which will be understood by the Cons. Party. Ashfield where a Lab majority of 22,915 was converted to a Cons majority of 264! on a 22% swing – a fantastic result[474]. The Libs were crushed, their vote cut at Grimsby from 9,487 to 3,128 and Ashfield from 7,959 to 4,830 both losing their deposits.

8.5.77

Tuesday Lords Reform Committee during which we interviewed Lord Carrington. At one stage he was talking about the role of PM and he said to Alec D-H "When were you PM was it 62/63?" Alec replied, "can't remember – yes, somewhere around then!" A glorious example of 'Alecism'. We went back together in his car to House of Commons and both had begun to conclude that an elected 2nd Chamber was not the answer – I think the Committee's views are beginning to firm up.

N. Ireland strike led by Ian Paisley started on Tuesday as a protest against Govt. handling of the security situation[475]. Altho' Paisley has a good point (and I agree) it is wrong way to go about it by calling a Protestant Loyalist strike. It fizzled out and so could Paisley! I think he was probably trying to get the leadership of N. Ireland but he may have dished himself in the process.

Wednesday was the start of the Silver Jubilee in UK and the Queen and Royal Family came to Parliament and addressed the joint sitting in Westminster Hall. <u>Superb</u> pageantry and timing and loyal address were presented to her. In her speech she talked about the understandable desire for devolution and then went on to say that she will never forget that she was crowned Queen of the <u>United</u> Kingdom - and she said it like a head mistress. The SNP feigned great anger – but everyone else thought it was well said. She got a great ovation as

---

[474] Austin Mitchell was returned as MP for Grimsby, with a majority of 520. Tim Smith, latterly MP for Beaconsfield who resigned over a cash-for-questions scandal in the 1990s, was elected in Ashfield. His Labour opponent Michael Cowan later defected to the Conservatives in 1998 and sat on Nottingham City Council.

[475] The second, and less successful, Ulster Workers' Strike, it lacked political support from the Ulster Unionists and Vanguard party.

she left. Scottish local elections on Tuesday showed a big swing away from Labour to SNP and Cons., the Libs being obliterated[476]. Thursday local elections to County Councils in England and Wales and there was a massive swing to Conservatives all over the country. In Oxfordshire we had 61 out of 69 seats to Cons. – the balance were 3 independents. In Banbury we swept the board – my ex-opponent Anthony Booth lost his seat and my Liberal opponent came well bottom at Bicester! Overall Conservative gained 1,138 seats and lost 3, Lab. gained 8 and lost 913, Libs gained 8 and lost 174, Independents gained 17 and lost 143 – net result 9 out of every 10 people now have Cons. C.C.'s. Swing about 16% to Cons. It might hasten in an election – but it might make Lab. hang on until things improve.

Summit conference all the w/end with Pres. Carter and others here trying to get the world economy right. Roy Jenkins (EEC) wanted to attend but Pres. Giscard d'Estaing of France said he could only attend when EEC matters were being discussed – a good example of France not recognising the EEC as a state[477]. Saw the PM for 15 mins. in the Cabinet Room and tried to get him to raise in Cwth. PM's conf. the question of raising a lump sum for CPA to propagate Parly. democracy. He wisely said it would be the wrong place to do it because some PMs would not agree with Parly. Democracy and would oppose it! So I must approach countries separately.

15.5.77

Peter Jay was nominated as Brit. Ambassador to Washington to succeed Peter Ramsbotham[478] who is going to be Governor of Bermuda. As he is son-in-law of Prime Minister there was an awful row – danger of nepotism etc., mainly from the Labour Party although the PM played it up no end!

---

[476] The SNP doubled its vote share from 12% to 24%. Labour fell from 38% to 31% and the Conservatives rose slightly from 26% to 27%. Marten is a bit unfair to the Liberals, their vote dropped from 5% to 4%.

[477] Or, rather, French national interest within the Community. Giscard drafted the European Constitution in 2004 to further extend Community powers.

[478] Sir Peter Ramsbotham (1919-2010), Ambassador to Unites States of America, 1974-77. Governor of Bermuda, 1977-80.

29.5.77

The week of the Cons. Women's Conf! 7 delegates to lunch and Benita Sullivan to stay in flat – but in Parliament a quiet week. My letter to *Times* (20 May) seems to have created an interest. I wrote that after 4½ years we should be able to judge the effect of CM - and then listed all the failures - and then suggested we should think about the future of CM particularly in view of its enlargement by Spain, Portugal and Greece. Margaret T read it and got hold of Patrick Cosgrave, one of her speech writers, and told him to contact me and get suggestions for her speeches so that she could point up 'stupidities' – a healthy sign! I also understand an ex-F.O. man who resigned from F.O. because he couldn't stand CM has been appointed to Margaret's private office! Cabinet Ministers have told me privately they thought it a good and timely letter – several Cons. MPs (pro-CM) also – I feel there is the beginning of an awakening in the Tory Party about CM – but a long way to go yet and still a lot of opposition to overcome. Margaret has sort of dropped devolution – can she drop direct elections in the same way? Still no sign of direct elections Bill – Cabinet very divided on it – I believe six of them oppose it – Foot, Shore, Silkin, Orme[479], Booth[480] and Varley – what will happen if they have a Second Reading? Will they resign? Or will the Govt. put Prop. Rep. in the long title and then they will claim to have a free vote on 2nd Reading. My own view is the antis want to delay it until we rise for Summer Recess and then Lab. Party Conf. will vote against it. Equally there is a CM Summit Conf. on 29 June at which Callaghan will be President/host and he will want to show that the legislation is on the way – all tactically very fascinating! Meanwhile a glorious row over pigs because the Eurocourt of Justice has told us to stop the pig subsidy 'forthwith'. This is being stopped early June and if the Commission doesn't agree to a substitute this will be another nail in the CM coffin because our pig industry will be clobbered, thanks to CM Commission and the Danes and the Dutch will be beneficiaries. I raised this in the House on Thursday and called for a national policy. Harold Wilson, who was sitting next to Tom Torney[481] and Geoffrey Robinson apparently said

---

[479] Stan Orme, Lord Orme (1923-2005), Labour MP for Salford West, 1964-83; Salford East, 1983-97. Minister for Social Security, 1976-79. Created Lord Orme of Salford, 1997.
[480] Albert Booth (1928-2010), Labour MP for Barrow-in-Furness, 1966-83. Secretary of State for Employment, 1976-79.
[481] Thomas Torney (1915-1998), Labour MP for Bradford South, 1970-87.

'NM is one of the best Parliamentarians in the House" – Geoffrey told me this as I left the Chamber! Kiss of death?!

12.6.77

Tuesday (7) was actual Jubilee Day. We stayed at home and watched it on TV. A superb presentation 10am – 3.30! The real pleasure in the last two days has been the tremendous loyalty to the Queen, particularly from the younger generation. Everywhere was decorated, and of course "the working class" showing their patriotism better than any other group. Council estates decorated to the nines! The crowds in London on the line were terrific and enthusiasm was unending. A wonderful, wonderful Monarchy. In the evening we went to Brompton Park to see the Banbury Jubilee Fete. Weather still far too cool, frost at night in some places. Meanwhile Commonwealth Prime Ministers Conference went on, Idi Amin[482] (Uganda) did not turn up and was roundly condemned by Africans as a cruel dictator! There seemed to be even a sort of consensus on Rhodesia.

26.6.77

Callaghan trying to restore discipline in his Party! He lectured them at a meeting of PLP after two Lab. MPs had voted against Govt and altered Healey Finance Bill in Committee[483]. Tues./Wed. an all night sitting on the Price Commission Bill – the major issue was that Lab. wanted it to be permanent and Cons. only for 1 year renewable. So we 'lost' Wednesday and it ran from 3.30 Tues. to about 9pm Wed.

3.7.77

Monday lots of EEC meetings to do with direct elections Bill published over the w/end – it contains PR as the method with first-past-the-post as the alternative. A division in the Party. The anti-PR lot who are pro direct elections – the anti-market lot who are anti both, the pro-market pro PR and pro-direct elections! We saw Margaret (i.e., 1922 Exec.) on Tuesday and it was raised. I proposed a reasoned amendment to decline a 2nd reading to a Bill which contains PR – but she couldn't

---

[482] Idi Amin (1925-2003), President of Uganda, 1971-79.
[483] The Rooker-Wise amendment named after its proposers Audrey Wise and Jeff Rooker. This linked income tax thresholds with inflation.

agree because that would split the Party even more! So there is a 3-line whip for the 2nd reading of the Bill – but few will pay much attention to it! However I expect it will get through. The idea is quite dotty to have a 2nd Reading and then it will go down the drain when this session is over and have another 2nd Reading in Nov! The antis will then keep it running for a long-time until it is too late to have the elections in May.

10.7.77

Wednesday debate (2 days) on direct elections Bill to Euro Assembly. I spoke early first day and it went quite well – the whole thing really is a farce. Then the vote came Labour had a free vote including Ministers and we had a 3-line whip. The result was 394 for the Bill, 147 against. 6 Cabinet Ministers voted against, Shore, Benn, Silkin (John), Orme, Foot, Booth and 26 Junior Ministers plus about 100 Lab. MPs. 14 Cons. (incl. me) voted against and a number abstained. The Committee Stage will be very, very lengthy!

17.7.77

Tuesday saw Margaret T and briefed her on Blenheim Rally following Saturday week on Crime and Criminal Law Act and a day on Finance Bill. An amusing Foreign Affairs Parly. Committee on Tues. to discuss the future of CM – quite a shift in opinion seems to be taking place and a general recognition that it will never be the same when it is enlarged by accession of Spain, Portugal, and Greece and possibly Turkey. Even Reggie Maudling sees it coming back to a Free Trade Area! That is where he started!

24.7.77

Monday debate on EEC budget. I spoke and attacked the expenditure on the Assembly, the racket of expenses, etc. – not too popular with some, naturally. Also as way of saving money on translation etc. I suggested everyone should speak French! Anyhow, got it off my chest. Wednesday tennis and lunch City Livery Club and then major debate on Healey's latest mini-budget. Phase III is now almost non-existent, Unions already shouting about massive claims and Govt. says not more than 10% - Libs are again two-faced having said there must be a statutory control of wages and prices now vote with the Govt. on a non-existent Phase III. Margaret T was a resounding success and made a superbly argued and aggressive speech and got a good press. She spoke again at the 1922 (end of term) in a friendly way and was again successful. John Cordle[484], under censure from the Select Committee Report to be debated next week, decided to resign from the House after the Poulson Affair – big drama – but next week's debate is a nasty one.

31.7.77

Tuesday was the debate on the Select Committee on Cordle, Maudling, Roberts[485] who, said the committee, fell below the standards expected of MPs. Cordle had already resigned so the debate focused on Reggie. His speech was very powerful and critical of the Select Committee; and its Chairman, Michael Stewart, couldn't answer Reggie's questions. However, in the end, all the nasty motions seeking to censure, suspend, and expel Reggie were defeated – even the one to approve the Report was defeated and the only one to be carried was the one to 'take note' which was the least possible – no one tried to reject it! The same result for Roberts. The ones to come out of it worst were Michael Stewart, the Father of the House George Strauss who wanted to suspend and Willie Hamilton who wanted to expel! The Labour so-called moderates mostly voted with the Conservatives. Perhaps John Cordle need not have resigned? However he has – but will he stand again? I doubt it. I did not attend the debate having agreed to take Maggie[486] to the Garden Party at Buckingham Palace – it was a lovely sunny day and a nice breeze and Maggie was presented to the Duke of Edinburgh. Then later a cocktail party given by Margaret T at the Carlton Club and Maggie met the politicians – and dinner at House of Commons – all in all a good day for her! Just as we were leaving for the Palace Peter Smedvig telephoned from Norway to say that Torolf had died – he had been ill for a year with cancer poor fellow – aged 60. It is a great loss – one of our dearest friends. So I

---

[484] John Cordle (1912-2004), Conservative MP for Bournemouth East and Christchurch, 1959-74; Bournemouth East, 1974-77. Embroiled in the Poulson Affair, he admitted to receiving payments of £5,628 from two of Poulson's companies to promote interests in West Africa. He resigned from parliament thereafter.

[485] Albert Roberts (1908-2000), Labour MP for Normanton, 1951-83. Roberts had also worked for Poulson.

[486] The wife of Neil's son, Anthony.

flew to Stavanger Thursday evening with Frederick and Peggy Newman for the funeral on Friday.

Back on Saturday and the recess had started 29 July to 26 Oct. – that's better. The Cons. have done very well – but the Lib-Lab pact has kept the Government afloat and has now been renewed and will continue unless the Govt. fails to stand up to wage settlements of 10% – I doubt they will – even then they are ultimately to be defeated in Parliament. But if wages explode they could run for cover in a spring election.

30.10.77

To Blackpool for Cons. Party Conf. – went primarily to speak in CM debate but was not called – the whole thing was rigged in the most odious way but Margaret made a great speech on the last day. Lots of constituency engagements the following week. Had a private meeting with Margaret T over the CM and found her <u>almost</u> sharing my views – I asked her to make her own views more known – she believes in the nation state and national parliamentary control and no extra powers for Euro-Assembly, anti-PR etc! Good if <u>only</u> she will say so! Parlt. re-assembled on Wed. 26th for Healey's mini-Budget and prorogation – he "gave away" £1bn but it didn't raise much excitement. Polls show Cons. and Lab. level pegging – but that is not unusual after a long recess.

6.11.77

Thursday Queen opened Parliament with a speech which was dull and known beforehand. Most of the session will be taken up with devolution and direct election to Euro-Assembly. Miners rejected pay offer on Tuesday[487], stock exchange fell, funds began to leave UK, power cuts by electricians also in dispute over pay. Blackout for 2 hours in Westminster area! Confrontation again?! Thorpe on the rack again over shooting of Scott question – apparently rumour has it that Roy Jenkins, then Home Secretary, called off the investigations two or three years ago!!

---

[487] And instead sought £135 per week, which was near double the current rate they were on.

Spoke to PM about his letter to Labour Party on EEC[488] and congratulated him on it – he said Margaret should do the same thing and that he had pre-empted her! I did <u>warn</u> her by letter when I sent her the latest NOP[489] that this would happen. PM said she was surrounded by people who wouldn't let her agree!

20.11.77

Devolution Scotland, Monday – Devolution Wales, Tuesday and oddly a guillotine motion on Wednesday for both Bills! And we lost all the votes by about 25-30 as the rebels on the previous voting were not prepared to do it again or PM had 'let it be known' that there would be an election if they were defeated – shades of Heath.

Firemen's strike goes on but so far nothing too awful has happened – PM won't allow the Forces to use Fire Service equipment because it would be strike breaking – how wet!

27.11.77

Monday had a meeting with Secretary to Canadian Cabinet on the techniques of referendum *vide* Quebec. In the evening Enoch Powell said he wanted to have a talk with me – this really was interesting – it was a different Enoch! Slightly more humble than usual! He started by referring to the night when he came to the flat in Feb '74 and told me he was not standing again as he couldn't honestly stand under Heath's leadership. He started by referring to that meeting and then a long and 'historical' discourse on his relations with the Cons. Party and the CM. He said that this relationship depended much on the Cons. view of CM and that unless it was positive about being anti-federal and retaining control by British Parliament (as Jim Callaghan had been in his recent letter to Ron Hayward – Lab. chief agent – in Sept.) he would have no alternative but to advise people to vote Lab. at next election as he did in '74. On the other hand if, in the debate later in the week on direct elections to Euro Assembly, the Cons. spokesman was to say that there would be no extension of the powers of the Assembly without a positive Act of Parliament rather than

---

[488] On 1 October James Callaghan published a letter to Labour General Secretary Ron Hayward on the EEC. In it he emphasised the authority of the nation state and governments, and more powers for the House of Commons to scrutinise EEC legislation. All things Marten couldn't disagree with.
[489] Opinion poll.

rushing it through by Sec. 1 and 2 of EC Act '72, he would not do so. Actually he wanted it to be more than that, i.e., that if there was any extension then the Euro elections Bill would be inoperative – but I advised against that as going too far and too complicated. I had the impression that he wanted the Ulster Unionists to rejoin the Cons. Party at some stage and this was the first overture. I immediately went to see Airey Neave (Margaret's Chef de Cabinet) and he sensed the same thing. He said if I would prepare a note on it for Margaret he would place it before her that evening and would be discussed by Shadow Cab. next morning. It worked! In his opening speech Willie Whitelaw made the precise point – at which Ted Heath walked out of the Chamber!! So, maybe we have reached the turning point over the CM – we are now anti-federal and pro keeping Parliamentary control. We shall have to see – if, at one stroke, we can block federalism and unite with the UUU's it will have been a good days/nights work!

4.12.77

Monday spoke on EEC and the way we handle our business, i.e. to make Govt. debate recommended documents before they are discussed in Brussels. Hitherto it is only a convention that they do so but Nigel Spearing wanted, rightly, to make it a resolution of the House. Motion withdrawn on the understanding that the Govt. was doing a major re-think on the whole of EEC legislation process – I wonder what they have in mind! Tuesday went before the Rent Officer about an attempt to put up rent of flat from £1,450, to £3,500 – he was sympathetic! (I hope). Meeting in afternoon with fishermen who were unanimous in demanding a 50 mile limit – Cons. have at last said they support an exclusive 50 mile economic zone – so did Libs and SNP – only the Govt. have said "up to 50 miles" – but John Silkin will I hope stand for a 50 mile exclusion limit when he meets Council of Ministers next week.

Thursday, the first day of Committee stage of Direct Election to Euro Assembly Bill – 2 hours of points of order to start with! Then Enoch Powell's amendment to insert a restraint on the Assembly taking any more powers. We lost that and then went on to debate Clause stand part[490] and during that the Govt. gave an assurance that they would introduce a clause to that effect – they said the clause

---

[490] That the Clause 'stand part' of the Bill. This means that no other amendment to the clause can be proposed.

would be to the effect that no powers would be <u>taken</u> from UK Parlt. but we wanted it the other way round that no extra powers would be given to Euro Assembly without an Act of Parliament. We shall see what happens. We really do seem to be moving things our way and we seem to have got things rolling at last with the Govt. and the Cons. Party in retreat – what a tonic it is when a General Election is on the horizon. Eventually, by 11.30pm, the Govt. had not got enough people there to keep it going and we said we would sit all night if necessary, so they gave in and adjourned the proceedings, not having finished Clause 1 – they had hoped to complete Clauses 1 and 2!

11.12.77

Big row on Monday when House of Commons overruled the Government who wanted to have a private inquiry into the Crown Agents[491] £200m losses – we won the vote for a public inquiry and this was subsequently agreed. Two days on Scottish devolution – one defeat for the Govt!

Something rather nice on Tuesday (6). David Ennals[492] (S/S Soc. Security) announced a new scheme for disabled drivers to commute their mobility allowances and lease a car. This was my original idea which I discussed with the Minister for Disabled (Alf Morris) about 2 years ago. I based it on the financing of the Abbeyfield Society. And now it has come to fruition - being an MP <u>does</u> serve a purpose! It will enable disabled to get the car of their choice (within limits) and have 4 wheels if they want them – particularly important for family disabled.

18.12.77

Monday we had a debate on the Polish shipping order where the Govt. got the contract to build 52 (?)[493] ships for Poland, in which the Poles got 100% credit from UK and the Unions in some of our yards refused the order for a variety of reasons! Then in the evening we completed

---

[491] The Crown Agents had invested vast sums in property that were hit by the property bust of the early-mid 1970s. This involved the government spending millions to keep the Agents solvent.

[492] David Ennals, Baron Ennals (1922-1995), Labour MP for Dover, 1964-70; Norwich North, February 1974-83. Secretary of State for Social Services, 1976-79. Created Baron Ennals, 1983.

[493] It was, in fact, a contract for 24 ships.

Clause 1 of the Euro Elections Bill after which the Government moved and got a motion to take Clause 3 out of order before Cl. 2 because Cl. 3 was the vital one about Proportional Representation or first-past-the-post. PR was defeated decisively by 97 votes and 317 voted against it – a majority of MPs – the Libs were furious and now there is talk of the Libs breaking the Lib-Lab pact. The debate on Cl. 3 took place on Thursday and by cooperating with the Chief Whip the anti-marketeers caused the vote to be at 10pm so there was a good turn-out. 4 Cabinet ministers voted against PR in spite of a 3-line whip!

Lunched by chance with Margaret T in canteen and we had a heart to heart over the CM – she certainly will not give any powers to the new Assembly!

15.1.78

Direct elections debate on Thursday on the alternative vote which was defeated and then the Irish UUU amendment to delete STV for NI – there was supposed to be a vote on this but, by 'devious' means, we got the Govt. to report to move progress at 10pm and the vote was postponed until the next sitting on the Bill – there was a considerable amount of cooperation from un-enthusiastic Ministers over this! At the next sitting I hope we can get a Cons. 3 line to support the amendment – rumours of a guillotine coming in the Bill – that will be interesting!

22.1.78

Thursday Michael Foot announced the guillotine on the Euro Assembly Bill – very odd as we have only had about 4 days on Committee stage and only about 6 more to go and it need not have Royal Assent until July. Labour Party is _furious_ and have convened a special meeting next Tuesday to try and get them to withdraw it. We are to have a free vote on it – how very odd when it is our duty to oppose and not give Govt. time to bring in more Socialism. I think the reason is that the Party is divided 3-ways and certain Shadow Cabinet people want to vote for it – a 3 line whip would be awkward for them! However, some Lab. MPs think it is better for _them_ if we have a free vote as it will enable them to vote freely, too – we will discuss it next week.

29.1.78

Scotland Bill on Tues. and Wed. and on Wed. we had some excitement. We had organised to support a Labour amendment (John Cunningham[494]) to make the Bill operate only if 40% of the electorate voted 'Yes'. This required 2 divisions and the next division was to separate Shetland and Orkneys from the Bill. Labour Whips, not wanting this amendment, lingered too long in the lobby and in the end Myer Galpern[495] sent the Serjeant at Arms to clear the lobby. More delay so he called in the tellers to announce the result of the division just in the nick of time. With 2 minutes to go before the guillotine fell Jo Grimond was able to move his Shetland motion in the shortest ever speech! So we won all 3 divisions which has successfully weakened the Bill unless the Govt. tries to restore the original clauses on Report stage – it will be difficult to win this as so many have already voted already on this point and how can they change?

Thursday was a horrible day – a guillotine motion on the European Assembly. Quite astonishingly the Shadow Cab. voted for the guillotine! I was <u>furious</u> and attacked them in my speech. Enoch, too. This has, temporarily I hope only, ruptured our relations with the Ulster Unionists which I have been patiently trying to build up. It was really a <u>sickening</u> sight. The vote was 314-137 – of the 314 in favour of the guillotine there were 155 Labour 151 Cons. and 8 others – against 60 Cons. 63 Lab 14 others. I felt really <u>terribly</u> sad.

Next day Friday off to N. Ireland with Harold McCusker[496] MP for Armagh. Raining hard we toured the bandit IRA areas of S. Armagh and the frontier, crossing the frontier several times completely unguarded and no control whatsoever. Met the military commander who was good but very inflexible – the troubles are starting up again – they have been re-organising and, cheered on by the Irish PM Lynch[497] and O'Keef the Bishop, they will now step it up. Mistake of Roy Mason to have said he is getting on top of IRA – it acts

---

[494] Marten has his names mixed up here. The amendment was put down by George Cunningham (1931-2018), Labour MP for Islington South West, 1970-February 1974; Islington South and Finsbury, 1974-82; SDP MP for Islington South and Finsbury, 1982-83.

[495] Sir Myer Galpern, Baron Galpern (1903-93), Labour MP for Glasgow Shettleston, 1959-79. Created Baron Galpern, 1979. Deputy Speaker, 1976-79.

[496] Harold McCusker (1940-1990), Ulster Unionist MP for Armagh, February 1974-83; Upper Bann, 1983-90.

[497] Jack Lynch (1917-1999), Irish Taoiseach, 1966-73 and 1977-79.

as a challenge. Then over to Enniskillen to speak for Harry West[498], leader of UU's, at his AGM.

12.2.78

Monday we had an interesting Party Committee meeting on Immigration after Margaret T's TV interview[499]. All the Govt. are trying to make out that she is racist which she isn't – she has brought the subject up for discussion which is healthy as many people are worried by it – but we must be careful. The Party was fairly sensible and well balanced. We did not want to dishonour our obligations yet it is absurd to let people in as we do with such high unemployment.

Tuesday a major debate on the Government's misuse of powers, i.e., the blacklist of companies which breached their voluntary pay guidelines. It all went well and we made our point. Afterwards, a champagne party given by the Tapsells – good old fashioned stuff! Wed., the last of 2 days guillotine on Euro elections Bill Committee Stage – pretty boring when the guillotine is in operation. Thursday a dull day – 1922 Exec. we discussed if we should change the Chairman of the Party[500] – will we?!

19.2.78

Tuesday we saw Margaret T (1922 Exec.) and had a general discussion which revolved around the weakness of the Front Bench and party unity – not a very good meeting – the Exec. is too ingratiating! Jobs?! Thursday report and 3rd Reading of Euro Assembly – guillotined - and we took the opportunity of making a lot of criticism of the pay and work of Assembly – also of nagging Geoffrey Rippon who had previously said in Luxembourg that if the EEC could not agree on fishing and enlargement it would break down – (uproar in Cons. Party!). 3rd Reading carried – but the French and Luxembourgers, with a vested interest in the Assembly being at Strasbourg and Luxembourg, have said they would veto direct elections if the Assembly was built at Brussels!

---

[498] Harry West (1917-2004), Ulster Unionist MP for Fermanagh-South Tyrone, February 1974-79. Leader of the Ulster Unionist party, 1974-79
[499] Broadcast on 30 January 1978, in an interview with ITV's 'World in Action', Mrs Thatcher said that British people feared being 'rather swamped by people of a different culture'.
[500] Lord Thorneycroft.

26.2.78

Monday morning off to visit EEC with my Select Committee – 2 members couldn't come as they were totally snowed in in the West Country – terrific snow storms. First visit was to the Hague – usual drill, visit to Ambassador, cocktail party given by him and supper by Counsellor. Next day meetings with Upper House and then Lower House – impression is that the Labour Party (the biggest) is moving against the EEC or at least having doubts about it. Then Wednesday a.m. to Brussels – lunch with Sir David Maitland our Ambassador, meeting with UK reps and of COREPAIR[501]. Next day, Thursday, we spent the day interviewing a series of directors-general of various Commission departments - it was somewhat terrifying to see the theories of the bureaucrats, out of touch with humanity wasting away in their 'chicken coups' in the Berlaymont[502], 1984 coming nearer! These theoreticians seem to have everything weighed up in their own minds – regional policy, economic and monetary union etc. It made my blood boil. With us were 2 excellent anti-marketeers – Ronnie Bell and Bryan Gould and the 3 of us nagged the Commission mercilessly – Tom Arnold[503] (pro) was heard to say "why do we always have to fight this on the anti-marketeers' ground?"

5.3.78

Thursday N. Ilford bye-election – Cons. won the seat from Labour with 7% swing which would give us an overall majority of about 70 in a General Election. Seeing that a recent poll actually put Labour ahead it was a good result. Callaghan tried to bring immigration into it and castigated Margaret T for her views for the last 3 weeks – but it had no effect on the bye-election. MT has hit a sensitive spot for the electorate who <u>are</u> worried about the immigration problem and Labour is obviously very worried. What effect this will have in a general election is anyone's guess but at this point of time the economic black clouds seem to be blowing up again – so he is boxing himself in about the timing of the election.

---

[501] COREPER, the Committee of Permanent Representatives to the European Community.
[502] The office building of the European Commission in Brussels.
[503] Sir Thomas Arnold (1947-2023), Conservative MP for Hazel Grove, October 1974-97. Knighted, 1990.

16.4.78

Mon./Tues. – snow storms and v. cold – a fascinating country of seasons! Mon. more money to British Leyland – where will it end? Tuesday Budget – after a lot of press build up of tax reliefs it was really a damp squib – it was Healey's 13th Budget in 4 years – Stock Exchange reaction was to wipe off £1,500m of value in shares! It was an attempt at an Election Budget but has really done nothing to restore confidence of industry and so do anything for unemployment. Wednesday went to Rent Tribunal to defend an attempt by landlords of 12 Gayfere Street to raise our rent to £3,500pa.

23.4.78

Another dreary Parliamentary week! End of Budget debate on Monday and Wales Bill Tues. and Wed. On Wed. the Govt. was defeated on a clause which made a nonsense of the Bill and we also put in the Bill the proviso that it would be inoperative unless 40% of the electorate voted positively for it – so it is unlikely to come into being! Wednesday we lunched with PM at No. 10 for Dr Banda of Malawi – he was very good after lunch making a short speech – what a difference from poor Ted! An agreeable occasion. Thursday Lambeth bye-election which Labour held with a much reduced majority[504] – Cons. vote up. Nat. Front finished 3rd and Libs 4th both losing deposits.

30.4.78

Monday went canvassing at High Wycombe bye-election[505] on the way up to London. Glorious warm day but few people at home. Tuesday Wales Bill last day of Committee Stage thank goodness. Wed. cross-examined Wedgwood-Benn on oil at Scrutiny Committee and served him up some good long hops on the EEC! Most people seem to feel a great sense of boredom about Parliament; as usual in the run up to the General Election. Great discussions on our amendments to Finance Bill and whatever the Libs and UUU's will join us in defeating Govt. on reduction of taxation. Bye-elections went well. Conservative votes

---

[504] John Tilley (1941-2005), held the seat for Labour until 1983 when his constituency disappeared. He failed to regain Southwark and Old Bermondsey from the SDP-Liberal Alliance at the 1983 election.
[505] Caused by the death of Sir John Hall.

up Labour votes down with about 8% swing to Cons[506]. Liberals faded right out losing deposit at Wycombe. I called in to do 3 hours of work on polling day at Wycombe and was struck by the disorganisation of the Cons. committee rooms! Epsom did well, too[507]. Friday was constituency AGM at Blenheim which went well. Len Edwards retired as Chairman (thank goodness!) and John Pritchard was elected in his place. Voting was close Robin Moffat 100 and John P. 101 – I would have been happy with either – Robin was the "county's" nominee! I suggested in my speech some form of National Service – I wonder how it will go down!

7.5.78

Tuesday we debated the enlargement of the CM – a debate which was preceded by a debate on the reference to the Committee of Privileges of the "Colonel B' case, i.e., whether the Press should have published the real name of an MI5 witness in a trial after it had been mentioned on as the privilege of the House – a nice point! The debate on enlargement was therefore truncated and not satisfactory – I got in a speech and one or two interviews one of which gained some publicity namely that I wanted the Spaniards to open the Gibraltar frontier before starting negotiations to enter EEC – subsequently did a broadcast on it – a point worth hammering home.

Thursday an inconclusive debate on Rhodesia – I feel the Cons. Party is going too far on this – David Owen should have the support of Cons. in his negotiations instead of which the Cons. seem to be harrying him.

GLC and metropolitan Boro' elections that evening – a muddled result – Cons. did well in London but not so well in the North – although it seems, overall, we gained 60 seats and Lab. lost 27 seats and Libs lost 8. – it is difficult to interpret. The Scottish elections were a revival of Cons. and Lab. support and a falling away of SNP!

14.5.78

Monday meeting at York Trust re Viking excavations, then lunch with Lloyds Bank followed by Committee Stage of the Finance Bill when

---

[506] Ray Witney was returned for the Conservatives and would sit for the seat until 2001.
[507] Archie Hamilton was elected for the Conservatives and held the seat until 2001.

we defeated Govt. and Parlt. decided to reduce Income Tax by 1p. Libs and all Parties joined us in this defeat – signs of Lib-Lab pact heating up – we jointly defeated the Govt. again on Wednesday to raise the bands of tax. But, rightly, no sign of resignation. Tuesday, up at 6am and to Manchester by air to debate CAP with Roy Jenkins at a seminar organised by the *Sun* and the Co-op: it was a good opportunity to hammer CAP in front of Jenkins.

21.5.78

Thursday evening 1922 Exec. met CBI for routine meeting. Also Peter Thorneycroft, Chairman of Party, came to 1922 Exec. and said that all MPs who were standing for EuroParliament must declare their intention to do so shortly before General Elections! This will frighten some of them and surely put them off.

28.5.78

Another dull week – debate on Armed Forces Pay on Monday – Winston Churchill wound up well – he is greatly improving! Tuesday the debate to ratify the direct elections to the Euro-Assembly – a messy debate and it was ratified by 111-52 – few Conservatives voted for it!!

11.6.78

On Tues. 6 June we reassembled after the 1 week Whit recess. There was no whipping that week so sparse attendance. Did Canadian Broadcast TV on Thursday, on Wed. Mr Desai[508] PM India came to meet us and, although 82 and modelling his existence somewhat on Mahatma Gandhi, he put up a good performance, very relaxed and philosophical! 'Bank rate' up during the week and a credit squeeze – so we are to debate it next Wed. on the censure motion – talk about 'stop-go' economy!

18.6.78

Apart from Wednesday (14th) it was a quietish week. Monday, tea with Turkish MPs then a meeting with a delegation of Soviet lawyers

---

[508] Shri Moraji Desai (1896-1995), Prime Minister of India, 1977-79.

– it was terrifying to hear them answer questions about Soviet political trials such as Orlov[509] - I should hate to get caught up in the Soviet legal system accused of anything!

Wednesday lunch with Norwegian Ambassador to meet Chairman of Norwegian Conservative Party – enjoyable occasion. Later that day we had a motion to cut the salary of the Chancellor Exchequer by half (a censure motion) due to his economic policies. PM decided to make it a vote of confidence in the Govt. and won by 5 votes, the Liberals abstaining! If they had had the guts to vote against the Govt. we would have had an election now – they are just clinging on to their seats! We came out of it well. So it now looks like 12 Oct. for General Election. Peter Thorneycroft to 1922 to talk about election.

25.6.78

Wednesday a debate on Housing. In the evening I was invited to speak at the memorial meeting to John Mendelson[510], a left wing Tribune MP who recently died. It was a very nice thing to be asked to do! It was because I had voted with him so many times over the CM. There I was on the platform, in a crowded 'leftie' room, with Ian Mikardo, Michael Foot, Eric Heffer[511] and others! But it went well and it was appreciated that a Conservative MP was there.

2.7.78

Friday a meeting with local magistrates to discuss law and order. The same magistrates, a week earlier, had fined me £24 for speeding!

9.7.78

Tuesday we went to Isle of Man for the 999th Anniversary celebrations of the foundation of their Parliament, the Tynwald – a fascinating occasion. Reception at Lt. Governor's House in evening and then ceremony next day. We all drove out to St. John's where we attended a Church Service and then out to the Tynwald in the open – an earth mound on which sat the MPs of IoM, judges, bishops etc. and all sorts

---

[509] Alexander Orlov had been a Soviet spy and defected to the USA in 1938. His book *The Secret History of Stalin's Crimes* was an expose of the Stalinist purges.
[510] Labour MP for Penistone who had died on 20 May.
[511] Eric Heffer (1922-91), Labour MP for Liverpool Walton, 1964-91. Challenged for the Labour deputy leadership in 1988 on a left-wing slate with Tony Benn.

of odd old Viking-titled men. The laws of the previous session were read out (titles only) in Manx and then in English – this over the Governor then asked if anyone wanted to present a petition and, amidst great cheering, one was presented to continue the use of the birch for punishment (it had recently been condemned by the European Court of Human Rights) – then back to Church which by then had been converted to a 'Tynwald' and all the Acts were signed by a quill pen! Lunch with Governor (Sir John Paul[512]), up a mountain and then a banquet in evening at which I had to reply for the guests – return Thursday a.m. A remarkable affair, much of it out of fairy land!

16.7.78

Monday drove to Birmingham to do a TV programme on direct elections to Euro Assembly and then down to London – awful sweat for a short appearance but was amazed how many locals had seen it! Later that day a debate on EEC preliminary budget when the Government accepted the amendment which we anti-marketeers put forward deploring the amount of money spent by EEC on surplus food. Why the Conservative opposition did not put it forward beats me – obviously Margaret cannot carry her Shadows on this sort of thing. Anyhow it was a fairly hilarious debate and was good for the Euro-nuts to hear – they could not have been very proud of their EEC!

Thursday, on to Foreign Affairs Committee, John Davies gave an account of his visit to Rhodesia and Zambia and came firmly to the conclusion that sanctions should not be lifted and that we must go on trying for a settlement etc. Thus dealt quite a blow to the right wing – John was excellent. Then in the 1922 on Thursday they all tried again – same arguments etc! I was so incensed I drafted an amendment to their motion on the order paper signed by 80 Tories saying sanctions should <u>not</u> be lifted – but John Davies and Chief Whip did not want it put down – so I didn't. I think it was wrong and regretted it afterwards. They argued that it revealed a split in the Party but it was true so who revealed the split.

Bye-elections on 13th in Moss Side Manchester and Penistone – Labour held both but 9% swing to us in Penistone. Polls put us some 6% ahead. Public support for EEC is now only 29%.

---

[512] Sir John Paul (1916-2004), Lt. Governor of the Isle of Man, 1974-80. The post of Governor of the Isle of Man was abolished in 1828.

23.7.78

Wed. tennis against Livery Club and lunch in the Lords after – we lost but good tennis. In the evening I got together about 30 MPs who do not feel that sanctions on Rhodesia should be lifted and we got John Davies and Humphrey Atkins to come and hear our views. It went well and we put down our marker and made our view clear that we would not vote to lift sanctions. We wanted to put down a motion but were dissuaded by Chief Whip – so we are meeting again next week to discuss it.

30.7.78

This was a week of good parliamentary activity once again. Our group returned to the charge of Rhodesia, several of us spoke at the Foreign Affairs Committee against lifting sanctions and then had a meeting of our 'A' (African) group again when strong views were expressed against lifting sanctions and Terence Higgins[513] and I went to see John Davies again to reflect these views. We agreed to see him again on the eve of the debate when he will have formalised his form of words. We will put down a motion if they are not good enough. The Party, as usual, is very divided, but Margaret T is very keen that we should not be divided and vote against Govt. on its handling on Rhodesia. It is interesting politics to have a 'group' operating again. 1922 Executive saw Margaret T on Wednesday a routine visit which went well. Then I saw her again for ½ hour about the Common Market, showing her the latest opinion polls and discussing it in relation to the Election and begging her to say that "as long as she leads the Party she will not condone any move towards a Federal State" – she took the point but will she say it?[514]

6.8.78

Tuesday was the Consolidated Fund debate which went on until lunchtime Wednesday. Terence Higgins and I went to see John Davies again about Rhodesia and tried to pin him down to a form of words

---

[513] Sir Terence Higgins, Baron Higgins (1928-), Conservative MP for Worthing, 1964-97. Financial Secretary to the Treasury, 1972-74. Knighted, 1993. Created Baron Higgins, 1997.

[514] She said it at Bruges in 1988. Sadly Marten was not there to hear it, he passed away in 1985.

about sanctions. Although not totally satisfied about his comments we nevertheless supported the Party because it was all really rather a silly exercise – the real test will come in November when the sanctions order will have to be renewed; John said that if free and fair elections were realistic "I cannot see the Cons. Party voting to renew sanctions" – we shall see – the situation may well have changed by then. Wednesday lunched with the Fishermen and discussed the CM – it seems that they are more than ever worried about the outcome of the EEC negotiations if the Conservatives return to office.

Thursday (3rd) the House adjourned for the summer recess – it has not been an agreeable session – in the last few months it has been all electioneering much encouraged by the broadcasting of Parliament. On Friday the news broke that Jeremy Thorpe had been charged with conspiracy to murder Norman Scott with whom, it is alleged, he had a homosexual affair some time ago. Four were charged one of them being an ex-hon. Treasurer of the Liberal Party. If true (and we must await the verdict) it is really a fantastic thing to have done: it will do no good to the Liberals in the elections and a row has broken out between the Lib. MPs as to whether he should stand at the election or not. His constituency want him to! Now for the recess and teeing up for an October election.

Undated entry

Great build up for the Election on 5 Oct. But, on Thursday 7th [September] PM came on TV and said no election! He treated it as though he was enjoying the job of having fooled the nation and the press and he was very smug. He got a very bad press for it and his image has greatly suffered. Margaret T was very restrained and dignified in reply the next day. The TUC whom he had led to believe that there was to be an immediate election were furious[515] and so were the Liberals. Now we shall be electioneering for some months?

8.10.78

The Labour Party Conference at B'pool on 2 Oct. and conference voted against Govt. pay policy! Left wingers voted on to Executive! On 11 Oct. I went to Cons. Party Conference at Brighton and delivered a

---

[515] It was at the TUC Congress Callaghan said, 'I have promised nobody that I shall be at the altar in October'.

speech to a fringe meeting of Trident Group attacking the European Monetary System for its Federalist pretences and also the European Movement for its bogus propaganda. Well attended but no press coverage in spite of a hand-out to every national paper! One day was enough at Brighton. The rank and file wanted sanctions on Rhodesia, Heath divided the party on incomes policy and put himself further out of court, and rejected PR. The Heath row continued when he made further speeches elsewhere supporting the Government's 5% incomes policy.

5.11.78

Queen opened Parliament on Wed. 1 Nov. – speech from Throne was a mass of fairly uncontentious proposals giving the impression that the Govt. would run its full course – but it had no proposals for dealing with inflation or unemployment. Ted Heath blew off again on his pay policy on TV earlier in the week and is now almost unanimously criticised by the Party in Parliament and in the country for the way he is behaving. Rhodesia came to the fore again as it is to be debated next week in Queen's Speech and we have to vote on sanctions. We had a meeting of the 'A' group to discuss it and then in the 1922 it was discussed for over an hour – some of the contributions were really neo-fascist – the Amery lobby is well organised! They will vote for the removal of sanctions (so they say) and the Party's line is to abstain altho' it thinks sanctions should remain on! How wet – compromise to help keep Party unity!

12.11.78

Tues. and Wed. the debate on Queen's Speech concentrated on Rhodesia. Partly on the Bingham Report (revealing the oil sanctions busting by oil companies and Govt?) in which Harold Wilson made a dreadful speech implying that he knew nothing about it! Amazing how he is held in such little respect by his party – he got no support from anyone and was attacked and contradicted by many of his own Party – same as Ted Heath over pay policy yet on oil sanctions he was good and respected in that particular.

Wednesday was the vote on sanctions and the Party was in its annual tizzy – Margaret and Shadow Cab. (unanimously) agreed to abstain and advised the Party to do so on a one-line whip! But 118 Tories voted to lift sanctions and made a lot of noise about it. Julian

Amery did himself no good threatening to resign the whip. John Biggs-Davison, front bencher on N. Ireland (No. 2) resigned honourably beforehand but Winston Churchill did not and was sacked, which was probably something he wanted for the publicity and in his grandfather's image. In the 1922 there was an effort to heal the wounds on both sides and all ended well but Julian A. put his foot in it again! I was re-elected to the 1922 Exec. although I must say I did not expect it as having led the keep-sanctions on lobby I thought 118 would not vote for me – but all was well.

19.11.78

Very dull in Parliament, except for question time! 'Bank Rate' up to 12½% and one way or another it looks as though things are not going so well for the Government. The much heralded agreement between TUC and Govt. was rejected by TUC Council which was a big setback to Govt. PM spoke at Lord Mayor's banquet and castigated our contribution to EEC etc. European Monetary System – still much discussed and the stupid Cons. Shadow Cab says it is in favour!

3.12.78

1922 Executive met Margaret T on Tuesday and had a good meeting. I warned her not to go overboard on backing the proposed European Monetary System as Callaghan was likely to turn it down and we should look silly if we were too "pro-EM'; also had at her for a clear statement of her views on a federal Europe – I followed this up with a letter setting it out clearly. Wednesday we had an inconclusive debate on EMS – we didn't really know the details! Anyhow it is a nasty move to EMU and another strand in the build up to a federal Europe and I hope it is thrown out next week by PM at Summit meeting.

10.12.78

On Wednesday PM made his statement on EMS on conclusion of Summit meeting. He decided Britain should not join because it would not benefit us. This was generally well received and he put it in the very best "patriotic" light. Margaret T opened her reply by saying "This is a sad day for Europe" – groans – it was very unwise – it made Labour seem the patriotic party and the Conservatives the anti-British pro-European party – it won't do us any good in an election. The

Italians and Irish did not join either largely due to the French objection to giving them too much money! Giscard D'Estaing is certainly building himself to take a great lead when he is President of the Council of Ministers next year - the French attitude to CM is getting intriguing.

Thursday we were supposed to debate the Government's sanctions on Fords for breaking the pay code. But it all went wrong as some Labour backbenchers refused to vote on the supplementary defence estimates which were 'supposed' to go 'on the nod' - fair enough, it is just what everyone complains of that Parliament does not control expenditure and here they were doing it and voting on it. This delayed the main debate on economic sanctions on Fords until 7.30 when the opposition called the debate off and asked for another day's debate. To add to this confusion a woman threw a pot of red paint on to the floor of the House to protest at the education of her child! We really should have a fine mesh net – next time, bombs?! Luckily I sit half way down the Chamber away from the public gallery! To what extent the delaying tactics of the 'left' were connived at by the Govt., because they would almost certainly have lost the vote, is a matter of speculation.

17.12.78

This was our final week before Xmas – a month's recess – the Govt. clearly prefers it when Parlt. is not sitting! The main event of the week was the postponed debate on sanctions against Fords – this took place on Wednesday and the Government was defeated on the Conservative amendment and defeated again on the motion as amended. PM took the right decision and accepted the will of Parliament and called for a vote of confidence the next day – this he won by 10 votes, the dissident Tribune MPs having returned to the Party on the confidence issue. But it could have been an election if all the minority parties had voted.

My next choice for the General Election is Mar/April 79 – new register, inflation not fully returned. Jeremy Thorpe standing trial at Old Bailey on conspiracy to murder!

24.12.78

Meanwhile the Iranian situation just about staggers on, pay claims pour in and an election looks likely in April (5th?). Petrol lorry drivers went on strike for a few days and there was a shortage of petrol in many pumps – anyhow that was settled bit by bit and then the lorry drivers had an official strike and chaos ensued with food held up in docks due to pickets, many lay offs as supplies were not getting through to factories and the railways too going to strike next week. This demolishes the claim that Labour only can work with the Unions. The public is getting fed up and Margaret T is talking about stopping strikers' Social Security and tax relief – she is showing up well and feels the public mood well.

21.1.79

This week was dominated by strikes, the most serious being the transport drivers where pickets were operating at the ports and factories and depots so that food was not being imported and supplies were dwindling to shops. We debated this in the House on Tuesday and Margaret T made an excellent opening speech and was even congratulated [by] the PM when he rose to reply. She also made an excellent TV broadcast when she outlined what should be done and said if the Government wanted to do these things they would have the full support of the Conservatives – there was no political yah-boo in her broadcast – she appealed for the nation to unite etc. She has obviously made a big impression on the country. She proposed ending secondary picketing and a strict code of practice on peaceful picketing and amending the law of the closed shop, secret ballots etc. and 'no-strike' agreements for essential services.

The Govt. refuses to bring in a state of emergency because they are clearly afraid of the Unions – our view is that they should take the powers now and use them as and when needed – we accuse them of being complacent. On the weekend I visited stores, etc, in the constituency to find out what the form is locally and they have enough food for next week but after that it will get tough. But the immediate and serious problem is food for animals who need protein which is being held at the Docks. Nasty stories about pickets demanding money to let vehicles through – bribes! The railways went on strike for 2 days and more to come – ambulance drivers, NUPE. The transport drivers' strike is beginning to collapse at the fringes over the weekend. Meeting at Woodstock in the evening – it was all about the strike situation.

28.1.79

The strike situation continued all week - and so did the stories about secondary picket abuses. The Govt. still did not introduce emergency powers. But things seem at the moment to be getting marginally "better" with further rail strikes postponed for the moment and lorry driver employers giving in to pay demands here and there – they should not deliver like this, and this is the weakness of so many employers. Standing Order No. 9 debated almost every day as the strikers hit at hospitals etc. Now the teachers have put in for a 35% rise compared with Govt's. stated 5%. Wednesday spoke at anti-CM meeting in London and Thursday evening spoke in House against EEC steel proposals which gave more powers to the Commission.

4.2.79

Meanwhile the strikes go on and on and the Govt is clearly the prisoner of the TUC. Standing Order No. 9 every day is requested as strikes by NUPE cause cancer patients to be sent home from hospital, bodies not buried because of strike by grave diggers, schools close because of strike by caretakers etc. The lorry drivers drift back to work as settlement @ £65 a week basic which the employers told us a week ago they would not accept! Oh dear, the country is in an awful mess – lack of leadership by Callaghan. Margaret asked him if he would encourage volunteers to man the stricken hospitals – but he wouldn't. No guts at all. I cannot see how the Govt. can now have any chance of winning the next election. We must hang round their necks, to remind electorate, that 1979 was Labour's year of capitulation.

11.2.79

Monday another S.O.9. debate and Lab. won by 6. In Parliament there is little apparent progress over the strikes – no sooner has the Govt. given into one lot then another lot strikes. Govt. is retreating fast from 5% and is cooking up another Social Contract with the Unions – I doubt if it can be much different than the last disastrous one (1975). Friday was at Bloxham all day with Jack Jones debating nominally the question of 'Pressure Groups' but it all came back to strikes, etc. Jack is looking older (he is?)[516] and not too clear, I thought. Also with us

---

[516] Jones was 65.

was T. E. Utley[517] of *Daily Telegraph*. On Sunday p.m. TV on a programme called 'Parliamentary Reform' Robin Day was interviewing Dennis Skinner, the left wing Labour MP, who had said he didn't admire many Conservatives etc. etc. and said he only admired those who stuck to their principles through thick and thin – in trying to drag out of DS the sort of person he referred to Robin suggested N.M.! Yes, said DS, because he had suffered in politics for sticking to his views on the CM! Dubious accolade from him!

18.2.79

Monday Dennis Skinner approached me saying he hoped I didn't mind and hoped it hadn't harmed me! We shall see. And still the wages battle goes on! The Govt. seems to have moved away from 5% and now is around 9½% of increases plus productivity deals which will probably be bogus but will allow settlements up to 15% - all the follies of an incomes policy are being displayed. Tuesday a.m. had a meeting with Francis Pym now our shadow Foreign Sec. about the Commonwealth and the Common Market – he said he is pro-Commonwealth and not a Eurofanatic – we'll see! Attended the Euro election Exhibition of the EEC's programme of informing the public about the election – a gross violation of our internal affairs! Ugh – they are a vile lot of smoothies.

25.2.79

Mon. and Tues. we debated the Procedure of the House – an unsatisfactory debate in many ways as no decisions were taken and we do need to improve our procedures. Wednesday Parliamentary Scientific Committee lunch at Savoy where Prince of Wales castigated communications between management and employees and blamed managers – he was right but they were hopping mad! Spoke on EEC budget debate in evening and the mood of the House was to deny any more budgetary powers to the Assembly.

---

[517] T. E. 'Peter' Utley (1921-88), journalist and author. In February 1974 Utley stood for the Ulster Unionist party against Ian Paisley in North Antrim.

4.3.79

This is devolution recess week – nice to feel the campaign going on and me not taking part in it. The result of the referenda left the Government's face covered in egg! <u>Scotland voted 32.5% yes and 30.4% No. Wales 11.9% Yes and 46.9% No.</u> The Scottish Yes campaign had told the voters that if they did not vote it would count as a No vote, so many did this – so really the vote was a pretty overwhelming No on that basis. The Govt. has been made to look foolish – the origin of their proposals arose because of the Scottish support for the Scot. Nats., the fear that Labour would loose [sic] seats to SNP and a 'deal' with SNP to support Labour minority Govt and so keep them in office. An amendment to the Bill stated that 40% of those entitled to vote must positively vote yes otherwise the Govt. would have to bring in an order to annul the Act. Now, on both Acts, 40% has not been achieved so they must lay the order. The question is whether they will whip their Party to vote down the order and set up the Assemblies. The SNP want them to do this. Unless they do it soon they will vote against the Govt. in a motion of confidence and possibly cause an election. Wheeling and dealing is rife!

11.3.79

Reassembled and much speculation about what the Govt. will do about devolution – answer is Callaghan will play it long and cool but will the SNP be prepared to wait? If the Govt. try and fiddle the Assemblies it seems that enough Lab. MPs will vote against their party to annul the Acts.

1922 is getting anxious about Euro elections – amusing! Friday lunch at County Council – extravagant – why?! Constituency Exec. in evening – some awkward question for me on Euroelections! There is a small gang of Sullivans and Colegraves still stirring it up over CM – but the rest of the Exec. seem more relaxed now – the atmosphere is changing. But Euroelections might present some problems if held on same day as General Election – but I'll take that when it comes.

18.3.79

A dull political week's manoeuvring still going on over Scottish devolution with SNP threatening a vote of no confidence if the Govt. does not do something quickly – Conservatives holding fire to see what happens but eager for the devolution order to be passed and then a vote of confidence. Callaghan back from EEC Summit is obviously preparing to make it an election issue. Margaret still makes the mistake of attacking him on every issue on CM when she ought to be supporting him on such things as reducing our net contribution and freezing agricultural prices. I got in a useful supplementary to PM on Tuesday on his statement and said that it was Cons. policy to reduce Govt. expenditure and therefore we must support him if he reduces the net Govt. contribution to EEC budget. Also next day at Agriculture questions underlined that Cons. Party supported Labour in price freeze. I must get her to "put Britain first" – the fault arises from those who brief her, i.e., the pros.

25.3.79

Went to Prime Minister's party at No. 10 for CPA delegates on Mon. evening - even there he looked a lot less confident than he used to – not quite the 'Big Jim' any more! Meanwhile the wheeling/dealing went on about devolution and in order to 'buy' the Welsh Nats. support he promised to bring in a Bill for compensation for industrial disease for the Welsh slate quarry workers! Oh it is all so obvious that he is just trying to cling on to office from hand to mouth and buying time. He made a Ministerial Broadcast on Thursday (why?) explaining, rather weakly I thought, his proposals for inter-party talks on devolution and it all sounded very silly. Why he did it I cannot imagine because he gave Margaret a wonderful opening to reply the next day which she did very well.

So the vote of confidence will take place on Wednesday 28th and the Press is all agog playing the numbers game. It seems, as at today, that the Libs. will vote with us, the SNP, some Ulstermen and ? the Welsh – we might <u>just</u> do it but I am doubtful – anyone's guess – an excellent example of why we should not have proportional representation leading to bargaining and horse trading of the worst kind.

1.4.79

Mon. and Tues. were the Defence Debate days much overshadowed by the vote of no confidence on the Wednesday. Waking on Mon. morning the snow was sweeping past the window like a blizzard – but it didn't settle merely added to the general flooding! In Parliament the numbers game was in full spate and on Wednesday evening at 6.30 the Chief Whip, Humphrey Atkins, forecast a victory for us by one vote. Everyone seemed very relaxed about it and after a brilliant wind up speech by Michael Foot we voted. After 20 minutes the Labour Whip came in and gave the thumbs up sign and there were roars of cheers from the Labour side, then the Cons. Whip Spencer le Marchant[518] came in and gave the sign for a tie which he soon altered to thumbs up for us! It was then announced as a victory for us 311-310. Roars from us again! PM then said he would see the Queen the next day which he did. Margaret said we would help through suitable business of the House and so we departed well satisfied. The Irish (except 2), the SNP and the Libs all voted with us and the Welsh against us – the two Irish Lab (SDLP) abstained. And so this Parliament ended. Back to Banbury Thursday evening, saw Joan Fri morning, M-L back from Italy, a quick meeting to decide on Adoption etc, then a meeting with Councillors to brief them for Local Elections on 3 May, same day as General Election!

8.4.79

Thursday lunch given by 1922 at Lockett's for Margaret T and then to large meeting of MPs and Councillors, (a meeting of 1922) when Peter Thorneycroft briefed us followed by keynote speech by Margaret and so back to Banbury to fight the election. Friday to Airey Neave's funeral – seem to have left it out of last week's diary. On Friday 30th March at 3pm he was leaving the House of Commons underground car park, driving up the ramp, when a bomb placed under his car went off and killed him. A really tragic loss, a good and charming friend, with a fine political and military record, who would have made a very good S. of S. N. Ireland - and that was why the IRA got him. His funeral on 6 March was at Longworth at Midday – Margaret particularly wanted me to go so I did – I had thought it was private so didn't intend going. Police abounded for miles around – security terrific – a beautiful service but, oh, so sad – a lovely day but cold – wretched for family.

---

[518] Sir Spencer le Marchant (1931-86), Conservative MP for High Peak, 1970-83.

15.4.79

Adoption meeting on Monday evening 8pm Chipping Norton Town Hall. Full House over 200. We had taped music to cheer it up! With Elgar's Enigma and Land of Hope and Glory as I walked to the platform with Chairman, John Pritchard – quite a success and it added good cheer. I spoke on Labour's failures and our hopes – not long, only 25 mins and then was smartly adopted! Only one question! Then the usual briefing by me and agent and away. A very enjoyable meeting – Joan and M-L came and Ruth.

It is interesting how the campaign is going nationally. Labour started early and could only offer the same old remedies as before which has put the country in a decline plus a few worse things like nationalisation, wealth tax, etc. and then attack Cons. by putting out a lot of bogus things they <u>thought</u> the Cons. would do – it was nauseating. Cons. started late and the better for it – hope we can keep it up: we have an average of 10% lead in the polls, although *Observer* gives us a 16% lead. It was very nice having the Easter break of 5 days not campaigning to collect oneself and get organised. But it is oh so boring – almost a repeat of the Feb. 1974 election, economy and TU and left wing! I am pressing the left wing take over of Lab. party and asking Lab. voters not to vote Labour as they would be voting for a 'Marxist' Govt. I will switch to 'positives' in last week.

22.4.79

Campaign still going well but it really hasn't sparked yet – it will no doubt end up in smears as Lab. is not doing well and they will probably resort to this towards the end as their only tactics. Started the week off again on Tuesday but Gillie had 5 puppies on Sunday night and this was the main attraction for the Press (plus me gargling with port!). Canvassing <u>very</u> slow in coming in but what <u>has</u> come in is a fraction better than 1970 showing 62% supporting Conservatives – this probably means about 50% or just above on polling day. Meetings very well attended and good and intelligent questions. Polls jump about a bit – RSL given a 20% lead and Gallup 5½%! But the average about 10% lead so there has not been much shift in the last week.

29.4.79

The main interest in the press is the polls – the gap has been closing but erratically although, as in 1970 election, my canvas returns show good swing to Cons. – on 27 April 23,000 canvassed was showing 55% pledged Cons. votes whereas at same time in 1970 it was only 51%. Many Lab voters have said they will vote for Cons. either fed up with Labour or fear Marxist developments! But on TV it is all presented as a presidential gladiatorial contest between 'Jim and Maggie'.

6.5.79

Started the last lap on Monday – canvassing, press conference and 3 meetings. On Tuesday, May Day, it snowed quite a bit and it was cold. Meetings at Chipping Norton and Banbury – fairly well attended and the animal lobby was out in force in Banbury and stormed out in anger at my answer to fox hunting – that was the only thing which the press reported! Wednesday 3 more meetings – at Milton-u-Wychwood 91 turned up! Last meeting at Leafield.

Thursday polling day, started at 8am driven by Mary Louise (v. well) and toured half the constituency visiting polling stations. Except at Banbury, Bicester and Woodstock no sign of Labour or Liberal tellers which showed a complete lack of organisation. In the evening, the Pritchards, the Dowsons came and together with Ruth and M-L we all watched TV, a good meal and plenty of drink (thoroughly boozed by 3am) and with the swingometer settling at 4.5% swing to us and a forecast majority of about 50 – so to bed.

Next day Friday to the count at Spiceball Park where until 11.30 they had been sorting Parliamentary and District Council ballot papers – both in the same box. The count looked good, with my votes piling up and in the event the result was Cons 31,137 (54.7%) ['74 elections 24,210 47.3%] Lab 16,623 (29.2%) ['74 18,019 35.2%] Lib 8658 (15.2%) ['74 8352 16.3%] majority 14,514 (25%) ['74 6,191 12.1%] swing +6.7% ['74 -6.15%]. A very good result. But the count was not declared until 3.15pm after which home for a snooze – won £100 betting 10-1 on majority over 10,000. In the evening the family came over for dinner and the w/end and we went after dinner to the Club and the Moffatt's victory party. Saturday and Sunday days of rest. Was sleeping in the garden (wrapped up in rugs) when the Chief Whip telephones and asked if I would accept a job as Minister of State Foreign Office in view of my anti-market views and my Commonwealth experience – I agreed. Then Margaret rang and confirmed it and said she particularly wanted to use my experience and said something about us both having come into Parliament together – nice chat and that's that! Children delighted!

It is clear from all my canvassing returns and experiences that a lot of Labour voters, traditional types, were fed up with Labour because it had let them down and because they were worried by the Marxist element in the Lab party. Also Margaret T did a wonderful job on TV etc. whereas Callaghan was the same boring and smug 'Uncle Jim' with nothing fresh to offer. Many will be the verdicts of the result but we have a lot to thank MT for.

Contributors

Dr Tim Aker is the Academic Director of the Margaret Thatcher Centre. He has a PhD and MA from the University of Buckingham. Formerly he was a Member of the European Parliament and a borough councillor. He lives with his family in Kent.

Anthony Marten is the son of Neil Marten. He spent his working life in the Brewing and Pub industries at Courage, Midsummer Leisure, Marstons, Morlands and Gales. He has been actively involved in Conservative politics in East Hampshire as successively Deputy Chairman, Chairman and President of East Hampshire Conservative Association.

During his father's foreign postings in the Foreign Office he lived in Egypt, Turkey and Germany. He was educated at St Edward's School, Oxford. He is married with 2 sons and five grandchildren.

Index

1922 Committee, 15, 22, 45; debates EEC, 45; NM encouraged to stand for chairman, 88; 50th anniversary party, 104; row over devolution, 179-80
1922 Executive Committee, 47, 63; NM re-elected 1971, 62; NM raises reversal of policies, 91; NM re-elected 1973, 110; meets new Chief Whip, 115; discusses February 1974 election result, 117-8; agree Heath should go, 140; Heathite challenge to, 141-2; meets Margaret Thatcher, 177, 182, 186, 206, 215, 222, 225; meets with Francis Pym, 193
1970 Group, 71

Aitken, Max, 91
Aircraft and Shipbuilding Industries Bill, 168, 181-3, 184, 186, 188, 190, 192, 193, 194, 199, 200
Agnew, Spiro, 107
Allen, Sir Philip, 158
Alison, Michael, 11
Amery, Julian, 149, 180, 189, 224-5
Amin, Idi, 206
Andrews, Eamonn, 37, 47
Anstruther-Grey, Lord, 27
Arab-Israeli War 1973, 108
Arnold, Tom, 216
Ashfield by-election (1977), 202
Ashley, Jack, 21, 40
Atkins, Humphrey, 60, 115, 117, 177, 182, 232
Ayrshire by-election, 13

Balneil, Robin, 24
Banbury Guardian, 66, 71
Barber, Tony, 15, 25, 26, 43, 52, 74, 97, 101, 111, 118
Beamish, Tufton, 27, 36, 46
Beckenham constituency EEC referendum, 58
Bell, Ronald, 29, 158, 174, 186, 216
Benn, Tony [see *Wedgwood-Benn, Anthony*]
Bennett, Air Marshall Don, 147
Berry, Lady Pamela, 138
Bessel, Peter, 9
Biafra, 8
Biffen, John, 65, 78
Biggs-Davison, John, 74, 225
Birmingham Stechford by-election (1977), 201
Blaker, Peter, 58
Boardman, Tom, 142
Body, Sir Richard, 64, 83, 84, 85, 95, 143
Bolton, Sir George, 97, 146
Booth, Albert, 205, 207
Borten, Per, 41
Bow Group, 97
Boyd-Carpenter, John, 32-3, 174
Boyle, Lord Edward, 103
Braine, Bernard, 92, 134
Brandt, Willy, 12, 45
Brezhnev, Leonid, 109
British Leyland, 169
British Overseas Airways Corporation (BOAC), 13
British United Airways (BUA), 13

Bridgewater by-election (1970), 13
Bromsgrove by-election (1971), 48
Brook, Lord, 26,
Bryan, Paul, 11, 88, 142
Bryant, Sir Arthur, 16, 49
Buchanan-Smith, Alec, 195
Budgen, Nick, 174
Budget: 1970, 14; 1971, 43; 1972, 73-4; 1973, 97-8; 1974, 121-2, 143; 1975, 154; 1976, 178; 1977, 202; 1978, 217
Budget (mini): July 1974, 138; July 1977, 207
Bullus, Eric, 65, 79
Burden, Frederick, 38
Butler, David, 160
Butler, Rab (Lord), 26

Callaghan, James; discusses Common Market with NM, 36; appointed Foreign Secretary, 120; criticised by left wing, 135; edges towards remaining in EEC, 144; NM dines with, 150; EEC Summit, 153, 205, 231; Lunch with NM, 160; NM comments on, 168; Russians criticise, 171; stands for Labour leadership, 176, elected Labour leader, 178; calls for reconciliation after aircraft and shipbuilding nationalisation vote, 183; EEC Summit statement, 186; meets with NM, 210; manages party splits, 206; letter to party on EEC, 210-11; attacks Thatcher on immigration, 216; does not call election, 223; refuses to enter European Monetary System, 225; loses vote of confidence 1979, 232
Cambodia, 16, 17
Cambridge by-election (1976), 193
Cambridge University, 10
Campaign for the Protection of Rural England (CPRE), 89
Campbell, Bruce, 65
Canavan, Denis, 182
Carlisle, Mark, 142, 182
Carr, Robert, 30, 89, 118, 121
Carrington, Lord Peter, 194, 203
Carshalton by-election (1976), 175
Carter, Jimmy, 197, 204
Carvel, Robert, 38
Castle, Barbara, 52, 157
Catherwood, Sir Fred, 39
Chaban-Delmas, Jacques, 81
Chalfont, Lord, 11
Channel Tunnel, 110, 111, 142
Chattaway, Chris, 31
Chrysler, 169
Churchill, Winston (1874-1965), 52
Churchill, Winston (1940-2010), 121, 225
Clark, William, 34, 60
Clark Hutchison, Michael, 41
Clarke, Kenneth, 156
Clegg, Walter, 133
Coal strike, 68
Colombo, Emilio, 51
Coleraine, Lord, 26
Common Market: 1970 White Paper, 10, 11; European Free Trade Area, 14; NM organises antis in parliament, 29;

Commons Debate, 36; preliminary discussions on Conservative Anti-Common Market Information Service (CACMIS), 44-5; The 'Great Debate', 53-4; Conference 1971 activity, 59-60; Commons motion on principle of entry, 61-2; Denmark fails to get parliamentary approval, 66; Labour blocking motion, 66; enabling legislation introduced, 67; Second Reading of EEC Bill, 69-70; Clause 2, 71; NM referendum amendment result, 77; guillotine announced, 77; Ireland votes to join, 78; CACMIS, 79, 84; Third Reading, 82; Norway votes 'No', 85; Denmark votes 'Yes', 85; 'snake in the tunnel', 90, 176; 'Fanfare for Europe', 92; NM discusses renegotiation, 120, 135; Scrutiny Committee, 137; sugar imports, 142; referendum White Paper, 151; referendum day and result 1975, 158; Select Committee on European Legislation, 167-8, 216; direct elections to the European Parliament, 176-7, 205, 207, 213-14; Labour NEC votes against direct elections, 186; EEC passports, 192; enlargement debate, 218; European Monetary System, 224, 225
Common Market Safeguards Campaign, 9

Commonwealth, 9, 44, 52, 66, 89, 90, 109, 119, 139, 142, 204
Commonwealth Parliamentary Association (CPA), 27, 40, 134, 153, 156, 160, 202, 204, 231
Commonwealth Sugar Agreement, 29, 46
Concannon, Don, 11
Confederation of British Industry (CBI), 87, 90, 93, 101, 161, 219
Conservative leadership election (1975), 145-151
Cordle, John, 208
Corfield, Fred, 13, 146
Cosgrave, Liam, 104
Cosgrave, Patrick, 157, 205
Couve de Murville, Maurice, 83, 199
Coventry by-election (1976), 173-4
Cowdrey, Colin, 112
Cox, Lord Roxbee, 153
Crawshaw, Lord, 22
Crawshaw, Richard, 163
Crosland, Tony, 11, 176, 191-2, 198, 200
Crouch, David, 43
Crown Agents, 212
Cunningham, John, 214

d'Avigdor-Goldsmid, Sir Harry, 94, 95
D'Estaing, Giscard, 177, 204, 226
Daily Express, 29-30, 89
Daily Mail, 161
Daily Mirror, 41
Daily Telegraph, 17, 36, 66, 196, 229
Davidson, Arthur, 121

Davies, John, 74, 79, 106, 112, 157, 192, 221
Day, Robin, 101, 151, 229
de Freitas, Sir Geoffrey, 10, 46
de Gaulle, Charles, 29
Deakins, Eric, 95, 107, 119
Delargy, Hugh, 68
Deutschmark: 1971 crisis and floatation, 45
Devlin, Bernadette, 67-8
Devolution, 170, 195, 197-9; 210, 214; referendum and results, 230
Deedes, William (Bill), 27, 58, 59
Diamond, Jack, 121
Dimbleby, David, 158
Dock strike, 23, 25, 84
Docks Bill, 191
Dodds-Parker, Douglas, 23, 27
Douglas-Home, Sir Alec, 16, 21, 23, 28, 36, 39, 43, 46, 50, 61, 64, 79, 86, 88, 90, 184, 203
Dowty, Sir George, 14
du Cann, Edward: 88-9, 92, 95, 117, 140, 141, 145, 155, 164, 167
Duffy, Patrick, 98

Economist, 36, 164
Edelman, Maurice, 47, 104, 138, 174
Eden, Anthony (Lord Avon), 15
Edwards, Len, 102-3, 110, 122, 153, 160, 162, 166, 218
Edwards, Sir George, 31
Ely by-election 1973, 106
Emery, Sir Peter, 38
English, Michael, 9
Ennals, David, 212
Epsom by-election (1978), 218

European Economic Community (EEC) [see *Common Market*]
European Movement, 49
Evening Standard, 38

Farr, John, 29, 64
Faulkner, Brian, 75
Fisher, Nigel, 118, 182, 187
Foot, Michael, 16, 49, 71, 72, 77, 120-1, 158, 162, 176, 178-9, 181, 186, 202, 205, 207, 213, 220
Fraser, Hugh, 8, 32, 118, 145, 148
Frere-Smith, Christopher, 9, 64, 68, 95, 143, 153-6
Friends of Anguilla, 16
Friswell, Jack, 22, 45, 52, 55-7, 69, 93, 96, 102, 117
Fry, Peter, 60

Gale, George, 157
Galpern, Myer, 214
Galsworthy, Sir Arthur, 35
Gandhi, Indira, 165
Gardiner, George, 196
Get Britain Out, 146, 153, 155-6
Gilmour, Ian, 113
Gladwyn, Lord, 39
Godber, Joe, 99, 101
Goodhart, Philip, 27, 58
Goodman, Lord Arnold, 92
Gould, Bryan, 216
Grant-Ferris, Robert, 72
Grieg, Maurice, 11
Griffiths, Eldon, 10
Grimond, Jo, 39, 118, 183, 214
Grimsby by-election (1977), 203
Guardian, 38, 58
Guinness, Jonathan, 174

Gummer, John, 59

Hailes, the Lord, 26
Hall, John, 88-9
Hall, Lord William, 31
Hamilton, Willie, 28, 208
Hannam, John, 104
Harrison, Bob, 160
Harrison, Sir Geoffrey, 8
Hart, Judith, 157
Harvie Anderson, Betty, 157, 171, 196
Hastings, Stephen, 27
Hattersley, Roy, 48, 144, 157
Hayward, Ron, 210
Healey, Denis, 12, 54, 121, 138, 175, 176, 179, 195-6, 207
Heath, Edward, 9, 12, 15, 66, 101, 110, 115; offers Marten government role, 20-21; addresses 1922 Committee, 22, 54, 87, 100, 122, 143; 'full hearted consent', 33; meets NM and the 1922 Executive, 36-7, 52, 114; NM and pro-EEC propaganda, 41; calls NM 'Mr Europe', 43; 1922 lunch, 45; statement on EEC negotiations, 47-8; NM questions leadership of, 48-9; becomes 'Chief Whip' of EEC Bill, 69; meets Pompidou at Chequers, 73; announces Irish border referendum, 74; asks EEC rebels to stop their struggle, 77; gets bored with 1922 Executive, 83; increasing isolation, 84; gives statement on EEC Summit, 86-7; announces formal prices and incomes policy, 87-8; defeat on immigration rules 1972, 90; 1922 Executive dines with, 92; booed in NM's constituency, 93; introduces Phase II, 93-4; 'Presidential' approach, 94; losing confidence of the City, 96; meets 1922 over Stage III, 107; election speculation, 114; announces election February 1974, 115-6; February 1974 election, 117; fails to get agreement with the Liberals, 118; described as 'wet pudding', 134; NM criticises, 135; petition to remove, 136; fails to vote in parliament, 138; refuses to resign, 140, 142; public spat with du Cann, 141; sets up new procedure for electing a leader, 143; stands in leadership election, 145; resigns as leader, 148; referendum TV appearance with NM, 157; return of Heathmen, 161; rude to Mrs. Thatcher, 162; calls Joseph and Thatcher 'traitors', 164; speaks at 1976 party conference, 187-8; rebels on devolution, 194-5; storms out of the Commons, 211; speech on incomes policy, 224

Heffer, Eric, 220
Henderson, Douglas, 157
Heseltine, Michael, 59, 163, 182, 188
Higgins, Terence, 222
High Wycombe by-election (1978), 217-8
Hill, Graham, 22
Hill, James, 155

Hobart Race, 9
Holyoake, Sir Keith, 43
Hornsby-Smith, Dame Patricia, 47, 58
Hove by-election 1973, 108, 110
Howe, Geoffrey, 30, 149
Hunt, David, 85

Ilford North by-election (1978), 216
Industrial Relations Bill, 33, 36, 37, 38, 40, 41, 44, 54, 135; NM worries Heah will abandon, 83
Industrial Reorganisation Corporation (IRC), 74
Industry Bill, 78
International Monetary Fund (IMF), 182, 188, 195
Irish Republican Army (IRA): internment, 63; Bloody Sunday, 67-8; terrorist activities and motives, 80-1, 137, 143; bombs parliament, 135-6; government proscribes, 143; murders Airey Neave, 232

James, David, 32, 46, 136
Jay, Douglas, 8, 10, 14, 16, 25, 29, 36, 39, 84, 85, 95, 121, 153, 157, 158
Jay, Peter, 146, 204
Jellicoe, Lord, 11, 101
Jenkins, Roy, 14, 43, 69, 99, 157, 178, 199, 204, 209, 219; resigns as Labour deputy leader, 76; stands for Labour leadership, 176; becomes EEC Commission President, 192
Jessel, Toby, 61
Johnson, Paul, 157
Johnson-Smith, Geoffrey, 50

Jones, Aubrey, 31
Jones, Elwyn, 169
Jones, Jack, 158, 228
Joseph, Sir Keith, 71, 118, 122, 145; gets leadership momentum, 119; meets NM to discuss leadership, 140

Keep Britain Out, 65
Kershaw, Tony, 151
Kilfedder, James, 61
King, Horace, 21, 32
King, Tom, 104, 192
Kirk, Peter, 146
Kissinger, Henry, 109, 121, 189, 194
Kitzinger, Uwe, 93, 155
Kleinwort, Sir Cyril, 105
Knox, David, 147, 167

Lambeth by-election (1978), 217
Lambton, Lord Anthony, 101
Lane, David, 193
Langford-Holt, John, 121
Lauderdale, Earl of, 23
le Marchant, Spencer, 232
Legge-Bourke, Harry, 23, 33, 34
Lever, Harold, 52, 76, 137
Lewis, Kenneth, 173
Lincoln by-election (1973), 97
Little, Ken, 157
Lonrho, 102
Lloyd, Ian, 88
Lloyd, Selwyn, 22, 27, 119, 140; row over Speaker, 32-4; retires, 172
Lynch, Jack, 214

Mackintosh, John, 8, 151, 156, 191

Macleod, Iain, 23, 84
Macmillan, Harold, 15, 21, 115
Macmillan, Maurice, 52, 149
Maitland, Sir David, 216
Manchester Moss Side by-election (1978), 221
Maplin Airport, 95, 111
Marquand, David, 146
Marten, Anthony, 101, 164
Marten, Neil: 1970 election campaign plan, 18; 1970 election result, 19-20; refuses promotion to government, 20-21; arguments within Constituency Association, 22. 25-6, ; NM elected to 1922 Executive, 23; CM to become 'United States of Europe', 28; pushes referendum on CM, 33; sends Wilson anniversary card, 34; visit to New Zealand, 34-5; opposes incomes policy, 38; addresses Constituency Association on EEC, 45; refuses to speak at Banbury fete, 51; launches CACMIS, 51; wedding anniversary, 53; complains of arm twisting, 54; pressure from Banbury Constituency Association, 55-7; NM discusses rebels with Whips, 60; referendum result in Banbury constituency, 61; thoughts on Norway and Denmark, 62; restores temporary peace in constituency, 62-3; NM congratulated for whipping EEC vote, 64; abstains on blocking motion, 66-7; NM challenged at Association Executive, 69; NM criticises government tactics on EC Bill, 72; NM senses government U-turns, 74; abstains on direct rule, 75; places amendment for consultative EEC referendum, 76; visits Northern Ireland, 80; NM reacts to prices and incomes policy, 87-8; NM dismissed from Securicor Board, 90; threatens to stand against his own association, 97; re-adopted as candidate, 102; car bomb close to NM's flat, 113; describes February 1974 campaign, 116-7; blames Heath for election loss, 117; NM supports Keith Joseph, 118; constituency trouble re-emerges, 122-3; hernia operation, 137; election October 1974, 139-40; forms campaign organisation for Keith Joseph, 140-1; attempts to bring anti-EEC organisations together, 143; votes to restore capital punishment, 143, 168; NM made chairman of 'No' campaign, 144; meets with Margaret Thatcher, 147; views on leadership election, 148-9; row over constituency agent, 151-4; thoughts on referendum result 158-9; confronts constituency critics, 161-4; visit to India, 165-6; concerns on devolution policy, 170-1; sees Mrs Thatcher over European Parliament, 163-4, 187; anti-NM cabal routed from the Association, 180-1; visits

Brussels and Luxembourg, 185-6; 1976 party conference, 187-8; misses vote on Rhodesian sanctions (1976), 189; advises anti-devolutionists, 196; concerns on Rhodesia, 218; fined for speeding, 220; leads pro-Rhodesian sanctions lobby, 221-3; attends Airey Neave's funeral, 232; general election campaign 1979, 233-5; appointed to government, 235
Marten, Joan, 47, 62, 71, 73, 82, 101, 104, 157, 158, 190, 201, 232
Marten, Judith, 10, 15, 164
Marten, Margaret, 164, 208
Marten, Mary-Louise, 22, 82, 158, 165, 232
Martonmere, Lord, 11
Mather, Carol, 61
Maude, Angus, 9, 51, 89, 118
Maudling, Reginald, 49, 52, 54, 67, 102, 207; resigns from government, 84; becomes shadow Foreign Secretary, 152; referendum TV appearance, 157; Rhodesia debate (1976), 189; sacked as shadow Foreign Secretary, 192; debate on involvement with Poulson, 208
Mason, Roy, 171
Maxwell-Hyslop, Robin, 87, 118, 181, 199
McCusker, Harold, 214
McMaster, Stanley, 61, 64
Mellish, Bob, 68, 188
Mendelson, John, 220
Middle East: withdrawal from, 39
Mikardo, Ian, 156, 220

Miners' Strike 1973, 110-3
Mitchell, Colin, 60
Mitchell, David, 140
Moate, Roger, 51, 64, 79, 84, 121, 158
Molyneaux, James, 64
Monday Club, 43, 68
Montague, Victor, 115
More, Jasper, 27, 60, 61
Morgan, Geraint, 58, 61
Morris, Alf, 11, 29, 31, 34, 84, 85
Morris, Charles, 34, 197
Morrison, Charles, 147, 182
Mott-Radclyffe, Sir Charles, 26
Mountbatten, Lord, 22
Mudd, David, 65
Muzorewa, Abel, 202

Nabarro, Sir Gerald, 51, 61, 64, 79, 112
National Economic Development Council (NEDC), 39
National Farmers' Union (NFU), 8, 18, 47
National Referendum Campaign (NRC): NM launches, 144; meetings of, 146, 153, 154, 155; trouble with GBO, 146; final meeting, 161-2
National Union of Teachers (NUT): The case of Mrs Green, 13, 17, 21
Neave, Airey, 201, 211, 232
New Society, 184
Nicholls, Harmar, 29
Nigeria, 8
Nixon, Richard, 107
Northern Ireland, 203: protestor throws CS gas into the Commons chamber, 25;

direct rule imposed, 74; border poll 1973, 98; direct rule, 135; Government releases detainees, 168; civil disturbances, 170; NM visits, 214-5
Nott, John, 195
Nottingham University, 147

Oakley, Robin, 53
Onslow, Cranley, 192
Oppenheimer, Peter, 49, 53
Orme, Stanley, 205, 207
Orr, Willie, 134
Osborn, John, 104
Owen, David, 199
Oxford Motorway, 9
Oxford Times, 103

Page, Graham, 54
Paisley, Ian, 74, 203
Palme, Olaf, 14
Panufnik, Andrezj, 10, 23
Peart, Fred, 32, 119, 144, 169
Penistone by-election (1978), 221
Peyton, John, 27, 89, 149
Pincher, Chapman, 134
Pompidou, Georges, 46, 73, 80, 81, 85
Ponomarev, Boris, 189
Poulson, John, 84, 102, 208
Pounder, Rafton, 61
Powell, Enoch, 12, 36, 39, 51, 59-60, 68, 71, 73, 78, 79, 84, 85, 94, 96, 97, 106, 111, 115, 119, 136, 157, 211, 214: fears for Heath's mental health, 112; confides in NM, 114, 210; NM reveals Powell's election plans, 116; intention to return to parliament, 122, 134; NM can't work out his intentions, 138; NM charts path to leadership, 145-6; will not rejoin the Conservative party, 147; dines with NM, 151; congratulates NM on role in referendum, 158; influence over Ulster Unionists, 183; filibusters Race Relations Bill, 186; vote on censure motion, 201
Powell Barker, Sir William, 15
Ports Bill, 14
Prior, James, 149, 182
Prentice, Reg, 16, 196
Pressure for Economic and Social Toryism (PEST), 10
Prices and Incomes Policy: NM worries over introduction, 87; Stage II, 93; Heathmen support for, 161; Labour's iteration of, 162
Proudfoot, Wilfred, 110
Pym, Francis, 54, 69, 167, 193, 229

Queen Elizabeth II, 82, 141, 203, 206
Queen Mother, 30

Raison, Tim, 192
Ramsbotham, Peter, 204
Rawlinson, Peter, 161
Referendum: France announces referendum on enlargement, 73; Irish border referendum announced, 74; [for 1975 Referendum see *National Referendum Campaign* and for Scots and Welsh

devolution referendum see *Devolution*]
Regan, Gerald, 165
Renton, David, 88, 118
Rhodes James, Robert, 193
Rhodesia, 28, 63-4, 202, 218, 224; Pearce Commission, 67; Pearce Commission result, 79; Sanctions Order 1972, 88; Sanctions Order 1973, 110; Geneva negotiations, 188-9, 194; NM drafts motion to maintain sanctions, 221-2; Sanctions Order 1978, 225
Rhys-Williams, Sir Brandon, 33
Ridley, Nicholas, 190
Ringadoo, Sir Veerasamy, 35
Ripon by-election 1973, 106
Rippon, Geoffrey: statements on Common Market negotiations, 27, 32, 37, 41, 45-7, 50, 51; NM meets at Foreign Affairs Committee, 28; addresses Safeguards Committee, 33; dines with NM, 39; meets CM Ministers, 40; NM says not meeting expectations, 44-5; NM told assurances not enough, 48; NM does TV with, 52; the Six disagree with Rippon's terms, 63; statement on fishing, 64, 65; Discussion with NM on ratification, 66; NM mentions, 90; accused of misleading on sugar trade, 138; views on fishing, 215
Robinson, Geoffrey, 174, 205-6
Rodgers, William, 58, 70, 169
Rolls Royce, 30, 31; government nationalises, 37

Ross, William, 169
Rost, Peter, 104, 148
Rotherham by-election (1976), 184
Royle, Anthony, 42, 50, 134
Russell, Ronald, 64-5

Sandys, Duncan, 25, 102
Schuster, John, 22, 55-7, 93, 96, 116, 117, 151-2, 160-1, 163-4, 167, 180
Scott-Hopkins, James, 49
Securicor, 24, 43, 51, 63, 81, 90
Sharples, Sir Richard, 98, 104
Sheldon, Robert, 193
Shepherd, Lord Malcolm, 121
Shore, Peter, 29, 36, 42, 50, 52, 53, 76, 84, 85, 95, 119, 138, 154, 157, 205, 207
Short, Renee, 14
Short, Ted, 17, 121, 133, 146
Silkin John, 29, 42, 65, 205, 207, 211
Silkin, Sam, 196
Simmonds, Hugh, 161
Skinner, Dennis, 229
Smedvig, Nora and Torolf, 15, 42, 62, 76, 101, 112, 208-9
Smith, Cyril, 172
Smith, Ian Douglas, 28, 189, 194, 202
Smith, T. Dan, 133
Soames, Christopher, 145, 153, 155, 176, 183
South Africa, 196: arms to, 23, 24; relations with Rhodesia, 63; Southampton Itchen by-election (1971), 48
Spearing, Nigel, 142, 211
Spectator, 36, 50, 63, 99, 142
Sproat, Iain, 180

St. Alwdyn, the Earl, 15, 44
St. John-Stevas, Norman, 38
State of Emergency, 84, 110
Steel, David, 157, 201
Sterling, 179: floated 1972, 81; falls to $1.80, 182; falls to $1.57
Stewart, Michael, 17, 196, 208
Stokes, John, 174
Stokes, Lord Donald, 107
Stonehouse, John, 146-7, 187, 190
Strauss, George, 208
Strauss, John, 163
Summers, Spencer, 27
Sunday Times, 106
Sunningdale Agreement, 134
Sussex University, 8
Sutcliffe, John, 64
Sutton and Cheam by-election (1972), 91
Swann, Sir Michael, 150

Tapsell, Peter, 173, 192, 215
Taverne, Dick, 25, 33, 54, 97, 102
Taylor, Teddy, 64, 180, 195
Tebbit, Norman, 80
Thatcher, Margaret, 87, 177, 232: stands for Conservative leader, 145-51; crowned Conservative leader, 151; meets 1922 Executive, 156, 182, 186; drinks with NM, 162; 1975 conference speech, 164; speech on devolution, 170; 'Iron Lady' speech, 171; dines with NM, 172, 213; row over devolution, 179-80, 195; calls for re-vote on shipbuilding nationalisation Bill, 182; calls off pairing, 182-3; NM praises, 184, 188, 190, 202, 208, 235; meets with NM, 187, 207; 1976 party conference, 187-8; reshuffles front bench, 192; NM briefs on Europe, 198, 209, 222; calls for vote of censure, 200; interest in NM views, 205; interview on immigration, 215, 216; gets boxed in on EEC, 221; views on European Monetary System, 225; views on social security, 227
The Times, 33, 36, 38, 53, 182, 198, 205
Thomas, Peter, 45, 54, 55, 56, 121
Thomson, George, 76, 172
Thorneycroft, Lord Peter, 27, 219-220, 232
Thorpe, Jeremy, 116, 118, 191: wife's death, 23; manhandled in parliament, 70; October 1974 election, 140; canvassing for proportional representation, 156; rumours of scandal, 172; scandals emerge, 175, 209; charged with conspiracy to murder, 223
Time Life, 99
Todd, Garfield, 194
Torney, Tom, 205
Towler, James, 80
Trade Union Congress (TUC), 85, 87, 93, 114, 136, 179, 184, 223, 225
Tribune Group, 175
Trowbridge, Maurice, 147
Trudeau, Pierre, 152
Tugendhat, Christopher, 192
Turton, Sir Robin, 21, 29, 42, 47, 54

Tuzo, Sir Harry, 80

Ulster Defence Association, 80
Utley, T. E., 229
Uxbridge by-election 1972, 91

Value Added Tax, 78, 91, 95, 109, 110, 189, 193
Varley, Eric, 169
Vaughn, Gerry, 110
Vickers, Dame Joan, 43

Walden, Brian, 191
Walker, Peter, 161
Walker-Smith, Sir Derek, 16, 22, 23, 29, 36, 47, 49, 51, 54, 64, 65, 80, 110, 118
Walsall North by-election (1976), 190
Walters, Denis, 118
Ward, Christopher, 59
Webb, Harry, 51, 55, 96, 102, 108, 117, 122-3, 151-2, 160, 162, 167
Wedgwood-Benn, Anthony, 136, 158, 163, 176, 207
Weinstock, Sir Arnold, 120, 122
Welbeloved, Jim, 12
Wells, John, 43
West, Harry, 215
Whitelaw, William, 41-2, 43, 74, 118, 121, 163, 211; asks for calm from colleagues on Northern Ireland, 75, 77; different line to Heath on Northern Ireland, 83; introduces White Paper on Northern Ireland 98-9; becomes party chairman, 136; leadership ambitions mooted, 145; stands in second round of the leadership election, 149; row over devolution, 179-80, 195
Whiteley, Jack, 151, 167, 180
Wistrich, Ernest, 157
Wigg, George, 146
Wilkinson, John, 50
Williams, Shirley, 50
Wilson, Harold, 8, 12, 18, 19, 21, 23, 33, 36, 95, 110, 114, 118, 199, 224: calls election October 1974, 139; renegotiation statement, 144, 146; EEC Summit, 153, 168; pays tribute to NM, 159; 60th birthday, 175; resigns as Prime Minister 175-6; NM asks his last question as Prime Minister, 177
Williams, Sir Robin, 95
Williams, Sir Len, 35
Winnifrith, Sir John, 53, 154
Wirral by-election (1976), 175
Winter of Discontent, 226-9
Worsley, Marcus, 132
Wright, Sir Michael, 9, 95, 97, 146
Wright, Sir Oliver, 167

THE BRUGES GROUP

The Bruges Group is an independent all-party think tank. Set up in 1989, its founding purpose was to resist the encroachments of the European Union on our democratic self-government. The Bruges Group spearheaded the intellectual battle to win a vote to leave the European Union and against the emergence of a centralised EU state. With personal freedom at its core, its formation was inspired by the speech of Margaret Thatcher in Bruges in September 1988 where the Prime Minister stated, "We have not successfully rolled back the frontiers of the State in Britain only to see them re-imposed at a European level."

We now face a more insidious and profound challenge to our liberties – the rising tide of intolerance. The Bruges Group challenges false and damaging orthodoxies that suppress debate and incite enmity. It will continue to direct Britain's role in the world, act as a voice for the Union, and promote our historic liberty, democracy, transparency, and rights. It spearheads the resistance to attacks on free speech and provides a voice for those who value our freedoms and way of life.

WHO WE ARE

Founder President:
The Rt Hon. The Baroness Thatcher of Kesteven LG, OM, FRS

Chairman:
Barry Legg

Director:
Robert Oulds MA, FRSA

Washington D.C. Representative:
John O'Sullivan CBE

Founder Chairman:
Lord Harris of High Cross

Former Chairmen:
Dr Brian Hindley, Dr Martin Holmes & Professor Kenneth Minogue

Academic Advisory Council: Professor Tim Congdon
Dr Richard Howarth
Professor Patrick Minford
Andrew Roberts
Martin Howe, KC
John O'Sullivan, CBE

Sponsors and Patrons:
E P Gardner Dryden
Gilling-Smith
Lord Kalms
David Caldow
Andrew Cook
Lord Howard
Brian Kingham
Lord Pearson of Rannoch
Eddie Addison
Ian Butler
Thomas Griffin
Lord Young of Graffham
Michael Fisher
Oliver Marriott
Hon. Sir Rocco Forte
Michael Freeman
Richard E.L. Smith

MEETINGS

The Bruges Group holds regular high–profile public meetings, seminars, debates, and conferences. These enable influential speakers to contribute to the European debate. Speakers are selected purely by the contribution they can make to enhance the debate.

For further information about the Bruges Group, to attend our meetings, or join and receive our publications, please see the membership form at the end of this paper. Alternatively, you can visit our website www.brugesgroup.com or contact us at info@brugesgroup.com.

Contact us
For more information about the Bruges Group please contact:
Robert Oulds, Director
The Bruges Group, 246 Linen Hall, 162-168 Regent Street, London W1B 5TB
Tel: +44 (0)20 7287 4414 Email: info@brugesgroup.com

www.brugesgroup.com

c

www.ingramcontent.com/pod-product-compliance
Lightning Source LLC
Chambersburg PA
CBHW030257100526
44590CB00012B/424